Nadia Magnenat-Thalmann
Daniel Thalmann (Eds.)

Computer
Animation '90

With 143 Figures, Including 61 in Color

Springer-Verlag Tokyo Berlin Heidelberg New York
London Paris Hong Kong

Prof. NADIA MAGNENAT-THALMANN
Centre Universitaire d'Informatique
12, rue du Lac
CH-1207 Geneva
Switzerland

Prof. DANIEL THALMANN
Computer Graphics Lab.
Swiss Federal Institute of Technology
CH-1015 Lausanne
Switzerland

Cover picture: *Teddy Bears*
Design: Arghyro Paouri
Fur rendering software: André Leblanc
Artistic and technical directors: Nadia Magnenat-Thalmann and
    Daniel Thalmann
Copyright: MIRALab, University of Geneva and Computer Graphics Lab.,
    Swiss Federal Institute of Technology 1990

ISBN-13:978-4-431-68298-1   e-ISBN-13:978-4-431-68296-7
DOI: 10.1007/978-4-431-68296-7

Library of Congress Cataloging-in-Publication Data

Computer Animation '90 (1990: Geneva, Switzerland)
Computer Animation '90/Nadia Magnenat-Thalmann, Daniel Thalmann (eds.).
p.   cm   Conference held Apr. 25-27, 1990, Geneva, Switzerland.
ISBN-13:978-4-431-68298-1 (U.S.)   1. Computer animation — Congresses.
I. Magnenat-Thalmann, Nadia, 1946-   II. Thalmann, Daniel.   III. Title.
TR897.5.C656 1990 006.6–dc20

Preface

This book contains invited papers and a selection of research papers submitted to Computer Animation '90, the second international workshop on Computer Animation, which was held in Geneva on April 25-27. This workshop, now an annual event, has been organized by the Computer Graphics Society, the University of Geneva, and the Swiss Federal Institute of Technology in Lausanne. Many panels and discussions have also been organized in order to promote interactive links between the researchers, the end-users, and the artists.

During the international workshop on Computer Animation '90, the third Computer-Generated Film Festival of Geneva was held, this year in Lausanne as well.

The book presents original research results and applications experience to the various areas of computer animation including scientific visualization, human animation, behavioral animation, and motion control.

NADIA MAGNENAT-THALMANN
DANIEL THALMANN

Table of Contents

Part IV: Models, Systems, and Languages

Part V: Animation Techniques

Part I
Scientific Visualization and Animation

Animation of the Development of Multicellular Structures

F. DAVID FRACCHIA, PRZEMYSLAW PRUSINKIEWICZ, and
MARTIN J. M. DE BOER

ABSTRACT

This paper presents a simulation-based method for the animation of the development of cellular layers. The neighborhood relations between the cells are determined using a simulated developmental process, expressed by the formalism of map L-systems. The cell shapes result from mechanical cell interactions. Two types of forces are considered: the osmotic pressure and the tension of cell walls. The animation consists of periods of continuous growth separated by instantaneous cell divisions. The method is illustrated using the fern gametophyte *Microsorium linguaeforme*.

Keywords: mathematical modeling in biology, animation through simulation, visualization of development, map L-system, dynamic model.

1   INTRODUCTION

An important issue in developmental biology is the study of cell division patterns, that is, the spatial and temporal organization of cell divisions in tissues. This paper presents a method for the visualization of the development of single-layered cellular structures, such as those found in moss leaves and fern gametophytes [de Boer 1989].

The practical motivation for this work is related to two applications. As a *research tool*, graphical simulations make it possible to study the impact of cell divisions on cell arrangement and global shape formation. As a *visualization method*, simulations provide a tool for presenting features that cannot be captured using time-lapse photography. For example, pseudocolor may be introduced to distinguish groups of cells descending from a specific ancestor or to indicate cell age. Inconspicuous structural elements, such as new division walls, can be emphasized.

The underlying mathematical model consists of two components. On a *topological* level, the cell division patterns are expressed using the formalism of *map L-systems*. At this stage the neighborhood relations between cells are established, but the cell shapes remain unspecified. Next, cell *geometry* is modeled using a dynamic method that takes into account the osmotic pressure inside the cells and the tension of cell walls. The animation consists of periods of continuous cell expansion, delimited by cell divisions. The divisions are assumed to be instantaneous.

The paper is organized as follows. Section 2 describes the simulation of cellular development on the topological level. After a brief survey of methods for the parallel generation of graphs with cycles, attention is focused on map L-systems with markers (mBPM0L-systems). Section 3 is devoted to specifying the geometry of cellular structures given their topology. A brief survey of previous methods is given, and a new method, based on the concept of dynamic modeling, is introduced.

The geometry of a cellular structure is viewed as a result of forces acting on cell walls. It changes in time as the entire structure attempts to reach an equilibrium state. Section 4 applies the method to model and visualize the development of a real biological structure — the gametophyte of the fern *Microsorium linguaeforme*. Problems open for future research are outlined in Section 5.

2   MAP L-SYSTEMS

2.1   Maps as Models of Cell Layers

In order to simulate the development of cell structures, one needs a formalism that will capture the relevant aspects of the developmental process. Cellular layers are represented using a class of planar graphs with cycles, called *maps* [Tutte 1982]. According to Nakamura et al. (1986), maps can be characterized as follows:

- A map is a finite set of *regions*. Each region is surrounded by a boundary consisting of a finite, circular sequence of *edges* which meet at *vertices*.

- Each edge has one or two vertices associated with it.[1] The edges cannot cross without forming a vertex and there are no vertices without an associated edge.

- Every edge is a part of the boundary of a region.

- The set of edges is connected. Specifically, there are no islands within regions.

A map corresponds to a microscopic view of a cellular layer. Regions represent cells, and edges represent cell walls perpendicular to the plane of view. We abstract here from the internal components of a cell.

2.2   Rewriting Systems and Cell Layer Development

The process of cell division can be expressed as map rewriting. This notion is an extension of string rewriting used in formal language theory. In general, map rewriting systems are categorized as *sequential* or *parallel*, and can be *region-controlled* or *edge-controlled*. Since several cells may divide concurrently, a parallel rewriting system is needed. The second categorization has to do with the form of rewriting rules, which may express cell subdivisions in terms of region labels or edge labels. Both approaches are suitable for biological modeling purposes [de Boer 1989]. We have chosen an edge-controlled formalism of *Binary Propagating Map 0L-system with markers*, or mBPM0L-systems. It was proposed by Nakamura, Lindenmayer and Aizawa (1986) as a refinement of the basic concept of map L-systems introduced by Lindenmayer and Rozenberg (1979). The name is derived as follows. A *map 0L-system* is a parallel rewriting system which operates on maps and does not allow for interaction between regions. In other words, regions are modified irrespective of what happens to other neighboring regions (a *context-free* mechanism). The system is *binary* because that a region can split into at most two daughter regions. It is *propagating* in the sense that the edges cannot be erased, thus regions (cells) cannot fuse or die. The *markers* represent a technique for specifying the positions of inserted edges that split the regions.

---

[1]The one-vertex case occurs when an edge forms a loop.

The choice of mBPM0L-systems as a modeling tool has two justifications. First, they are more powerful than other interactionless map rewriting systems described in the literature [de Boer 1989, de Boer 1987, Culik 1979]. In addition, markers have a biological counterpart in preprophase bands of microtubules, which coincide with the attachment sites for division walls formed during mitosis [Gunning 1981].

2.3 Definition and Operation of mBPM0L-systems

An mBPM0L-system $\mathcal{G}$ is defined by specifying a finite alphabet of *edge labels* Σ, a *starting map* ω with labels from Σ, and a finite set of *edge productions P*. In general, the edges are *directed*, which is indicated by a left or right arrow placed above the edge symbol. In some cases, the edge direction has no effect on the system operation. Such an edge is called *neutral* and no arrow is placed above the symbol denoting it. Each production is of the form $A \to \alpha$, where the directed or neutral edge $A \in \Sigma$ is called the *predecessor*, and the string α, composed of symbols from Σ and special symbols $[,], +, -$, is called the *successor*. The sequence of symbols outside the square brackets specifies the edge subdivision pattern. Arrows can be placed above edge symbols to indicate whether the successor edges have directions consistent with, or opposite to, the predecessor edge. Pairs of matching brackets [and] delimit *markers*, which specify possible attachment sites for region-dividing walls. The markers are viewed as short branches which can be connected to form a complete wall. The strings inside brackets consist of two symbols. The first symbol is either + or −, indicating whether the marker is placed to the left or to the right of the predecessor edge. The second symbol is the marker label, with or without an arrow. The left arrow indicates that the marker is directed towards the predecessor edge, and the right arrow indicates that the marker is oriented away from that edge. If no arrow is present, the marker is neutral.

For example, in the production $\overrightarrow{A} \to \overrightarrow{D}\overleftarrow{C}\,[- \overleftarrow{E}]\,\overrightarrow{B}F$, the directed predecessor A splits into four edges D, C, B and F, and produces a marker E (Figure 1a). Successor edges D and B have the same direction as A, edge C has the opposite direction, and F is neutral. Marker E is placed to the right of A and is directed towards A. Note that this same production could be written as $\overleftarrow{A} \to F\overleftarrow{B}\,[+ \overrightarrow{E}]\,\overrightarrow{C}\overleftarrow{D}$ (Figure 1b). As an example of a production with a neutral predecessor, consider $A \to \overrightarrow{B}[-\overleftarrow{B}]x[+\overrightarrow{B}]\overleftarrow{B}$. In this case the result of production application does not depend on the assumed direction of the predecessor edge (Figure 1c).

A *derivation step* in an mBPM0L-system consists of two phases:

1. Each edge in the map is replaced by successor edges and markers using the corresponding edge production in P.

2. Each region is scanned for *matching markers*.

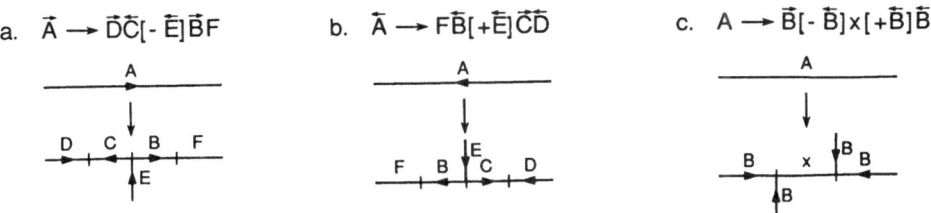

a. $\overrightarrow{A} \longrightarrow \overrightarrow{D}\overleftarrow{C}[\text{-} \overleftarrow{E}]\overrightarrow{B}F$ b. $\overleftarrow{A} \longrightarrow F\overleftarrow{B}[+\overrightarrow{E}]\overrightarrow{C}\overleftarrow{D}$ c. $A \longrightarrow \overrightarrow{B}[\text{-} \overleftarrow{B}]x[+\overrightarrow{B}]\overleftarrow{B}$

Figure 1: Examples of edge productions.

Two markers are considered matching if:

1. they appear in the same region,

2. they have the same label, and

3. one marker is directed away from its incident edge while the other is directed towards the edge, or both markers are neutral.

If a match is found, the markers are joined to create a new edge which will split the region. The search for matching markers ends with the first match found, even though other markers entering the same region may also form a match. From the user's perspective, the system behaves in a nondeterministic way since it autonomously chooses the pair of markers to be connected. The unused markers are discarded.

2.4 Examples of Map L-Systems

This section presents examples which illustrate the operation of mBPM0L-systems.

L-system 1

ω : ABAB
p_1 : A → B[−A][+A]B
p_2 : B → A

In L-system 1, production p_1 creates markers responsible for region division, while production p_2 introduces a delay, so that the regions are subdivided alternately by horizontal and vertical edges. The resulting sequence of maps is shown in Figure 2.

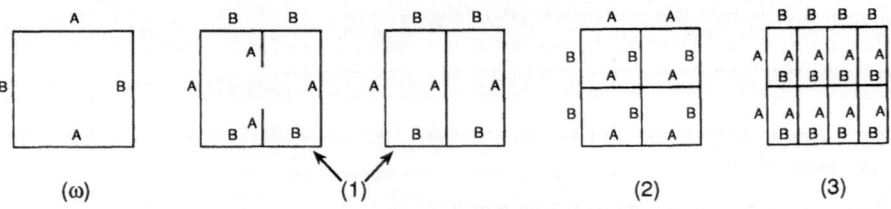

Figure 2: Developmental sequence defined by L-system 1. In the first step, a distinction is made between the edge rewriting phase and the connection of matching markers.

L-system 2

ω : ABAB
p_1 : A → B[−A]x[+A]B
p_2 : B → A

L-system 2 is a modified version of L-system 1. The only difference is the addition of an edge x which separates the markers in the successor of production p_1. This edge creates a Z-shaped offset between the inserted edges A (Figure 3). Z-offsets and symmetric S-offsets (Figure 4) can be observed in many biological structures [Lück 1988].

L-system 3

$$\omega : \quad \overrightarrow{A}\overrightarrow{B}\overrightarrow{C}\overrightarrow{D}$$
$$p_1 : \quad \overrightarrow{A} \quad \rightarrow \quad \overrightarrow{D}\,[-\overrightarrow{A}]\,\overrightarrow{B}$$
$$p_2 : \quad \overrightarrow{B} \quad \rightarrow \quad \overrightarrow{B}$$
$$p_3 : \quad \overrightarrow{C} \quad \rightarrow \quad \overrightarrow{B}\,[-\overleftarrow{A}]\,\overrightarrow{B}$$
$$p_4 : \quad \overrightarrow{D} \quad \rightarrow \quad \overrightarrow{C}$$

L-system 3 illustrates the operation of an mBPM0L-system with directed edges. Productions p_1 and p_3 create markers. Production p_4 transforms edge D into C, so that in each derivation step there is a pair of edges A and C to which productions p_1 and p_3 apply. Production p_2 indicates that edges B do not undergo further changes.[2] The resulting structure is that of a clockwise spiral (Figure 5).

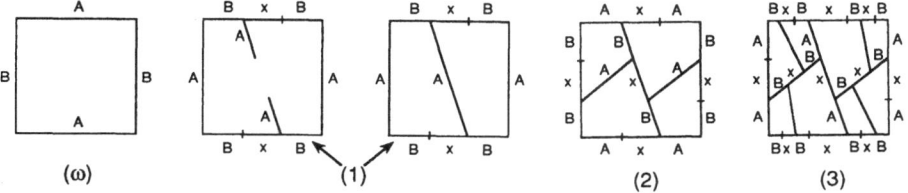

Figure 3: Developmental sequence defined by L-system 2.

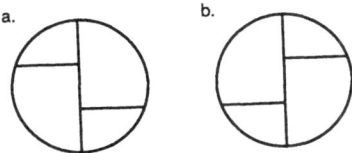

Figure 4: Offsets between four regions that result from the division of two regions sharing a common wall: (a) Z-offset, (b) S-offset.

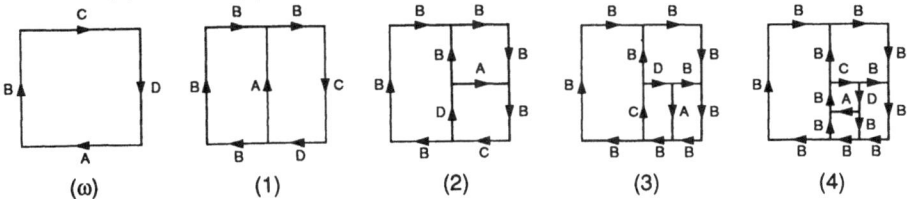

Figure 5: Developmental sequence defined by L-system 3.

[2]In further L-systems such identity productions are omitted.

3 GRAPHICAL INTERPRETATION OF MAP L-SYSTEMS

3.1 Previous Work

Maps are graphs or topological objects without inherent geometric properties. In order to visualize them, some method for assigning geometric interpretation must be applied. In the scope of this paper, we are interested in the representation of cellular layers. Consequently, we will use the biologically-motivated terms, cell and wall, instead of their mathematical counterparts, region and edge.

Siero, Rozenberg and Lindenmayer (1982) proposed a method which, in the simplest case, is expressed by the following rules:

- walls are represented by straight lines,

- the starting map is represented by a regular polygon, bounded by the walls specified in the axiom,

- when a production subdivides a wall, all successor walls are of equal length, and

- the position of a wall resulting from the union of two matching markers is based on the position of these markers.

This *wall subdivision* method was used to draw Figures 2, 3 and 5. However, in the biological context it creates cells whose shapes are seldom observed in nature.

De Does and Lindenmayer (1983) proposed a *center of gravity* method which produces more realistic shapes. The main idea is to place each interior vertex of the map in the center of gravity of its neighbors. Such positioning of vertices has a sound biological justification: it minimizes hypothetical forces acting along cell walls [de Does 1983], thus bringing the entire structure to a state of minimum energy. However, if all vertices were positioned this way, the entire structure would collapse. In order to prevent this from happening, the vertices on the map perimeter are pushed outwards by a fixed distance. Unfortunately, this approach lacks biological justification and introduces sudden shape changes which make it unsuitable for animation purposes.

3.2 The Dynamic Method

Assuming the dynamic point of view, the shape of cells and thus the shape of the entire organism results from the action of forces. The unbalanced forces due to cell divisions cause the gradual modification of cell shapes until an equilibrium is reached. At this point, new cell divisions occur, and expansion resumes.

The dynamic method is based on the following assumptions:

- the modeled organism forms a single cell layer,

- the layer is represented as a two-dimensional network of masses corresponding to cell corners, connected by springs which correspond to cell walls,

- the springs are always straight and adhere to Hooke's law,

- the cells exert pressure on their bounding walls; the pressure on a wall is directly proportional to the wall length and inverse proportional to the cell area,

- the pressure on a wall spreads evenly between the wall corners,

- the motion of masses is damped,

- other forces (for example, due to friction or gravity) are not considered.

The position of each vertex, and thus the shape of the layer, is computed as follows. As long as an equilibrium is not reached, unbalanced forces put masses in motion. The total force $\vec{F}_T$ acting on a vertex X is given by the formula:

$$\vec{F}_T = \sum_{w \in W} \vec{F}_w + \vec{F}_d,$$

where:

- $\vec{F}_w$ are forces contributed by the set W of walls w incident to X, and

- $\vec{F}_d = -b\vec{v}$ is a damping force, expressed as the product of a damping factor b and vertex velocity $\vec{v}$.

A wall $w \in W$ contributes three forces acting on X (Figure 6). The *tension* $\vec{F}_s$ acts along the wall, and its magnitude is determined by Hooke's law:

$$\vec{F}_s = -k(l - l_0)$$

where k is the spring constant, l is the current spring length, and l_0 is the rest length. The remaining two forces, $\vec{P}_L$ and $\vec{P}_R$, are due to the *pressure* exerted by the cells on the left side and on the right side of the wall. Each force acts in the direction perpendicular to the wall, and is distributed equally between its two incident vertices. The magnitude of the force $\vec{P}_L$ exerted by the cell on the left side of the wall equals $p_L \cdot l$, where p_L is the internal cell pressure and l is the wall length. A similar formula describes the force $\vec{P}_R$. The pressure is assumed to be inversely proportional to the cell area: $p \sim A^{-1}$. This assumption corresponds to the equation describing osmotic pressure, $p = SRT$, where S is the concentration of the solute (n moles per volume V of the solution), R is the ideal gas constant, and T is the absolute temperature [Sears 1985, Webster 1967]. Assuming that the cell volume V is proportional to the area A captured by the two-dimensional model under consideration ($V = Ah$), pressure can be expressed as

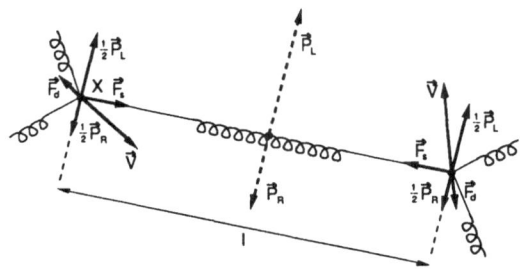

Figure 6: Forces acting on a cell corner X according to the dynamic method.

$$p = \frac{nRT}{Ah}.$$

Thus, $p \sim A^{-1}$, provided that the term nRT/h is constant.

A convenient formula for calculating the area A is:

$$A = |\sum_{i=1}^{M} (x_i - x_{i+1})(y_i + y_{i+1})/2|$$

where (x_i, y_i) are coordinates of the M vertices surrounding region A, $x_{M+1} = x_1$, and $y_{M+1} = y_1$ [Bronshtein 1985].

The force $\vec{F}_T$ acts on a mass placed at a map vertex. Newton's second law of motion applies:

$$m \frac{d^2 \vec{x}}{dt^2} = \vec{F}_T$$

where $\vec{x}$ is the vertex position. Assuming that the entire structure has N vertices, we obtain a system of $2N$ differential equations:

$$m_i \frac{d\vec{v}_i}{dt} = \vec{F}_{T_i}(\vec{x}_1, \cdots, \vec{x}_N, \vec{v}_i)$$
$$\frac{d\vec{x}_i}{dt} = \vec{v}_i$$

where $i = 1, 2, \ldots, N$. The task is to find the sequence of positions $\vec{x}_1, \ldots, \vec{x}_N$ at given time intervals, assuming that the functions $\vec{F}_{T_i}$ and the initial values of all variables: $\vec{x}_1^0, \ldots, \vec{x}_N^0$ and $\vec{v}_1^0, \ldots, \vec{v}_N^0$ are known. These initial values are determined as follows:

- Coordinates of the vertices of the starting map are included in the input data for the simulation.

- Positions of existing vertices are preserved through a derivation step. New vertices partition the divided walls into segments of equal length. The initial velocities of all vertices are set to zero.

The system of differential equations with the initial values given above represents an *initial value problem*. It can be solved numerically using the *forward (explicit) Euler method* [Fox 1987]. To this end, the differential equations are rewritten using finite increments $\Delta \vec{v}_i$, $\Delta \vec{x}_i$ and Δt:

$$\Delta \vec{v}_i^k = \frac{1}{m_i} \vec{F}_{T_i}(\vec{x}_1^k, \cdots, \vec{x}_N^k, \vec{v}_i^k) \Delta t$$
$$\Delta \vec{x}_i^k = \vec{v}_i^k \Delta t$$

where the superscripts $k = 0, 1, 2, \ldots$ indicate the progress of time, $t = k\Delta t$. The position and velocity of a point i after time increment Δt are expressed as follows:

$$\vec{v}_i^{k+1} = \vec{v}_i^k + \Delta \vec{v}_i^k$$
$$\vec{x}_i^{k+1} = \vec{x}_i^k + \Delta \vec{v}_x^k$$

The iterative computation of the velocities $\vec{v}_i^k$ and positions $\vec{x}_i^k$ is carried out for consecutive values of index k until all increments $\Delta \vec{v}_i$ and $\Delta \vec{x}_i$ fall below a threshold value. This indicates that the equilibrium state has been approximated to the desired accuracy, and a derivation step can be performed. A system of equations corresponding to the new map topology is created, and the search for an equilibrium state resumes. In such a way, the animation of a developmental process consists of periods of continuous cell expansion, delimited by instantaneous cell divisions. Continuity of cell shapes during divisions is preserved by the rule which sets the initial positions of vertices.

Color plate 1 illustrates the expansion of a structure generated by L-system 2. Plate 1a shows the structure immediately after the insertion of division walls. Plate 1b superimposes consecutive wall positions, with colors changing from blue to red as time progresses. Plate 1c describes the final structure at equilibrium. A smooth progression of shapes simulating the growth process can be easily observed.

4   A BIOLOGICAL EXAMPLE

In this section we apply the described simulation method to visualize the development of the fern gametophyte *Microsorium linguaeforme*. Fern gametophytes represent the sexually reproducing life stage of fern plants. They show no differentiation into stem, leaf, and root, forming a plant body called a *thallus*. The development of a thallus can be conveniently described in terms of two types of activities: the activity of the *apical cell* giving rise to cell clones called *segments*, and the development of these segments. The modeling process captures repetitive patterns of cell divisions, so that large cellular structures can be described using a small number of productions.

4.1   Apical Activity

The apical cell is the originator of the gametophyte structure. It divides repetitively, giving rise each time to a new apical cell and a primary (initial) segment cell. The segment cells subsequently develop into multicellular segments. The division wall of an apical cell is attached to the thallus border on one side and to a previously created division wall on the other side. Thus, the division walls are oriented alternatingly to the left and to the right, yielding two columns of segments separated by a zig-zag dividing line (Figure 7). The recursive nature of the apical activity can be expressed by the following *cell production system*:

$$A_L \rightarrow S_L \mid A_R \qquad\qquad A_R \rightarrow A_L \mid S_R$$

This notation means that the cell on the left side of the arrow sign produces two daughter cells separated by a wall.

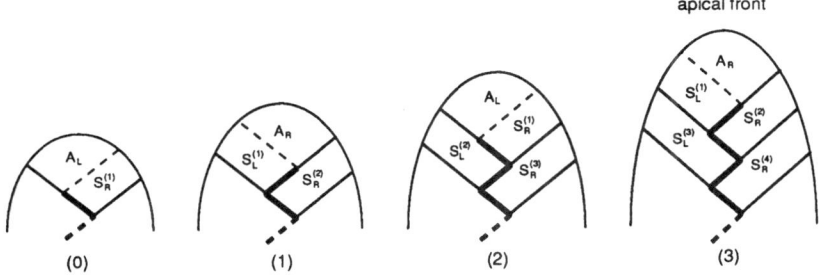

Figure 7: Apical production of segments. The labels A_R and A_L denote apical cells producing right segment S_R and left segment S_L, respectively. Dashed lines indicate the newly created division wall. The superscripts represent segment age. The internal structure of segments is not shown.

4.2   Division Pattern of Segments

In describing the structure of a segment, we distinguish between *periclinal* and *anticlinal* walls. Intuitively, periclinal walls are approximately parallel to the *apical front* of the thallus, and anticlinal walls are perpendicular to this front. A more formal definition is as follows:

- In a primary segment, the apical front wall and one or more walls opposing it are periclinal walls. The remaining walls are anticlinal walls.

- A division wall attached to the periclinal walls is an anticlinal wall, and vice-versa.

In *Microsorium*, a wall is never attached to a periclinal wall on one side and an anticlinal wall on the other side, so the above definition comprises all possible cases.

Microscopic observations of growing *Microsorium* gametophytes reveal that all segments follow the same developmental sequence, shown diagramatically in Figure 8. The primary segment cell S_1 is first divided by a periclinal wall into two cells, S_2 and S_3. Subsequently, the basal cell S_3 is divided by another periclinal wall into two "terminal" cells T which do not undergo further divisions. At the same time, the cell S_2 lying on the thallus border is divided by an anticlinal wall into two cells of type S_1. Each of these cells divides in the same way as the primary cell. Consequently, the recursive nature of segment development can be captured by the following cell production system:

$$S_1 \rightarrow \frac{S_2}{S_3} \qquad S_2 \rightarrow S_1 \mid S_1 \qquad S_3 \rightarrow \frac{T}{T}$$

In the above rules, a horizontal bar denotes a periclinal wall between cells, and a vertical bar denotes an anticlinal wall.

4.3   The Development of the Entire Thallus

The development of the *Microsorium* thallus is a result of concurrent divisions of the apical and segment cells. A single division of the apical cell corresponds to a single step in the segment development. A developmental sequence which combines the activity of the apex and the segments is shown in Figure 9. This figure also reveals offsets between neighboring walls. On the basis of observation, it is assumed that periclinal division walls form S-offsets in the segments on the right side of the apex, and Z-offsets in the segments on the left side.

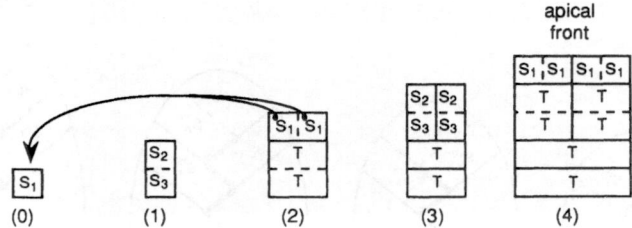

Figure 8: Developmental sequence of a *Microsorium* segment.

4.4 Expressing the Development Using a Map L-System

In order to capture the development of *Microsorium* using the formalism of map L-systems, it is necessary to identify all combinations of cells which may lie on both sides of a wall. Careful examination of these combinations yields the wall labeling scheme shown in Figure 9. Two walls have the same label if and only if they divide in the same way.[3] The uppercase letters apply to right segment walls, and the corresponding lowercase letters denote symmetric walls in the left segments. By comparing pairs of subsequent structures, we arrive at the following map L-system.

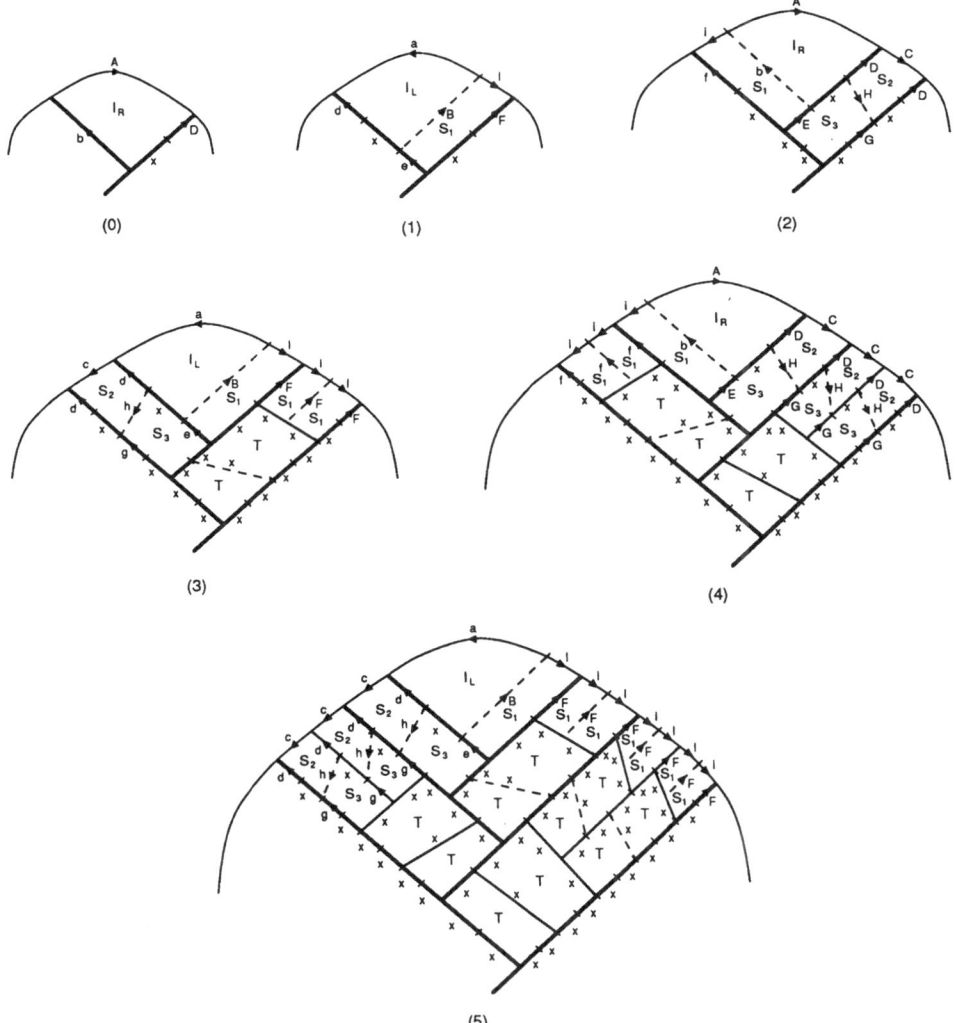

Figure 9: Developmental sequence of a *Microsorium* gametophyte.

---

[3]It is conceivable to formulate an algorithm which would assign labels consistent with the above rule automatically. However, the labeling scheme given in Figure 9 was obtained "by hand".

L-system 4: Microsorium 1

$\omega:\ \vec{A}\overleftarrow{D}x\vec{b}$

$l_1:\ \vec{a}\ \rightarrow\ \vec{A}\,[+\overleftarrow{b}]\,\vec{i}$ $r_1:\ \vec{A}\ \rightarrow\ \vec{a}\,[-\overleftarrow{B}]\,\vec{I}$

$l_2:\ \overleftarrow{b}\ \rightarrow\ \vec{e}\,[-\overleftarrow{B}]\,x\,[+\overleftarrow{h}]\,\vec{d}$ $r_2:\ \overleftarrow{B}\ \rightarrow\ \vec{E}\,[+\overleftarrow{b}]\,x\,[-\overleftarrow{H}]\,\vec{D}$

$l_3:\ \overleftarrow{d}\ \rightarrow\ \vec{f}$ $r_3:\ \overleftarrow{D}\ \rightarrow\ \vec{F}$

$l_4:\ \vec{f}\ \rightarrow\ \vec{g}\,[-\overleftarrow{h}]\,x\,[+\overleftarrow{h}]\,\vec{d}$ $r_4:\ \vec{F}\ \rightarrow\ \vec{G}\,[+\overleftarrow{H}]\,x\,[-\overleftarrow{H}]\,\vec{D}$

$l_5:\ \overleftarrow{h}\ \rightarrow\ x\,[-\vec{f}]\,x$ $r_5:\ \overleftarrow{H}\ \rightarrow\ x\,[+\vec{F}]\,x$

$l_6:\ \vec{i}\ \rightarrow\ \vec{c}$ $r_6:\ \vec{I}\ \rightarrow\ \vec{C}$

$l_7:\ \vec{c}\ \rightarrow\ \vec{i}\,[+\vec{f}]\,\vec{i}$ $r_7:\ \vec{C}\ \rightarrow\ \vec{I}\,[-\overleftarrow{F}]\,\vec{I}$

$l_8:\ \vec{e}\ \rightarrow\ x\,[+x]\,x$ $r_8:\ \vec{E}\ \rightarrow\ x\,[-x]\,x$

$l_9:\ \vec{g}\ \rightarrow\ x\,[-x]\,x\,[+x]\,x$ $r_9:\ \vec{G}\ \rightarrow\ x\,[+x]\,x\,[-x]\,x$

The apical cell divisions result from the application of productions $r_1 - l_2$ (creation of a right segment) and $l_1 - r_2$ (creation of a left segment). The subsequent segment cell divisions proceed in a symmetric way in right and left segments; we describe in detail the development of a right segment.

Concurrently with the insertion of wall segment B which creates segment $S_R^{(1)}$, wall D on the opposite side of the segment is transformed into F. This transformation introduces a one-step delay into the application of production r_4 which, together with r_2, is responsible for the insertion of the first periclinal wall H into segment $S_R^{(2)}$. As the derivation progresses, production r_4 inserts subsequent periclinal walls H between pairs of anticlinal walls F. Production r_3 introduces a delay needed to create walls F which are inserted between periclinal walls H and apical walls I, using productions r_5 and r_7. Production r_6 plays a role analogous to r_3 — it introduces a one-step delay into the cycle of creating markers F at the apical front of the segment. Thus, periclinal walls H and anticlinal walls F are produced alternatingly, in subsequent derivation steps. The last two productions, r_8 and r_9, create terminal walls x which do not undergo further changes. The first such wall is inserted between walls labeled D and E during derivation step 3. Wall D separates segment $S_R^{(2)}$ from $S_L^{(1)}$. Wall E lies on the border of the thallus. The subsequent walls x are inserted every second step between pairs of walls D; only production r_9 is applied in these cases.

4.5   Including Basal Segments in the Model

L-system 4 was formulated under the assumption that all segments develop in the same way. However, in a real organism the first two segments, situated at the thallus base, form a modified pattern with less extensive cell divisions. The developmental sequence of a right basal segment is shown in Figure 10. The corresponding cell production system is given below.

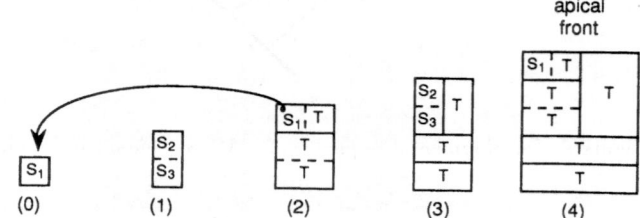

Figure 10: Developmental sequence of a basal *Microsorium* segment.

$$S_1 \rightarrow \frac{S_2}{S_3} \qquad S_2 \rightarrow S_1 \mid T \qquad S_3 \rightarrow \frac{T}{T}$$

The map L-system describing the development of a *Microsorium* gametophyte including basal segments has the following productions:

L-system 5: Microsorium 2

$$r_1: \ \overrightarrow{A} \ \rightarrow \ \overleftarrow{a} \ [- \ \overleftarrow{B}] \ \overrightarrow{I} \qquad\qquad r_9: \ \overrightarrow{G} \ \rightarrow \ x \ [+ \ x] \ x \ [- \ x] \ x$$

$$r_2: \ \overrightarrow{B} \ \rightarrow \ \overrightarrow{E} \ [+ \ \overrightarrow{b}] \ x \ [- \ \overleftarrow{H}] \ \overrightarrow{D} \qquad r_{10}: \ \overrightarrow{J} \ \rightarrow \ \overleftarrow{L}$$

$$r_3: \ \overrightarrow{D} \ \rightarrow \ [- \ \overrightarrow{m}] \ \overrightarrow{F} \qquad\qquad r_{11}: \ \overleftarrow{K} \ \rightarrow \ \overleftarrow{N}$$

$$r_4: \ \overrightarrow{F} \ \rightarrow \ \overrightarrow{G} \ [+ \ \overrightarrow{H}] \ x \ [- \ \overrightarrow{H}] \ \overrightarrow{D} \qquad r_{12}: \ \overleftarrow{L} \ \rightarrow \ x \ [- \ \overleftarrow{M}] \ x$$

$$r_5: \ \overrightarrow{H} \ \rightarrow \ x \ [+ \ \overrightarrow{F}] \ x \qquad\qquad r_{13}: \ \overrightarrow{M} \ \rightarrow \ x \ [- \ \overleftarrow{L}] \ x$$

$$r_6: \ \overrightarrow{I} \ \rightarrow \ \overrightarrow{C} \qquad\qquad\qquad r_{14}: \ \overleftarrow{N} \ \rightarrow \ \overrightarrow{0}$$

$$r_7: \ \overrightarrow{C} \ \rightarrow \ \overrightarrow{I} \ [- \ \overrightarrow{F}] \ \overrightarrow{I} \qquad\qquad r_{15}: \ \overrightarrow{0} \ \rightarrow \ x \ [- \ \overleftarrow{L}] \ \overleftarrow{N}$$

$$r_8: \ \overrightarrow{E} \ \rightarrow \ x \ [- \ x] \ x$$

Only productions describing the development of the right side of the thallus are given. Their predecessors are denoted by uppercase letters. The corresponding lowercase productions, which complete the L-system definition, can be obtained by switching the "case" of letters and the orientation of markers. The wall direction remains unchanged. For example, the right-side production

$$r_x: \ \overrightarrow{P} \rightarrow \overleftarrow{A} \ [- \ \overrightarrow{b}] \ c$$

corresponds to the left-side production

$$l_x: \ \overrightarrow{P} \rightarrow \overleftarrow{a} \ [+ \ \overrightarrow{B}] \ c$$

For more examples, see L-system 4.

A simulated developmental sequence generated by L-system 5 using the dynamic method to determine cell shape is given in Plate 2. Different colors are used to indicate the apical cell, the alternating "regular" segments, and the basal segments. A comparison of a developmental stage farther from the equilibrium (Plate 3) with a photograph of *Microsorium linguaeforme* (Plate 4) shows good correspondence between the model and reality with respect to structure topology, the relative sizes and shapes of cells, and the overall shape of the thallus.

5 CONCLUSIONS

This paper presented a modeling method for single-layered cellular structures, suitable for the animation of developmental processes. The topology is captured using mBPM0L-systems. The geometry results from a dynamic model that takes into account internal cell pressure and wall tension. The method is illustrated using a model of the gametophyte of *Microsorium linguaeforme*.

There are many possible refinements and extensions.

- The assumption that cell divisions occur after the structure has reached an equilibrium simplifies the computation, but is not essential to the modeling method. Cell divisions could also occur while the vertices are still in motion. In that case, velocities of existing vertices, as well as their positions, should be preserved.

- The described method is based on the assumption that cell divisions throw the structure out of an equilibrium state, and the subsequent process of reaching a new equilibrium describes the structure expansion. A physiological justification of this approach is an open problem.

- The assumption that wall strengths and solute concentrations defining osmotic pressure are the same for all walls and cells, and remain constant in time, may have to be relaxed for some structures.

- The method also assumes that cell states are not affected by the states of neighboring cells — the model is context-free. In some cases, cell interaction plays an important role in the control of development. To model this effect, a *context-sensitive* extension of map L-systems is needed.

- During the *cleavage* stage of embryo development, the structure consists of a single layer of cells which covers the surface of an imaginary sphere, called the *blastula* [Balinsky 1970]. By extending the method presented in this paper to a surface of a sphere, it was possible to model the development of worm and snail embryos [de Boer 1988]. For example, Plate 5 shows a ray-traced image of the embryo of *Patella vulgata*, modeled according to data in [van den Biggelaar 1977]. Nevertheless, both planar and spherical models operate on surfaces. Many cellular tissues and organs require truly three-dimensional models. A study of three-dimensional map systems, termed *cellworks*, was initiated in [Lindenmayer 1984]. Application of this theory to graphical simulation of development remains an open problem.

ACKNOWLEDGEMENTS

We are deeply indebted to Professor Lindenmayer for inspiring discussions and comments on earlier versions of this paper. The reported research has been supported by an operating grant, equipment grants and a scholarship from the Natural Sciences and Engineering Research Council of Canada, and by an equipment donation from Apple Computer, Inc. Facilities of the Department of Computer Science, University of Regina, were also essential. All support is gratefully acknowledged.

REFERENCES

Balinsky BI (1970) *An introduction to embryology.* W. B. Saunders Co., Philadelphia, 3rd edition.

Bronshtein S (1985) *Handbook of mathematics.* Van Nostrand, New York.

Culik II K, Wood D (1979) A mathematical investigation of propagating graph 0L-systems. *Information and Control*, 43:50–82.

de Boer MJM (1989) *Analysis and computer generation of division patterns in cell layers using developmental algorithms.* PhD thesis, Theoretical Biology Group, University of Utrecht, the Netherlands.

de Boer MJM, Lindenmayer A, Fracchia FD (1988) Analysis and simulations of spiral cleavage patterns. Abstract in *European Journal of Cell Biology*, 47:18. Supplement 24.

de Boer MJM, Lindenmayer A (1987) Map 0L-systems with edge label control: comparison of marker and cyclic systems. In H. Ehrig, M. Nagl, A. Rosenfeld, and G. Rozenberg, editors, *Graph-grammars and their application to computer science*, pages 378–392. Springer-Verlag. Lecture Notes in Comp. Sci. 291.

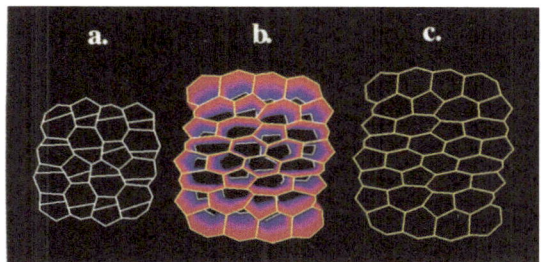 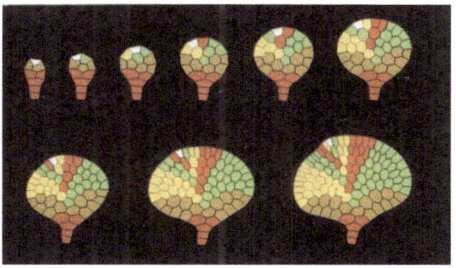

Plate 1: Layer expansion simulated using the dynamic method.

Plate 2: Simulated developmental sequence of *Microsorium linguaeforme.*

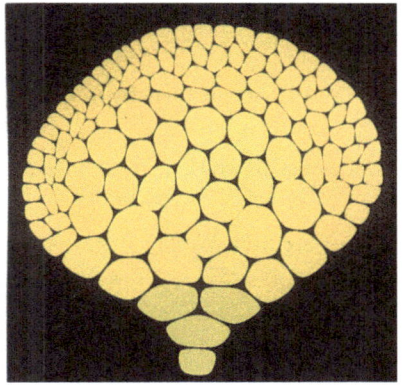 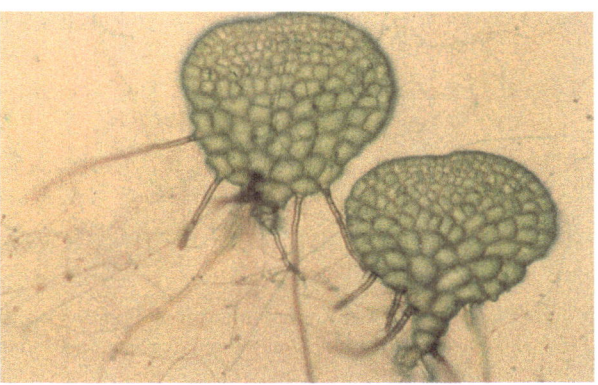

Plate 3: A model of *Microsorium linguae-forme.*

Plate 4: Photograph of *Microsorium linguae-forme* at magnification 60x.

Plate 5: Ray-traced image of a modeled embryo of the snail *Patella vulgata.*

de Does M, Lindenmayer A (1983) Algorithms for the generation and drawing of maps representing cell clones. In H. Ehrig, M. Nagl, and G. Rozenberg, editors, *Graph-grammars and their application to computer science*, pages 39–57. Springer-Verlag. Lecture Notes in Comp. Sci. 153.

Fox L, Mayers DF (1987) *Numerical solution of ordinary differential equations*. Chapman and Hall, London.

Gunning BES (1981) Microtubules and cytomorphogenesis in a developing organ: the root primordium of *Azolla pinnata*. In O. Kiermayer, editor, *Cytomorphogenesis in plants*, pages 301–325. Springer-Verlag, Wien. Cell Biology Monographs 8.

Lindenmayer A (1984) Models for plant tissue development with cell division orientation regulated by preprophase bands of microtubules. *Differentiation*, 26:1–10.

Lindenmayer A, Rozenberg G (1979) Parallel generation of maps: developmental systems for cell layers. In V. Claus, H. Ehrig, and G. Rozenberg, editors, *Graph-grammars and their application to computer science and biology*, pages 301–316. Springer-Verlag. Lecture Notes in Comp. Sci. 73.

Lück JL, Lindenmayer A, Lück (1988) Models of cell tetrads and clones in meristematic cell layers. *Botanical Gazette*, 149(2):127–141.

Nakamura A, Lindenmayer A, Aizawa K (1986) Some systems for map generation. In G. Rozenberg and A. Salomaa, editors, *The Book of L*, pages 323–332. Springer-Verlag, Berlin.

Sears FW, Zemansky MW, Young HD (1985) *College physics*. Addison-Wesley Publ. Co., Reading, 6th edition.

Siero PLJ, Rozenberg G, Lindenmayer A (1982) Cell division patterns: syntactical description and implementation. *Computer Graphics and Image Processing*, 18:329–346.

Tutte WT (1982) *Graph theory*. Addison-Wesley Publ. Co., Reading.

van den Biggelaar JAM (1977) Development of dorsoventral polarity and mesentoblast determination in *Patella vulgata*. *Journal of Morphology*, 154:157–186.

Webster HC, Robertson DF (1967) *Medical and biological physics*. University of Queensland Press, Queensland.

F. David Fracchia received his B.Sc. from the University of Regina, Canada, in 1986 and a M.Math degree from the University of Waterloo, Canada, in 1988. He is currently pursuing a Ph.D. degree at the University of Regina. His research interests lie in the area of computer graphics, specifically the modeling of natural phenomena, scientific visualization, and physically-based modeling. Mr. Fracchia is a member of the ACM.
Address: Dept. of Computer Science, University of Regina, Regina, Saskatchewan, Canada S4S 0A2

Przemyslaw Prusinkiewicz is an associate professor of Computer Science at the University of Regina, Canada. His research interests include computer graphics, interactive techniques, and computer music. Dr. Prusinkiewicz received his M.S. in 1974 and Ph.D. in 1978, both in computer science, from the Technical University of Warsaw. He is a member of the ACM and IEEE CS.
Address: Dept. of Computer Science, University of Regina, Regina, Saskatchewan, Canada S4S 0A2

Martin J. M. de Boer received his B.Sc. in Biology in 1979, and M.S. in Mathematical Biology in 1984, both from the University of Amsterdam. From 1985 to 1989, he worked with Prof. Lindenmayer as a research assistant with the Theoretical Biology Group at the University of Utrecht, The Netherlands. He received his Ph.D. from the University of Utrecht in 1989.
Address: Theoretical Biology Group, University of Utrecht, Padualaan 8, Utrecht 3584 CH, The Netherlands

Computer-Animated Chemical Models

JACQUES WEBER, PETER FLUEKIGER, and MARTIN J. FIELD

ABSTRACT

Among the vast number of applications recently developed in computer-assisted chemistry, the animation of chemical models is by no means the least important, as it allows one to perform realistic simulations of the properties of gases, liquids and solids. In this context, we report in the present paper two applications dealing with the construction and representation of computer-animated chemical models simulating the following processes: (i) the unimolecular rearrangement of piperidine, a cyclic amine which undergoes interconversion between two conformers; (ii) the harmonic dynamics of urea and L-alanine, two molecular crystals exhibiting independent motions along the normal modes of vibration.

Keywords : molecular graphics ; animated chemical models ; dynamic modeling ; molecular rearrangements ; harmonic dynamics

INTRODUCTION

Through their ability to build, display and manipulate realistic models of chemical objects, molecular graphics techniques play nowadays an important role in molecular sciences (Dubois and others 1985 ; Frühbeis and others 1987). They indeed provide the essential tools in a vast number of applications ranging from drug design (Marshall 1987) to quantitative structure-activity relationships (QSAR) (Hansch and Klein 1986), the search for new materials such as heterogeneous catalysts (Ramdas and others 1984), etc..., all of them fully exploiting the enormous potential of today's supercomputers and powerful graphic workstations.

Molecular graphics (MG) may be defined as the application of computer graphics techniques to investigate molecular structure, function and interaction. In the last few years, MG has known a spectacular development mainly due to considerable progress in both hardware and software available in computer-assisted chemistry. MG techniques have indeed evolved from the static representation of wire-frame molecular architectures to the construction and display of molecular surfaces, volumes and properties allowing the modelization of complex phenomena such as organometallic reactivity or protein docking (Weber and others 1989).

A recent and very important application of MG consists in animating computerized models representative of dynamic chemical processes so as to simulate in vitro or in vivo situations. Indeed, as the collection of atoms constituting one or several molecular structures never remains rigid in normal conditions, real-time dynamic modeling is of prime utility. In this respect, MG is an ideal tool through which to visualize the changes of a system as a function of time and a standard application of computer animation lies today in the dynamic modeling of the atomic trajectories along molecular rearrangements or chemical reaction paths (Weber and others 1983 ; Jefford and others 1984 ; Weber and others 1987). To this end, structural data bases containing the different conformations of the molecular systems along the reaction path must first be calculated using reliable quantum chemical models and the difficulties of such computations should not be underestimated. However, such dynamic modelization has considerable potential for understanding reaction mechanisms and for teaching complex rearrangements which are difficult to preceive using the standard techniques of conformational analysis.

Another group of computer-animated chemical modelization is concerned with thermodynamic and transport properties in liquids and in solids which can be investigated using molecular dynamics simulations. In this case, the aim is to calculate the motions of particles constitutive of matter using potential energy functions describing their interactions (Fincham and Heyes 1985; Wilson 1986). For example, these calculations are used to simulate the normal modes of vibration of molecular crystals or the motion of a substrate entering the active site of an enzyme (White and others 1989). The real-time visualization of the results of molecular dynamics simulations is important as it allows the chemist to comprehend at the microscopic scale the cooperative effects which are responsible for the macroscopic properties of proteins in solution and complex materials as well.

These examples show that the use of dynamic chemical models is of invaluable help in rationalizing and understanding the molecular bases of many chemical processes and material properties as well. In this paper, we present two applications we have recently developed in the field of computer animation in chemistry. The first one is devoted to the representation of a typical rearrangement of piperidine, a cyclic molecule, namely its interconversion from the so-called chair to boat conformation. The second one is the visualization of the harmonic dynamics of the urea and L-alanine crystals.

TECHNICAL ASPECTS

Basically the problem consists in displaying sequentially a large number of conformations previously calculated using a theoretical model and corresponding to the structures obtained through the dynamic process. The animated sequences are then generated on an Evans & Sutherland PS-390 graphics system, using our own function-network. A function-network is a series of commands in a language which is unique to the PS and which builds up hardware-like connections between the input devices (like dials and function-keys), the existing internal functions (which perform for example mathematical or viewing operations), and the display. Unlike a program which is executed step-by-step, a function-network treats all incoming informations instantaneously.

Our function-network is kept very general in order to visualize any kind of animated pictures, such as changes in molecular conformations or orbitals, variations of 3D-plots and so on. The use is, however, restricted to vector-models, because this equipment is not able to animate raster-images.

The pre-calculated objects, which represent one single step of the animation, can be downloaded from the host-computer (in our case a VAX 780) into the local memory and stored in the display list of the graphics system by using the appropriate graphics support routines. To each of these steps is assigned one non-negative integer, and only the step whose number corresponds to the internal 'level of detail' is displayed on the screen. By increasing (or decreasing) this level, one can switch from one step to another and thus run through the whole sequence. As all the steps are in the local memory, their number is limited by the size of the memory, but 6 MB are sufficient to hold more than 100 steps consisting of 4000 vectors each. For smaller objects there is place for more steps and vice versa.

Using dials and function-keys, it is possible to interact with the animated scenario: step-by-step or automated forward or backward sequencing (or both alternating), in one shot or in a loop (for which one can determine the starting- and end-points), and varying the speed from one up to fifty steps per second. In addition, dials can be used for translating, rotating and scaling of the 'moving' objects. Finally, it is possible to generate images made of both animated and static objects, thus including titles, rigid structures, 2D-curves and so on.

APPLICATIONS

1. Dynamic Representation of the Interconversion of the Piperidine Molecule

Among the large number of intramolecular rearrangement processes, the interconversion of cyclic molecules has been the subject of a vast number of experimental and theoretical investigations. In particular, such processes have been studied in detail for six-membered rings because of the interest these compounds present in the chemistry of natural products. As an example, piperidine, a cyclic amine of $C_5H_{11}N$ formula, can exhibit several stable conformations to which correspond different molecular energies (Lambert and Featherstone 1975). The most stable form is the so-called chair conformation, in which the C-H bonds of two adjacent carbon atoms are staggered, whereas in the less stable boat conformation the C-H bonds of the same carbon atoms are eclipsed.

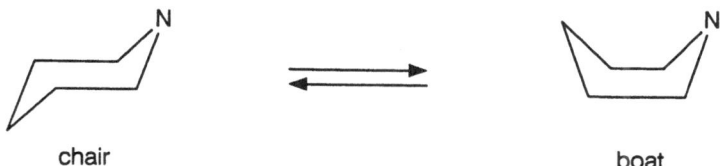

chair   boat

Interconversion from the chair to the boat form, which is a high energy process almost nonexistent at room temperature, requires jumping over the barrier of potential energy separating these different conformers.

The application of dynamic modeling we have developed is designed so as to simultaneously display the deformation of the molecular skeleton and the associated energy curve (figs. 1-3). During the molecular rearrangement, a cursor moves along the energy path and indicates the energy of the displayed conformation. Nineteen well-defined conformations preserving a vertical mirror plane, which ensures a C_s molecular symmetry, have been calculated as intermediate points on the minimum energy reaction path (MERP) between the chair and boat forms, which represents the starting- and end-point of the MERP, respectively. As mentioned in the previous section, the full control of the sequential display of these 21 images allows us to dynamically

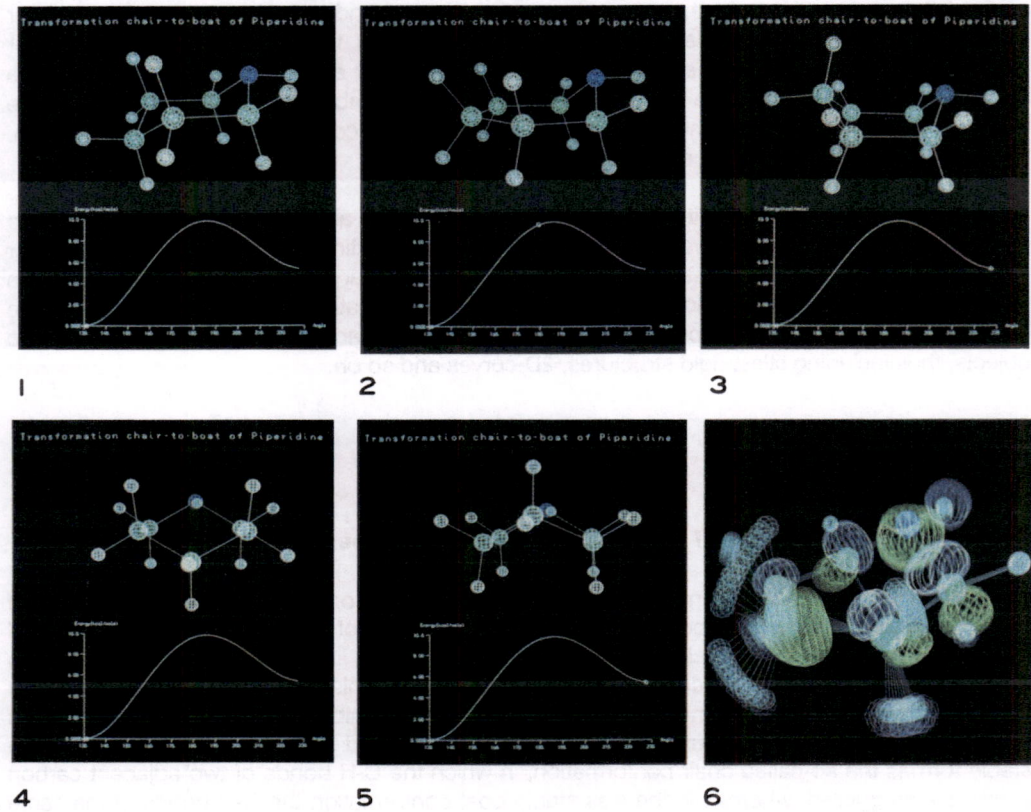

Fig.1   Molecule of piperidine displayed in the chair conformation together with the minimum energy reaction path. The color coding of the atoms is the same for all figures : hydrogen: white, carbon: green, nitrogen: blue and oxygen: red.

Fig.2   Piperidine in an intermediate conformation.

Fig.3   Piperidine in the boat conformation.

Fig.4   Same as fig.1 using a different viewpoint allowing to visualize the staggered C-H bonds.

Fig.5   Same as fig.3 using the viewpoint of fig.4 to visualize the eclipsed C-H bonds.

Fig.6   The lowest unoccupied MO of piperidine represented in blurred motion as iso-amplitude lobes (0.1 atomic units) along the chair-to-boat MERP (positive lobes in yellow, negative ones in pink).

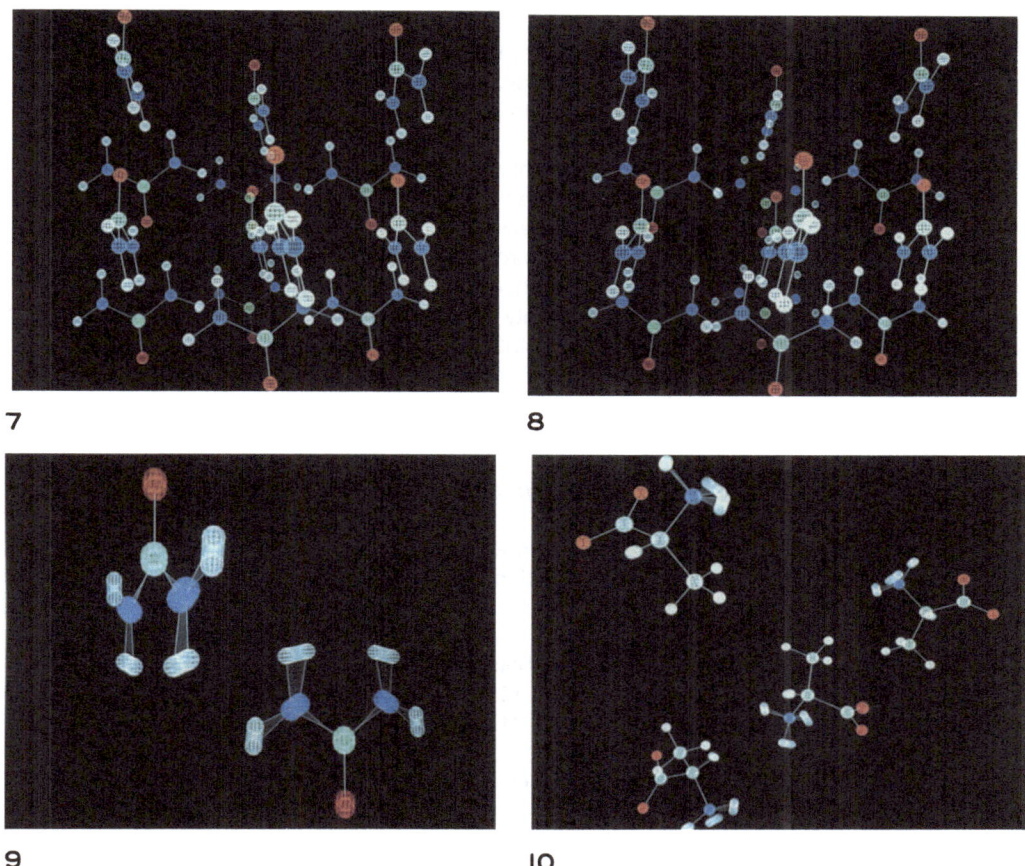

7

8

9

10

Fig.7   Mode 9 shown for 8 unit cells of the urea crystal consisting of 16 molecules. The mode is an out-of-plane bending motion for one of the molecules in the unit cell and an in-plane rocking for the other. The figure displays the atomic positions for one extremum of the motion.

Fig.8   Same as figure 7 but for the other extremum of the motion.

Fig.9   Mode 16 for one unit cell of the urea crystal blurred so as to show the full range of movement for the mode. The mode is an antisymmetrically coupled in-plane N-C-N bend for each molecule.

Fig.10   A blurred picture of mode number 128 for one unit cell (4 molecules) of the L-alanine crystal. The motion for the mode consists primarily of ammonium group H-N-H bending within the molecules.

visualize the rearrangement in any viewing conditions. As any translation, rotation and scaling can be performed on the rearranging structure, the user is able to place the emphasis on any particular stereochemical feature of the process, such as the rotation of the C-H bonds from staggered (fig. 4) to eclipsed (fig. 5) positions along the chair-to-boat reaction path.

In order to also display the changes in electronic properties of the piperidine molecule along its rearrangement process, we simultaneously can represent any of its most reactive molecular orbitals (MOs), which are known to be spatial wave functions describing the behavior of electron pairs within the molecule. To this end, 3D wire-frame lobes corresponding to iso-amplitude values of the MOs are generated and superposed to the rearranging skeleton, allowing us to visualize the deformation of electron density associated with the chair-to-boat reaction mechanism (fig. 6). The simultaneous representation of both structural and electronic features of such rearrangements provides the chemist with a powerful tool for the investigation of reaction mechanisms.

2. The Harmonic Dynamics of Molecular Crystals

Molecular crystals are important because they are of interest in their own right and because they can act as models of more complex, aperiodic systems, such as proteins. There is an abundance of high quality experimental data for crystals and the theoretical methods used to describe them are among the most highly developed for any condensed phase system. Therefore, their study provides an ideal "test-bed" for the application and testing of theoretical techniques (Kitaigorodskii 1973; Wright 1987). Molecular graphics is essential when attempting to visualize the structure or dynamical behavior of even the simplest of molecular crystals.

In the present study the harmonic dynamics, i.e. the analysis of normal modes of vibration, of two crystals, urea and L-alanine, was investigated using an empirical potential energy function model. Urea and L-alanine were chosen because they are important biomolecules and so can be used to test parameters for a protein or nucleic acid force field. Each of them possesses an excellent low-temperature crystal structure (Destro and others 1988; Swaminathan and others 1984) and there is extensive data on their infrared and Raman spectra and other aspects of their dynamics (Kosic and others 1984; Durman and others 1988). The behavior of the crystal is particularly sensitive to the non-bonded parameters (atomic partial charges and van der Waals parameters) in the potential energy function.

A full dynamical simulation of a crystal is very complicated and so a useful first step is to look at the harmonic dynamics instead (Brooks and others 1988). In the harmonic approximation the full dynamics of a crystal can be approximated as a sum over independent motions along the normal modes for the zero wave-vector (the infrared and Raman sensitive modes) and for all other wave-vectors within the Brillouin zone (the phonon modes of the crystal). Calculation and visualization of these modes is important because motions of individual modes (or combinations of them) help determine how a crystal will respond to externally-applied stresses or what reactions will occur within it. Such studies are very useful as tools for engineering crystals to exhibit particular properties or to undergo specific reactions (Wright 1987).

All the dynamics calculations presented here were performed using the CHARMM molecular mechanics program (Brooks and others 1983), which includes the recent developments of Field and Karplus (1989) for the analysis of normal modes of vibration of crystals. The dynamics trajectories for each normal mode were generated with the following procedure :

a.   The crystal was constructed using the experimentally determined structure with the CHARMM program.

b.   The geometry of the crystal was optimized to give a minimum energy structure subject to the constraint that the symmetry remained the same. The minimizations were performed for all intramolecular degrees of freedom. The lattice was kept fixed at the experimental value.

c.   The normal modes of the crystal were calculated for the minimum energy structure by computing and diagonalizing the dynamical matrix at the zero wave-vector (Born and Huang 1954; Maradudin and others 1971; Warshel and Lifson 1970).

d.   Dynamics trajectories were computed for selected normal modes or combinations of them. The amplitude of motion of the mode was set so as to represent the motion at a temperature of 300K and each mode cycle was represented by 50 frames of dynamics.

We viewed a large number of the dynamics trajectories for the 48 modes of urea and the 156 modes of L-alanine but we have chosen to display in the paper only two modes for urea and one for L-alanine. The urea modes are number 9 (figs. 7 and 8) which is one of a pair of degenerate E-symmetry modes with a calculated frequency of 126 cm^{-1} and mode 16 (fig. 9) which has a frequency of 445 cm^{-1} and is of A symmetry. The L-alanine mode is number 128 (fig. 10). It is of B2 symmetry and has a frequency of 1637 cm^{-1}.

CONCLUSIONS

In this paper, we have presented two applications of dynamic molecular modeling recently developed in order to display computer-animated chemical models. This technique is very useful for representing complex processes such as molecular rearrangements and for investigating the harmonic dynamics of molecular crystals. It is seen that, in each case, the use of animated chemical models is an ideal tool for an in-depth perception of such dynamical processes. In addition, it may be used to simulate processes of activation such as enzymatic reactions and ligand binding in proteins. Finally, computer experiments allowing the investigation and the prediction of the dynamic properties of liquids and solids may be performed today on a routine basis. They enable chemists to investigate transport properties of liquids, for example, leading thus to a so-called computer-assisted molecular engineering with an almost unlimited range of new applications such as drug design and the conception of new materials.

ACKNOWLEDGEMENTS

The authors are grateful to Drs. P.Y.Morgantini and R.Houriet for fruitful discussions. This work is part of project 20-25317.88 of the Swiss National Science Foundation.

REFERENCES

Born M, Huang K (1954) Dynamical theory of crystal lattices. Clarendon Press, Oxford

Brooks BR, Bruccoleri RE, Olafson BD, States DJ, Swaminathan S, Karplus M (1983) CHARMM : A program for macromolecular energy, minimization and dynamics calculations. J. Comput. Chem. 4 : 187-217

Brooks III CL, Karplus M, Pettitt BM (1988) Proteins : A theoretical perspective of dynamics, structure and thermodynamics. Adv. Chem. Phys. 71 : 1-259

Destro R, Marsh RE, Bianchi R (1988) A low-temperature (23K) study of L-alanine. J. Phys. Chem. 92 : 966-973

Dubois JE, Laurent D, Weber J (1985) Chemical ideograms and molecular computer graphics. Visual Computer 1 : 49-64

Durman R, Jayasooriya UA, Kettle SFA (1988) LO-TO effects in the single-crystal Raman spectra of urea. J. Phys. Chem. 92 : 620-622

Fincham D, Heyes DM (1985) Recent advances in molecular-dynamics computer simulation. Adv. Chem. Phys. 63 : 493-575

Frühbeis M, Klein R, Wallmeier H (1987) Computer-assisted molecular design (CAMD) - An overview. Angew. Chem. Int. Ed. Engl. 26 : 403-418

Hansch C, Klein T (1986) Molecular graphics and QSAR in the study of enzyme-ligand interactions. On the definition of bioreceptors. Acc. Chem. Res. 19 : 392-400

Jefford CW, Mareda J, Combremont JJ, Weber J (1984) Dynamic molecular modelling. The case of rearranging C_8H_9 cations. Chimia 38 : 354-356

Kitaigorodskii AI (1973) Molecular crystals and molecules. Academic Press, New York

Kosic TJ, Cline, Jr RE, Dlott DD (1984) Picosecond coherent Raman investigation of the relaxation of low frequency vibrational modes in amino acids and peptides. J. Chem. Phys. 81 : 4932-4949

Lambert JB, Featherstone SI (1975) Conformational analysis of pentamethylene heterocycles. Chem. Rev. 75 : 611-626

Maradudin AA, Montroll EW, Weiss GH, Ipatava P (1971) Theory of lattice dynamics in the harmonic approximation. Academic Press, New York

Marshall GR (1987) Computer-aided drug design. Ann. Rev. Pharmacol. Toxicol. 27 : 193-213

Ramdas S, Thomas JM, Betteridge PW, Cheetham AK, Davies EK (1984) Modelling the chemistry of zeolites. Angew. Chem. Int. Ed. Engl. 23 : 671-679

Swaminathan S, Craven BM, McMullan RK (1984) The crystal structure and molecular thermal motion of urea at 12, 60 and 123K from neutron diffraction. Acta Cryst. B40 : 300-306

Warshel A, Lifson S (1970) Consistent force field calculations. II. Crystal structures, sublimation energies, molecular and lattice vibrations, molecular conformations and enthalpies of alkanes. J. Chem. Phys. 53 : 582-594

Weber J, Fluekiger P, Morgantini PY, Schaad O, Goursot A, Daul C (1988) The modelling of nucleophilic and electrophilic additions to organometallic complexes using molecular graphics techniques. J. Comput. Aid. Mol. Design 2 : 235-253

Weber J, Mottier D, Carrupt PA, Vogel P (1987) Dynamic modeling of chemical reactions : the Diels-Alder cycloaddition. J. Mol. Graphics 5 : 126-128

Weber J, Roch M, Combremont JJ, Vogel P, Carrupt PA (1983) Dynamic representation of quantum chemical results using computer graphics : molecular rearrangements, art or science ? J. Mol. Struct. Theochem 93 : 189-200

White DNJ, Ruddock JN, Edgington PR (1989) Molecular mechanics. In: Richards W.G. (ed) Computer-aided molecular design. IBC Technical Services, London, pp 23-41

Wilson S (1986) Chemistry by computer. An overview of the applications of computers in chemistry. Plenum, New York

Wright JD (1987) Molecular crystals. Cambridge University Press, Cambridge

Jacques Weber is currently a professor of computer-assisted chemistry at the Department of Physical Chemistry of the University of Geneva. After completion of his Ph.D. thesis in chemical physics in Geneva (1969), he spent two years as a post-doc in the USA, working at the Quantum Theory Project of the University of Florida and at the IBM Research Laboratory of San Jose (California). Back at the University of Geneva, he founded in 1975 the Laboratory of Computational Chemistry, which he has headed since then. His research interests include computational quantum chemistry, Monte Carlo and molecular dynamics simulations, and molecular graphics. In his recent research projects, supported by the Swiss Science Foundation, Weber is combining different techniques deriving from these various fields so as to develop interactive molecular graphics tools for the prediction and interpretation of organometallic reaction mechanisms. Weber was the organizer, or a member of the scientific committee, of several international congresses in computational chemistry and molecular graphics; in addition, he has authored and published over 130 refereed scientific papers in a broad range of chemistry and computer science journals.

Address: Department of Physical Chemistry, University of Geneva, 30 quai Ernest Ansermet, 1211 Geneva 4, Switzerland.

Peter Fluekiger received his M.Sc. in chemistry from the University of Geneva in 1987. He is now a graduate student in the Department of Physical Chemistry of this University. The main theme of his Ph.D. thesis is closely related to the calculation and representation of molecular properties on high-performance graphics equipments.

Address: Department of Physical Chemistry, University of Geneva, 30 quai Ernest Ansermet, 1211 Geneva 4, Switzerland.

Martin J. Field did his undergraduate education at Cambridge in England. He obtained his Ph.D in 1985 from Manchester University under the supervision of Professor Ian Hillier by investigating simple reactions using ab initio molecular quantum mechanics. The next four years were spent at Harvard with Professor Martin Karplus working on crystals and combined quantum mechanical/molecular mechanical potential energy functions. He is currently doing research in the chemistry and biochemistry laboratories at the University of Geneva where his main interest is the development and use of theoretical techniques for the study of reactions and excited state processes in chemical and biochemical condensed phase systems.

Address: Department of Physical Chemistry, University of Geneva, 30 Quai Ernest Ansermet, 1211 Geneva 4, Switzerland.

Applications of Scientific Visualization to Meteorological Data Analysis and Animation

Philip C. Chen

ABSTRACT

Multi-variate data analysis and scientific visualization techniques available on a supercomputer-workstation environment were applied for producing animations of meteorological parameters. Through experimenting, animations of individual and combined parameters were used to investigate evolutions of winter cyclone systems. The results indicate an animation with combined parameters reveals important cyclonic development mechanisms which could not have been seen by an animation with individual parameter.

Keywords: animation, meteorology, supercomputing, raytracing, volumetric rendering

1. INTRODUCTION

Traditionally, meteorological data have been analyzed with two-dimensional charts on pressure surfaces or height levels. Data were mostly presented by showing a single-surface or multi-layer view as exemplified by Klemp and Rotunno (1984). With this type of data representation, a three-dimensional structure is hard to grasp. Recently, some research has been done, for example by Hibbard (1987) and Grotjahn (1986), to use three-dimensional animation to study mesoscale severe weather phenomena, including thunderstorms and tornados. In this type of research, several meteorological parameters were displayed, and each parameter was depicted by a different color or symbol. By viewing the animation of these parameters a meteorologist infers the interactions among them. The type and number of meteorological parameters are not fixed. However, parameters often used are: wind vectors, streamlines, temperature, water vapor, cloud water and rain content. Occasionally, derived parameters such as vorticity and divergence are also incorporated into data display.

To look at parameters simultaneously is the first step toward understanding parameter interactions. However, choices of parameters are often undefined and somewhat arbitrary, and what is to be investigated is often ambiguous. This uncertainty in parameter selection for visualization may be due to the fact that habitually most meteorologists have been studying parameters separately. Therefore, parameters are still being viewed as separate entities without regard to underlying physical laws that control their interactions, even when several parameters are presented.

This paper presents a case study illustrating how to select and visualize important parameters. The important scientific discoveries in relation to the understanding of the evolution of cyclonic weather systems will be discussed. Additionally, computational environment, data preparation, and visualization techniques will be introduced.

2.   COMPUTATIONAL AND VISUALIZATION ENVIRONMENT

The major computations were done on supercomputers.   The advantage of using supercomputers for visualization has been discussed elsewhere by Chen (1988).   A provided database was originally generated from a CRAY X-MP/48.   Parameter dataset preparations were done on the CRAY complex including X-MP's, Y-MP's, and CRAY2.   The computations for generating visual images were conducted on a CRAY X-MP/18.

The original database was generated under CRAY Operating System (COS), all other remaining data processing activities were done under UNIX operating systems.

The graphics software system OASIS, which is the acronym of Our Animation-Simulation Interactive System, was provided to the author by the CRAY Research, Inc.   This software system has modeling, rendering, frame generation and animation capabilities.   This system was implemented on SUN and IRIS workstations as well as on CRAY machines, and it was used by the author to do the data analysis and visualization.   The OASIS rendering algorithm is using raytracing technique, and it has transparency feature capable of volumetric rendering.

The computers used in this research were networked, so that data could be transferred to/from any computer and software programs in OASIS could be executed from any computer.   In practice, however, each type of computer was used for special purposes: supercomputer for video frame generation, workstation for animation preview and image file storage, and the IRIS workstation with SONY U-Matic deck for video recording.

3.   DATA PREPARATION

A database containing 168 hours worth of forecast data was created by a numerical weather prediction model run on a CRAY X-MP/48 at the European Centre for Medium-Range Weather Forecasts (ECMWF), U.K.   The database includes meteorological parameter data of geopotential, temperature, specific humidity, vertical velocity, vorticity, divergence, relative humidity, and horizontal u, v wind components. The parameter data were recorded in World Meteorological Organization (WMO) Gridded Binary (GRIB) format, which is hourly data format.

The database size is portrayed as follows: each parameter, which has data for 91x47 horizontal grids and 14 pressure levels, has about 60K data values for each hour.   For 168 hours, there are about 10 Mega data values.   Provided that each data value is stored with 32 bits (4 bytes), the size of a 168-hour database is about 40 Mega bytes.   For 9 parameters, there are about 360 Mega bytes -- a formidable data size for any computer to accommodate.   The database was further processed by CRAY supercomputers, which are equipped with large storage devices, until each meteorological parameter had its own dataset.
With these individual meteorological parameter dataset available, further data processing and visualization became quite easy.   One did not have to go through voluminous sequential hourly multiple meteorological data to retrieve a particular meteorological parameter or parameters; instead one could obtain data from smaller processed datasets.   This is like retrieving data from a well-structured database.

4. DATA ANALYSIS AND VISUALIZATION

The data analysis and visualization involve parameter selection and derivation, image creation, pseudo-animation, and video production steps. These steps are clarified as follows:

4.1 Parameter Selection and Derivation

As a demonstration case, a minimum set of meteorological parameters, which includes kinetic energy, potential temperature and water vapor specific humidity, is chosen for studying weather phenomena. The kinetic energy and potential temperature are derived parameters which can be computed from parameter data provided by processed datasets. The kinetic energy is computed by using horizontal wind components u, v datasets. The potential temperature is computed by using pressure and temperature datasets. The exact formulas used for computing kinetic energy and potential temperature can be found in a basic meteorology text book. The water vapor specific humidity data need not be computed, as they are provided by a water vapor dataset.

The selection of parameters is based largely on energy conservation law and energy transferring between different energy forms. By selecting kinetic energy other than wind components u, v expressed in scalar (speed) or vector (arrow) form, one can perceive how the kinetic energy was transported horizontally and vertically, and how it would relate to cyclone formation. By selecting potential temperature rather than temperature itself, one can see how thermodynamic quantity -- entropy or heat content -- is related to the storm. By selecting specific humidity, one can visualize the outline and structure of a weather system.

4.2 Image Creation

This step is the beginning of data visualization. The outcome of this step will affect animation quality. In this research, an image was created considering contour values, viewing perspective, and object lighting.

An hourly data of a parameter with a try-out contour value was pre-processed to a data file with a format acceptable to an OASIS rendering program -- Clockwork. A graphic image file containing three-dimensional and rendered iso-contouring surfaces with a trial viewing perspective and lighting conditions was created by the Clockwork on a CRAY computer. This graphics image file was then downloaded to SUN or IRIS workstations for viewing, using an OASIS program -- Display. The image creation and viewing process was repeated until a satisfactory image was obtained.

Once determined, the contouring intervals, perspective, and lighting will be applied to all images to be generated for animation production.

4.3 Pseudo-Animation

Since the SUN and IRIS workstations used for this research did not provide fast playback capability, a pseudo-animation technique was used for preview. The pseudo-animation technique, which consists of viewing images at low frame rate and a low image resolution, is elaborated as follows:

A low spatial and temporal resolution animation with sequential video image frames produced by Cray machines were downloaded to a graphics workstation. Frames generated in this animation have typically 128x128 pixel resolution, and were produced by skipping every 5 time-step (hourly) records. Using a prescribed script file as an input to the Display program without human intervention, these frames were displayed automatically on a workstation. The motion of contoured features displayed with low raster rate -- about a frame per second -- could be perceived by paying special attention to feature displacements.

If the motion proved satisfactory, one proceeded to the next step. Otherwise, it was back to the previous step for determining contour levels, perspective, and lighting.

4.4 Video Production

In this step, the animation sequence of a parameter or parameters was produced on the CRAY computers with full spatial resolution (512x512 pixels) and fine temporal (hourly) images. This animation sequence consists of rendered video images generated by raytracing with volume transparency. Generated video images in tri-color (red,green,and blue) format were transported via network to workstations and recorded onto a video tape.

5. CASE STUDY

5.1 Background

The database used in this research was originally applied to weather prediction operations in the ECMWF. The database was generated by running the ECMWF numerical weather prediction model, using February 4, 1988, 1200 GMT global observation data as input. The model run provided 168 hours of predicted parameter data. A rapidly developed winter cyclone, which originated near Newfoundland, travelled across the Atlantic Ocean, became intensified, and remained stationary over the European Continent for several days. This winter cyclone was accurately predicted by the model. The two-dimensional line graphics visualization done by Soederman (1988), was showing good agreements between the observed and predicted temperatures and sea-surface pressures. Motivated by the successful numerical model prediction, the ECMWF staff prepared a fine-resolution database with area covering the Atlantic Ocean and part of European Continent for further studies. In this research, the graphics data analyses were done in three dimensions with animation, and the analyses were using more than basic parameters provided by the database.

5.2 Results of Parameter Animation

Due to time constraint and limited resources, not all available meteorological parameters were analyzed. However, as mentioned in section 4.1, as a minimum set, analyzed parameters include derived parameters kinetic energy and potential temperature; and basic parameter water vapor specific humidity.

Parameter animation results including kinetic energy, water vapor specific humidity and potential temperature will be shown during the video presentation at the conference. Highlights of animations in this paper are shown in Figs. 1 to 4. The base map, showing the geographical area coverage of the Atlantic Ocean and Western Europe, is shown in cyan. The outline of Greenland is visible, and the outline of the British Isles is masked by yellow.

Figures 1 to 3 show composite fields of kinetic energy and water vapor specific humidity at predicted hours of 113, 125 and 135. These hours correspond to hours on February 9 to 10, 1988 when the cyclone in question was in the fullest developmental stage. For the kinetic energy field: cloud-like white features, with some exhibiting red enclosures, are situated in middle and upper air and contain high energies. Two energy divisions, from 1,000 to 2,000 and from 2,000 to 3,600 m^2/sec, are colored in white and red. For water vapor specific humidity field: terrain-like, yellow and purple features near the surface of earth contain water vapor. Two water vapor specific humidity ranges, from 3 to 6 g/kg and from 12 to 22 g/kg, are colored in yellow and purple.

Figure 4 is a snap shot of potential temperature at the 120th hour when the cyclone became nearly stationary. The temperatures ranging from 295 to 305K are colored in white.

The case study deserves more detailed analyses together with other non-graphics quantitative assessment studies. However, preliminary results obtained from viewing repeatedly the video tape already reveal important cyclonic structural features relating to development mechanisms. The results that can be concluded are listed as follows:

• Kinetic energy field clearly shows tropospheric jet-stream structure in the middle altitude. The jet structure depicted by kinetic energy iso-contours is much more effective than that depicted by other meteorological parameters, such as momentum or wind vector. Examples of such structures are shown in Figs. 1-3, colored in white and red.

• Water vapor specific humidity field shows structures unknown to most meteorologists. A terrain-like summit indicates a cyclonic storm center, and a ridge/trough indicates a frontal zone in three dimensions. Examples of such storm structure are shown in Figs. 1-3, colored in yellow and purple.

• Potential temperature field and water vapor specific humidity field show near-circular structures associated with a cyclonic storm. Examples of such structure are shown in Figs. 3 and 4.

• Animation of kinetic energy shows that the jet structure changes shape constantly, as is shown in Figs. 1-3. The wedge-like configuration is generally associated with a cyclone.

• Animation of water vapor specific humidity shows that iso-surfaces are driven by winds, and the motion of surface is three-dimensional, with evidence of vertical oscillation relating to gravity waves.

• As realized in Figs. 1-3, composite animation of kinetic energy and water vapor specific humidity shows that the two fields are closely related. The evidence of a middle atmospheric jet feeding energy

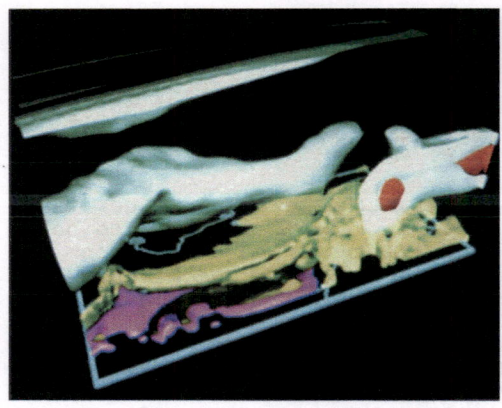

Fig. 1. Kinetic energy and water vapor specific humidity at hour 118.

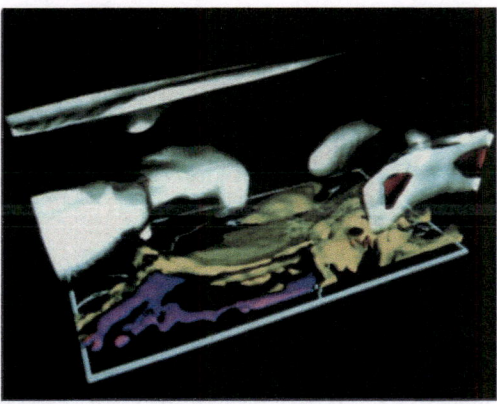

Fig. 2. Kinetic energy and water vapor specific humidity at hour 125.

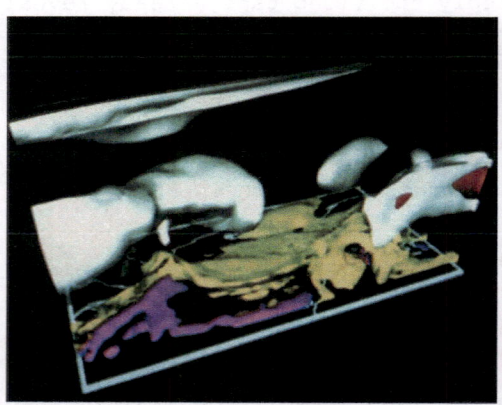

Fig. 3. Kinetic energy and water vapor specific humidity at hour 135.

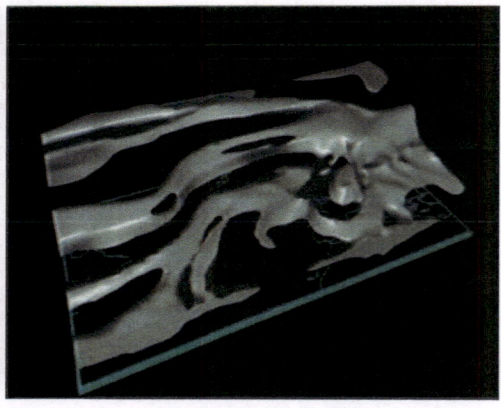

Fig. 4. Potential temperature at hour 120.

to a cyclone near the ground for its further development can be seen from the composite animation with a white-colored, funnel-like feature, as shown in Figs. 2 and 3.

• Animation of potential temperature shows that the near-circular structure at one time became nearly stationary, and motion was confined to a downward direction. This is evidence of an air subsidence during a later stage of cyclonic life cycle.

6. CONCLUSIONS

The supercomputer-workstation environment provided to the author was vital for completing this research in a short time. The production of this research project was accomplished within three months. If no supercomputers were used for object rendering and frame generation, a much longer time -- typically a year would be required.

This research demonstrates to meteorologists that with the proper computation and production environment, one can:

- do the undone: volumetric representation of a weather system with basic and derived meteorological parameters

- see the unseen: cyclone evolution in three-dimensional time animation

- know the unknown: middle atmosphere may supply kinetic and thermal energies and be responsible for triggering the growth of low-level cyclone

For future research, more parameters will be analyzed and more cases will be studied. Similar analyses of other meteorological parameters can be accomplished by the methods presented here, and they may shed more light on understanding the evolution weather systems in general.

7. REFERENCES

Chen, PC (1988) Computer graphics systems. Workshop of Graphics in Meteorology, November 31 to December 5. Proceeding, European Centre for Medium-Range Weather Forecasts, U.K.: 111-132.

Grotjahn, R, and Chervin, RM (1984) Animated Graphics in Meteorological Research and Presentations. Bull. Amer. Meteo. Soc., 65: 1201-1208.

Hibbard, WL (1986) Computer-Generated Imagery for 4-D Meteorological Data. Bull. Amer. Meteo. Soc., 67: 1362-1369.

Klemp, JB, and Rotunno, R (1984) Taking a Good Look at Data. NCAR Annual Report for 1984. Report NCAR/AR-84: 46-49.

Soederman, D (1988) Visualization of the development of an extratropical cyclone. Palmen Memorial Symposium on Extratropical cyclones, August 29 to September 2. Proceeding, Amer. Meteo. Soc.: 301-304.

ACKNOWLEDGEMENTS

The author wishes to thank the ECMWF's Graphics Project Leader Mr. J. Daabeck, who provided me with initial research time and a database. The author also wishes to thank Cray Research, Inc. for providing staff and material supports, especially Mr. G. Lorig, Ms. J. Ingle, Ms. N. Howe, and Mr. G. Phillips for their analyst support, and Mr. D. Blaskovich and Mr. B. Jastremski for their computer resources. Thanks are extended to Jet Propulsion Laboratory, Supercomputing Project staff's Dr. C. Kukkonen and Ms. P. Olsen who gave me free access to CRAY X-MP/18 during the project's shake-down and promotion period from August to October, 1989.

Philip C. Chen is currently engaged in supercomputing and scientific visualization. In winter, 1988, he worked as a consultant to the ECMWF in the area of scientific visualization and meteorology research. He participated in the ECMWF four-year plan for graphics system upgrading of supercomputing environment; set up guidelines for selections of graphics systems; and engaged in prototyping for a graphics system. He worked for Digital Productions from 1983-1987 in computer graphics software and system development. He was credited for working in the movies:
The Last Starfighter, The Year 2010 - A Space Odyssey, and Labyrinth. Prior to 1983, he worked as meteorologist in industry and in universities. Chen received his BSc in meteorology from National Taiwan University, and MS and PhD in meteorology from University of California at Los Angeles.
Address: 6959 Oakdale Ave, Canoga Park, California 91306, U.S.A.

Part II
Human Modeling
and Animation

Directing an Animated Scene with Autonomous Actors

Roberto Maiocchi and Barbara Pernici

ABSTRACT

PINOCCHIO is a motion control system for computer animation designed for the use by animators in controlling the motion of a puppet. The main goal in PINOCCHIO is to provide digital description of human movements for replication of real movements as closely as possible.

For this purpose, movements are digitized using Elite, a 3D vision system based on a two level architecture reflecting the hierarchical structure of vision in living beings. A general movement dictionary has been developed to classify movements and their attributes using entries from natural language, and each movement in the dictionary has been stored in a motion database where it is available for display. Sequences of movements of the characters acting in an animated scene are specified by the animator through an animation script, then the characters themselves take care of the coordination issues related to the scene.

In this paper we focus on two of the main features of PINOCCHIO: the movement database and the object-oriented mechanism for controlling transitions between sequences of motions specified by animators in a script.

Keywords: human movement, motion recording, movement sequences, animation script, object-oriented synchronization.

Art and Science meet when they both seek accuracy

Etienne-Jules Marey (1888)

1. INTRODUCTION

The complexity of the motion of the human body has attracted the attention of fine artists first, and then of scientists. Perhaps, Etienne-Jules Marey (1984) and Eadweard Muybridge (1955) can be chosen to mark the borderline between the artistic and the scientific approach to human movement.

At the end of the last century, through use of a newborn tool, the photographic camera, both studied human motion by taking stills of mimes performing everyday life actions, the former, Marey, visualizing the trajectories described by joints and limbs during the motion, the latter, Muybridge, observing motions from different points of view.

Since the beginning of the scientific inquiry of human motion, it became apparent that three prerequisites were needed for studying it (Badler 1979): a representation of the human body, a representation of movement, and a notation for movement description.

The general issues of human movement observation raised by Marey and Muybridge have been faced in the last century by various disciplines. For instance, in choreography different notations for recording human movement have been developed (Labanotation, Eshkol-Wachmann notation, Benesh notation) where the body has been viewed just as a set of joints and limbs. In robotics, on the other hand, the need for precise control of anthropomorphic robots makes necessary the use of dynamics for movement description; for this purpose, languages for motion specification that allow to set directly the values of the parameters in the movement equations have been implemented (Raibert 1986).

Modeling human motion is also one of the main challenges of computer animation (Badler 1979, IEEE Computer Graphics and Applications 1982, 1987). Two main approaches have been followed for animating the human figure, the kinematic approach and the dynamic approach. With the **kinematic approach**, motion control is achieved through the positioning of certain joints or limbs of a body model and computing algorithmically position and orientation of the others without taking into account the causes of motion; on the other hand, in the **dynamic approach** the body is manipulated by forces and torques rather than positions: the component segments of the figure are assumed to have a mass and the joints have springs to model the mechanical properties of muscles.

Major drawbacks of both approaches are not only the computational time required for solving the equations describing the motion, but also the difficulty in finding realistic movement laws, which causes movements that generally appear too regular, and the complexity in defining the movements through angles, torques, and forces.

In this paper, we present PINOCCHIO, a motion control system for computer animation under development at the Dipartimento di Elettronica, Politecnico di Milano, Italy. The main goal of PINOCCHIO is to provide digital descriptions of human movements for replication of real movements as closely as possible. For this reason, movements performed by real actors are recorded using Elite, a 3D vision system created at the Centro di Bioingegneria, Fdn. Pro Juventute, Politecnico di Milano, Italy.

Few motion recording systems have been proposed in literature in the past. For instance, the purpose of the system illustrated in Calvert, Chapman, and Patla (1980) was to obtain an animation system supporting the integration of analog inputs derived directly from actual movements through use of electro-goniometers with symbolic inputs (Labanotation commands) chosen to produce the desired movement, in order to overcome the disadvantages of each single approach in animating the human figure. In Ginsberg and Maxwell (1983), it was theorized that the most natural and effective way of accomplishing motion representation is to have an actor directly perform the motions that will be interpreted graphically. Then, the versatility of traditional character animation can be achieved by parametrizing the motion to produce effects that depart from realism.

With respect to these proposals, distinctive aspects of PINOCCHIO are the introduction of features that facilitate the user in designing an animation script and the autonomy of the characters in performing a specified scene. A **general movement dictionary** has been developed to classify **movements** and **movement attributes** using entries from natural language. Tokens of the dictionary correspond to **elementary motions**, i.e., motions that we consider not decomposable in submotions. Each elementary motion has been recorded with Elite and stored in a **motion database** where it is available for display.

An animation language allows sequences of motions to be described as a formal, written script. The language for specifying scripts is based on the movement dictionary mentioned above and allows animators to work in terms of body positions and movement database entries as "walk forward". An

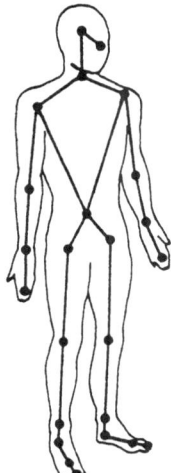

Fig.1. The stick model used for acquisitions with the ELITE 3D vision system

object-oriented mechanism is associated to the movements retrieved from the motion database for synchronizing the characters in a scene. This mechanism allows the animator to specify only high-level coordination constraints for the sequence of movements, without handling explicitly low-level movement descriptions.

In this paper, our main goals are to present the movement database developed in PINOCCHIO and to discuss the object-oriented mechanism for controlling a scene. The presentation is organized as follows.

In Section 2., we describe shortly the basic concepts and assumptions of PINOCCHIO, i.e., the representation of the human body, the representation of movement, the notation for movement description on which the movement database has been built, and the method for graphic interpolation between movements. Section 3. is dedicated to the introduction of an object-oriented environment for animation based on scripts. In Section 4., a detailed description of the coordination mechanism is given through the example of an animated scene requiring synchronization of various characters, i.e., the exchange of the baton in a relay race. Conclusions are finally drawn in Section 5., and future developments of the system are envisioned.

2. BASICS OF PINOCCHIO

2.1 Representing the Human Body

In PINOCCHIO we look at movements performed by the entire body. Animation of human movement requires a specification of the body as an object for display. In literature, there are three general methods for modeling the human body (Badler 1979): stick figures, surface models, and volume models.

For our purposes, a **stick figure model** is taken, i.e., a skeleton made up of a collection of body segments and joints arranged as in Fig. 1. To solve some of the problems inherent in this assumption, such as difficulties in visualizing depth, for display we can make the skeleton wear a 3D outfit (Fig. 2.) designed following the description of the puppet Pinocchio by the Italian writer Carlo Collodi in the book that gives the name to the system (Collodi 1883).

2.2 Representing Movement

In PINOCCHIO, movements are represented as sequences of positions of the joints of the stick figure. The tool used to collect and record movements is Elite (Ferrigno and Pedotti 1985), a 3D vision system aiming at the support of human movement analysis in biomedical applications. Such analysis is performed by marking joints on the human body with passive markers and following their trajectories during body movements. Depending on the particular analysis to be performed, a specific stick model of the parts of the body to be analyzed is to be chosen, placing markers at joints as, for instance, in Fig. 1.

Elite is based on a two level architecture reflecting the hierarchical structure of vision in living beings (see Fig. 3). The first level, hardware implemented, receives the image from a set of TV cameras and recognizes in real-time (10 msec) the markers on the scene. Markers are simple hemispherical pieces of reflective paper which are recognized only on the basis of their shape. The second level, software implemented, performs a more intelligent task, i.e., matching the surveyed markers coordinates to the arrangement predefined in the model. A specially designed program called KAT (Knowledge-based Automatic Tracking) automatically tracks down each marker frame by frame reconstructing the coordinates of each marker even when overlapping of body segments occurs. This procedure is based on trajectory prediction and on body modeling. After this procedure, a 3D reconstruction is carried out by means of a generalized triangulation algorithm starting from the images recorded by a couple of TV cameras. The system is then completed with the 3D resection and calibration algorithms. The first allows the recovering of TV cameras geometrical parameters requested in 3D reconstruction; the calibration algorithm, on the other hand, allows distortion correction and leads to a final high accuracy in the computation of 3D markers position.

2.3 Classification of Movements

Several authors are investigating the expressiveness of natural language for the specification of human movement. For example, the classification of English verbs of motion proposed in Miller (1972) has been used in Tsotsos, Mylopoulos, Covvey, and Zucker (1980) to realize a motion analysis system. More recently, in the attempt to represent the dynamic qualities of human movement for the purposes of animation, the so called "Effort-Shape" analysis has been proposed (Badler 1986).

In Camurri, Morasso, Tagliasco, and Zaccaria (1986), in the framework of robotics research, a general movement dictionary which lists entries from natural language is presented.

Natural language provides a large dictionary of movement-related terms which express **motor knowledge**. These terms are commonly used to define movements and their attributes; different forms of the same movement are distinguished through specification of different attributes related to a motion verb. Each verb of motion with its attributes may be considered as an elementary movement which is not decomposable in submotions.

The digital representation of each elementary movement is recorded using Elite as described in the foregoing subsection, and constitutes an entry of the motion database underlying PINOCCHIO. Additional annotations for each entry are its natural language description, its initial position in space and time, and other parameters characterizing the motion (e.g., speed).

A general movement grammar is used to classify movements in the motion database. The grammar has the aim of giving a **qualitative** description of human motion in natural language terms, and does not pretend to be an exhaustive dictionary for human movement description. Additional entries may then be entered following the general classification scheme.

In the grammar, every movement can be considered as an **elementary motion**, i.e., not decomposable in submotions, performed by humans. Motions, referred to as verbs or verbal expressions, are classified as follows:

Fig.2. The 3D character displaying motion

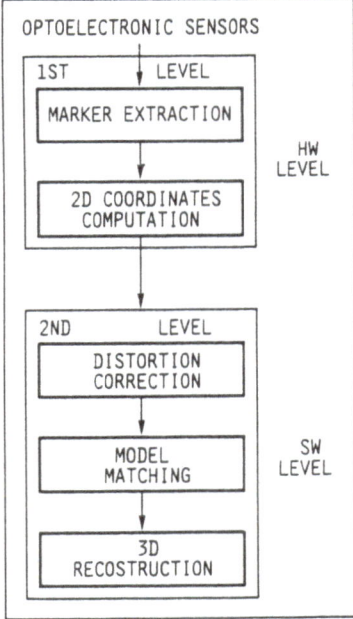

Fig.3. The hierarchical organization of ELITE vision system

- **transition**: verbs in this class describe motions that do not imply any displacement or direct interaction with the environment, but just on-site transitions from an initial posture to a different final posture, e.g., "Raise";

- **locomotion**: verbs in this class describe movements specifying a spatial displacement from an initial position to a final position, e.g., "Walk";

- **environment**: actions that imply manipulation of external objects, e.g., "Lift";

- **communication**: finally, in this class actions with paralinguistic meaning are specified, e.g., "Nod".

Additional parameters used to qualify an action are adjectives and adverbs classified as follows:

- **space** and **time** attributes relate to the description of locomotion, e.g., "Walk Forward Fast"

- **object** and **position** attributes describe the kind of interaction with the environment, e.g., "Lift Up Heavy"

- finally, in the class named **qualitative_aspects**, attributes specifying the way in which a motion is performed are classified, e.g., "Raise Slowly"

The movement grammar is presented in Appendix 1. For instance, the motion of a runner that starts his run in a race can be described as follows:

```
initial_position: Kneeled
locomotion: Run
space: Forward Straight Horizontal
time: Fast Accelerating Continuous
final_position: Erect
```

2.4 Interpolation between Movements

Elementary motions can be combined to describe complex actions if sequences or repetitions of motions are specified for a single character, as detailed in the next section of the paper. In this view, elementary motions can be considered as building blocks of the animation process, through which more complex actions can be specified. Interpolation between key-frame positions of elementary motions is then computed automatically by the system.

According to the classification of computer animation methods given in Thalmann (1989), PI-NOCCHIO can be classified as an image-based keyframe animation system, keyframe animation consisting of the automatic generation of intermediate frames, called in-betweens, of keyframes supplied by the animator.

The interpolation method adopted in PINOCCHIO is a splining technique that provides first and second derivative continuity of the motion. The choice of the set of keyframes controlling the interpolation is based on kinematic descriptions of human movements given according to the approach proposed in Zeltzer (1982). Such descriptions provide a means to identify the frame corresponding to a certain position during motion performance and to specify the initial and final positions assumed by the puppet during motion transition. For instance, in the transition from "walking" to "running" of the same character, interpolation is computed between the frame of the walking cycle corresponding to the left toe leaving the ground at the end of the stance phase of the left leg and the frame of the running cycle corresponding to right heel-strike, at the beginning of the next stance phase.

Transitions between sequences of motions is controlled by the object-oriented environment described in the next section of the paper.

3. AN OBJECT-ORIENTED ENVIRONMENT FOR SCENE ANIMATION

One of the biggest problems in computer animation is the enormous amount of information necessary to produce an animation sequence. For instance, if algorithmic animation is adopted, motion has to be described through a sequence of transformations, each one characterized by parameters that can change during the animation according to complex physical laws. This implies that the animator must be familiar with some of the details of the lower levels of the system hierarchy of motion control, where motion is actually determined.

In order to facilitate the task of describing an animation, various systems that provide higher levels of abstraction for specifying a scene have been developed. For instance, in systems such as ASAS (Reynolds 1982) and MIRA (Magnenat-Thalmann and Thalmann 1983) the concept of data abstraction for object modeling and motion specification and synchronization has been introduced. More recently, the object-oriented paradigm has been adopted in SOLAR (Chua, Wong and Chu 1988) to implement an easy-to-use interactive environment to compose and modify animation information. An example of use of temporal scripts for describing animated scenes can be found in Dami, Fiume, Nierstrasz, and Tsichritzis (1988).

In PINOCCHIO, we provide a high-level mechanism for describing and controlling a scene. A scene is a number of coordinated **movements** of several **actors** in given time and space constraints. Scenes are represented by means of **animation scripts** and are executed in an object-oriented environment. A **director** describes the general characteristics of the scene, and a **camera** views the scene. Distinctive features of objects to represent a scene in PINOCCHIO are the following:

a. the kinematic description of the objects corresponding to human movements is a recording obtained by acquisition with the Elite 3D vision system; such recordings can be retrieved from the motion database specifying the corresponding natural language annotation.

b. the scene is composed of objects to which movement are associated by the system according to the animation script given by the director.

c. objects in the scene are active, i.e., they actively participate in performing an animated scene by mutual *movement adjustment*.

The elements of a scene are described in Section 3.1, the composition of animation scripts in Section 3.2. An example of scene description is presented in Section 3.3.

3.1 PINOCCHIO Objects

In PINOCCHIO, we describe a scene using an object-oriented approach. Every entity in the system is an **object** and all the objects operate independently and concurrently. Objects belongs to classes, organized in a class hierarchy (Fig. 4). The behavior of objects belonging to a class is defined by the object interface, which is composed of a set of **methods** which can be called by other objects.

The most general class in PINOCCHIO is the OBJECT class, which represents any object involved in the scene. In the OBJECT class are defined all the methods for creating or destroying objects, and for assigning and inquiring values of local variables within an object. The OBJECT class is specialized in four subclasses, that describe the objects participating in a scene (each of these classes is described in detail in Fig. 5):

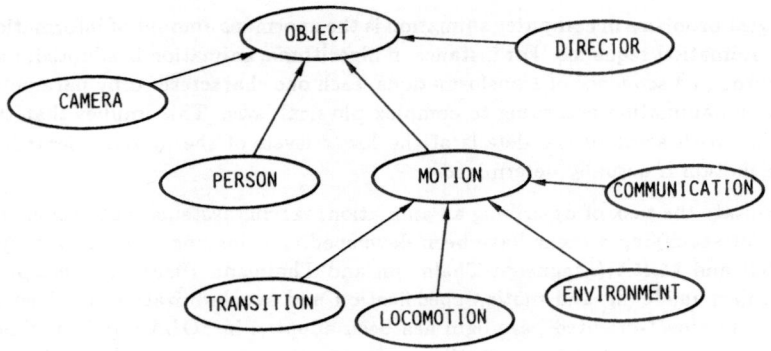

Fig.4. Object hierarchy in PINOCCHIO

- the **class DIRECTOR** specifies and then executes a scene by defining the **animation script** and by associating motions to the objects in the scene.

- The **class PERSON** contains a geometric description of the puppet, while its dynamics is defined associating to it various MOTION objects and a script controlling such associations.

- **class MOTION**: methods in MOTION class provide a mechanism for movement adjustment when a scene has to be animated. Movement adjustment basically consists of the coordination between MOTION objects of the initial and final position of their appearance in a scene; the dynamics of such mechanism is fully detailed in Section 4. According to the classification of movements described in the previous section, the MOTION class is specialized into the subclasses COMMUNICATION, TRANSITION, LOCOMOTION, and ENVIRONMENT.

- **CAMERA** class objects are used to manipulate the view of the world window where the animation takes place. Besides the animation script, the DIRECTOR specifies also a **camera script**, which defines the camera motion. The camera script is a time dependent law expressing the position of the camera point of view and as well as where the camera points to at any time during the scene. For the purposes of this paper, we do not give a description of camera scripts. An example of use of camera data types similar to the one that we adopt can be found in Magnenat-Thalmann, Thalmann and Fortin (1985).

3.2 Scene Description

A scene is specified by a DIRECTOR by defining what are the objects involved in a scene and what are the MOTION objects associated to them, and by describing their coordination requirements with a **general animation script**. The general animation script relates motions that must be performed by objects through a set of temporal operators. Temporal operators express constraints on motion execution that the characters in the scene must satisfy in order to fulfill the DIRECTOR's instructions.

Several MOTION objects can be associated to a single PERSON object, but only one MOTION can be active at a given time for a PERSON during the scene. Parallel execution of motions is defined only for distinct objects of the PERSON class.

```
class DIRECTOR

description
        general-script: SCRIPT
methods
        formulate-scene
            /* provides support to enter the description of scene
               in terms of the following messages:
               create-Motion (parameters) ==> MOTION
               motion-in-Scene(MOTION, parameters) ==> script
               add-Motion (MOTION) ==> PERSON
               add-Script(script) ==> PERSON
               add-script(script) ==> CAMERA

               instructions to prepare the scene are given to the
                  first coordinator with the message:
               generate-Scene(SCENE) ==> PERSON
            */
        computed-Motion
            /* message returned by each PERSON object with
               the result of generate-Scene */
        execute-Scene
            /* method called to actually execute the
               computed scene */




class PERSON

description
        person-script: script
methods
        add-Motion(MOTION)
        add-Script(script)
        generate-Scene
              /* coordination process is started
                 Messages sent are:
                 start-Coordination ==> MOTION
              */
        computed-Motion(MOTION)
              /* each motion returns the result of the computed motion */
```

Fig.5. Definition of object classes

```
class MOTION

description
        initial
           time
                 time-range
                 accepted-time
           space
                 space-range
                 accepted-space
           c-objects
        final
           time
                 time-range
                 accepted-time
           space
                 space-range
                 accepted-space
           c-objects
methods
        create-Motion
           /* sets the constraints on the initial
              and final description */
        start-Coordination
           /* the motion is computed, according to the given constraints;
              if motion cannot be computed due to the  constraints
              a request for adjustment of parameters is sent to
              coordinated objects (adjust-Motion message);
              if motion can be computed, the following coordinated objects
              are called with a start-Coordination message on them */
        adjust-Motion(parameters)
           /* the computed motion must be changed, to allow synchronization;
              all possible adjustments are tried one after the other */


class CAMERA

description
        camera-Script: CAMSCRIPT
methods
           /* general movements for synthetic camera control */
```

Fig.5. Definition of object classes (cont'd)

We introduce the following temporal operators for specifying animation scripts [1]:

1. **sequential execution** of motions: PM1 ; PM2

2. **parallel execution** of motions: PM1 & PM2

3. **repeated execution** of a motion: PM * n
   (motion PM is repeated n times)

4. **time delay:** PM1 ; t ; PM2
   (t expresses the minimum number of time units between the execution of two motions)

5. **grouping of motions:** (S)
   where S is recursively defined with rules 1-5 (e.g., PM1 and PM2 above can be groupings of motions).

It is relevant to point out that time constraints specified within an animation script are **relative times**, i.e., they relate temporally two or more MOTION objects with no reference to when the scene actually takes place. The actual starting time of the scene is set by the DIRECTOR when it receives the command "execute-scene" to execute the animation sequence.

The DIRECTOR specifies also the **initial and final constraints** for each MOTION object according to the following syntax:

initial constraints

time:	{ time constraints }
space:	{ space constraints }
objects:	{ coordination constraints }

Within the slot labeled **time** a relative time is specified, referred to the to the starting time of the scene. **Space constraints** refer to the world spatial positions where the motion begins and ends. **Coordination constraints** specify the list of other MOTION objects a given object should synchronize with. A similar syntax is used for final constraints.

3.3 Example of a Relay Race

We assume to have a scene specified as illustrated in the previous section: objects involved are a DIRECTOR, who builds the scene, a number of PERSON and MOTION objects created by the DIRECTOR, and a CAMERA object. The example describes a scene in which actors act autonomously in a coordinated way with respect to the director's instructions: a relay race. In a relay race, each runner runs in a relay and has to coordinate with the runner in the next relay. There are spatial constraints on where this coordination has to take place. After passing the baton to the next runner, each runner finishes his race, and can stop running.

For our purposes, we consider the moment of change of two runners (the mechanism can be easily generalized to the complete race). For sake of clarity, we do not specify in the following discussion all the parameters qualifying motions, but just the corresponding verbal expressions. There are several elements that must be coordinated in this scene:

---

[1]In the following, we indicate the instance of MOTION currently associated to an instance of PERSON as PM (short for PERSON.MOTION)

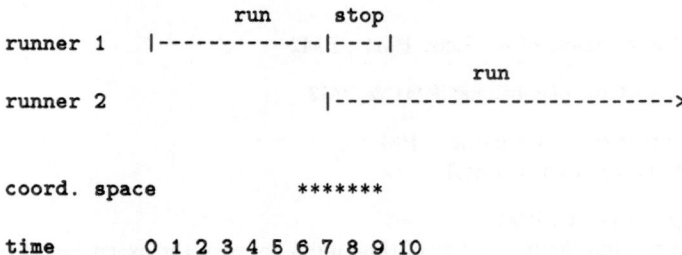

Fig.6. A relay race example

1. The first runner (RUNNER1) has to coordinate with the second runner (RUNNER2): they must run in one or more points of the part of the track where synchronization is allowed at the same time. It is beyond the purposes of this paper a discussion of another coordination problem, i.e., how RUNNER2 catches the baton from RUNNER1.

2. The first runner has to coordinate his own two movements: running and stopping.

In the description of this scene, we do not make any assumption on the runners' speed. We focus on the coordination mechanism, rather than on ways to get the best global result in the race, i.e., we concentrate on mechanisms for providing a correct relay race scene from the point of view of runners' movements, rather than on planning movements for improving the race performance.

Let us consider the relay race described in Fig. 6. The race starts (with RUNNER1) at time 0, at space 0 (assuming to have only the x axis). RUNNER2 has to coordinate with RUNNER1 between time 6 and time 9. After meeting RUNNER2, RUNNER1 can stop.

The director specifies where and when each runner starts moving, with which movements. Termination constraints, in terms of time and space limitations, are also specified for each movement. A general script is created by the director. The characteristics of a given scene are specified creating objects of the appropriate classes. In our case, we have the following objects:

- objects of the DIRECTOR class : DIRECTOR1
- objects of the PERSON class: RUNNER1, RUNNER2
- objects of the MOTION class: RUN1, STOP1, RUN2
- objects of the CAMERA class: CAMERA1

MOTION objects RUN1 and STOP1 are associated to RUNNER1, RUN2 is associated to RUNNER2.

In Fig. 7, we present the general script, associated to DIRECTOR1. DIRECTOR1 creates RUNNER1 and RUNNER2, and their motions. Fig. 7 presents also the constraints associated to motions RUN1, STOP1, and RUN2. For instance, the MOTION object RUN1 must start at time 0 and at position 0. RUN1 must terminate at any position between time 6 and time 9 and must coordinate with STOP1 and RUN2.

4. ANIMATION WITH AUTONOMOUS ACTORS

In this section we outline the basics of a technique for creating animated scenes with active participation of the objects involved in the scene. In most of the system for motion control presented so far in literature, coordination instructions for animating objects are given specifying exactly the different parameters of motion for each object and each motion.

We propose a mechanism internal to the objects themselves to achieve coordination once constraints on motion performance have been given, without further DIRECTOR's or external intervention. As in movie making the director gives general instructions to the actors and they figure out themselves how to act in the scene, so in our system the DIRECTOR object specifies the global scene and the related constraints just in terms of a script, leaving the coordination issues to be solved autonomously by the PERSON and MOTION objects involved in the scene through message exchange.

Messages can be of two types:

1. **Preparation messages** are exchanged between the director, and among moving actors, to agree on how to adjust movements at coordination points;

2. **Execution messages** are used to actually animate the scene.

General script

```
(RUN1*);(STOP1 & (RUN2*))
```

Motions constraints

```
object RUN1 in RUN
        description
            initial constraints
                time: 0
                space: 0
            final constraints
                space: 6-9
                objects: RUN2
                    STOP1


object RUN2 in RUN
        description
            initial constraints
                space: 6-9
                objects: RUN1

object STOP1 in STOP
        description
            initial constraints
                objects: RUN1
```

Fig.7. DIRECTOR's instructions for the relay race example

We focus here on preparation messages and on active creation of details of the scene by the participating actors. When executing the scene, objects simply perform motions as agreed by the participants in the scene, displaying the movements associated to the MOTION objects in the movement database according to the initial and final constraints derived from coordination with other MOTION objects.

Participants in a scene are a DIRECTOR object, a CAMERA object, and a number of PERSON and MOTION objects. The scene is described by a general script, associated to the DIRECTOR, which specifies how the actors interact in the scene. On the basis of the general script, personal scripts are created and sent by the DIRECTOR to each of the PERSON objects involved; also, the DIRECTOR associates MOTION objects to PERSON objects, with appropriate initial and final constraints. It is task of the MOTION objects to complete the scene according to the given constraints interacting with other MOTION objects.

The following methods are used by the objects to autonomously compute their motions:

- the personal scripts are received by each PERSON from the DIRECTOR with the message **add-Script**. For instance, the personal scripts of RUNNER1 and RUNNER2 are created (Fig. 8):

    RUNNER1 runs (motion RUN1 repeats itself any number of times) and then stops.
    RUNNER2 runs (motion RUN2 repeats any number of times).

This preparatory method is exchanged when still in the phase of scene formulation.

- **generate-Scene** (called from the DIRECTOR object on PERSON objects, to start the computation of the details of the scene).

- **start-Coordination** (called by PERSON objects to MOTION objects and from a MOTION object to a coordinated MOTION object)

- **adjust-Motion** (between coordinated MOTION objects, to request modifications of the initial or final constraints when they cannot be satisfied).

- **computed-Motion** (from MOTION objects to their coordinating MOTION or PERSON objects, from PERSON objects to the DIRECTOR; this message is used when movements can be computed according to the given constraints).

Scene execution can be obtained in two steps:

- **Step 1 - Starting scene computation**
  The director sends the **generate-Scene** message to all PERSON objects to have them start the computation of their motions. Computation of motion is started by the PERSON objects (RUNNER1 and RUNNER2 in the example) with a **start-Coordination** message which is sent to the first MOTION objects in the script.

- **Step 2 - Autonomous scene computation**
  Each MOTION object in turn starts coordination with following MOTION objects, as indicated in the animation script (in our case, RUN1 must coordinate with STOP1 and RUN2).

```
RUNNER1.script: (RUN1*;STOP1)
RUNNER2.script: (RUN2*)
```

Fig.8. Personal scripts of RUNNER1 and RUNNER2

```
start-Coordination
    compute motion;
    if motion can be computed
        if termination condition sent
            start-Coordination to coordinated objects,
    with additional initial conditions when required
            else /* no coordinated object */
                send compute-Motion(OK) to caller
        else /* motion cannot be computed */
            if caller is a PERSON object
                send compute-Motion(NOT OK) to caller
            else /* caller is a MOTION object */
                compute motion ignoring caller's constraints
                send adjust-Motion to caller

    adjust-Motion
        if retry-number <= S
/* max number of computations allowed
    for a motion object */
                recompute motion with new constraints
                restart coordination procedure with new state
                        number (see start-Coordination procedure */
        else /* number of allowed retries exceeded */
                send compute-Motion(NOT OK) to the PERSON object
    to which the MOTION is associated
```

Fig.9. Start-Coordination and adjust-Motion answering protocol

Fig. 9. details the methods **start-Coordination** and **adjust-Motion** briefly illustrated in Fig. 5. in the definition of the MOTION object. For instance, the actions taken after a start-Coordination message arrives to a MOTION object are described. The MOTION object first tries to compute its motion. Movement computation consists of setting time and space values for the initial and final positions of the motion that satisfy the given constraints. If a motion cannot be computed within the given constraints (for instance, given the second runner cannot meet the first runner in the allowed space because the first runner is too slow and does not reach the coordination space at the right time), the motion object will request possible modifications of the previous movement with an **adjust-Motion** message, indicating the new time and space constraints.

For instance, if RUN2 cannot compute its motion given the parameters sent by RUN1 when starting the coordination between the two objects, it can send an **adjust-Motion** message suggesting new time and space constraints. RUN1 will compute its motion again, and start over the coordination procedure with the new termination time and space constraints. If no agreement is found between two coordinated motions, the **computed-Motion** message reports the situation to the PERSON, which can ask the DIRECTOR to modify the script (with a negative **computed-Motion** message to the DIRECTOR).

We assume to limit the number of requests for adjustment that can be answered by a given MOTION object. Each **start-Coordination** and **adjust-Motion** message cause the MOTION object to change state. The number of allowed states (S) is computed as follows:

$$S = K * NO * \prod_{i=1,NO} NCO_i$$

where NO is the total number of MOTION and PERSON objects, NCO is the number of motion objects coordinated by a MOTION or PERSON object. The parameter K indicates the number of retries allowed for each case. The number of states is computed by the director and distributed to all the objects he creates.

If the movement can be computed, the object starts coordination with objects coordinated by it.

Fig. 10. illustrates the schema for message exchange in the case of the relay race. Assuming that coordination is achieved without any request for adjustment, we have the following sequence of messages:

RUNNER1	$\Longrightarrow$	RUN1:	**start-Coordination**
RUNNER2	$\Longrightarrow$	RUN2:	**start-Coordination**
RUN1	$\Longrightarrow$	STOP1:	**start-Coordination**
RUN1	$\Longrightarrow$	RUN2:	**start-Coordination**
STOP1	$\Longrightarrow$	RUNNER1:	**computed-Motion**
STOP1	$\Longrightarrow$	RUN1:	**computed-Motion**
RUN2	$\Longrightarrow$	RUNNER2:	**computed-Motion**
RUN2	$\Longrightarrow$	RUN1:	**computed-Motion**
RUN1	$\Longrightarrow$	RUNNER1:	**computed-Motion**

The director can then **execute** the scene when he receives a **computed-Motion** message by every PERSON object involved.

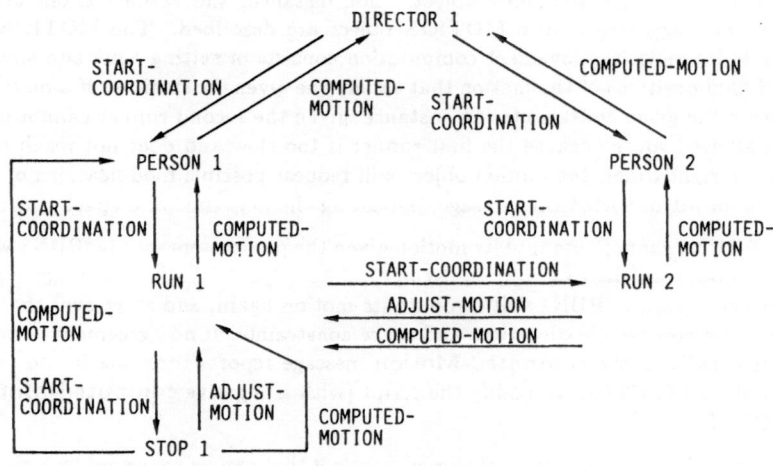

Fig.10. Message exchange schema for the relay race example

CONCLUDING REMARKS

In this paper, we have focused on two of the main features of PINOCCHIO: the movement database underlying the system and the coordination mechanism used for controlling transitions between motions. The system is currently under implementation on a workstation HP 9000, Series 800 using the C programming language, Unix operating system. Several movements have been recorded using Elite and are available for display in the movement database. The interpolation method has been tested in few cases, e.g., in the transition from walking to running and vice versa.

In the development of the project, we are facing some of the drawbacks of motion recording systems for motion representation outlined in Badler (1986), such as the difficulties in modifying a motion primitive in order to create animation effects and in applying the same motion to an individual with different body dimensions. Nevertheless, we think that the guiding mode can be integrated with higher level motion control systems, as suggested in Zeltzer (1985).

Starting from the results achieved so far, we are in fact developing a knowledge-based model for the synthesis of human movement consisting of kinematic rules describing the way in which a certain motion is performed and of gravity-dependent rules that impose constraints on the performance of the movement by considering factors such as inertia and dynamic balance. Future developments of the system include also the enhancement of the expressiveness of animation scripts through the specification of event synchronization operators and the introduction of time reasoning capabilities generally required in real-time systems (Maiocchi and Pernici 1988).

Acknowledgments

We would like to thank Prof. A. Pedotti and Prof. A. Polistina at Politecnico di Milano for their contribution in conceiving PINOCCHIO. We also acknowledge L. Dami at the Centre Universitaire d'Informatique of the University of Geneva for his detailed comments on the presentation of this work.

6. REFERENCES

Badler N (1979) Digital Representation of Human Movement. ACM Computing Surveys 11(1):19-38

Badler N (1986) Animating Human Figures: Perspectives and Directions. In: Proceedings Graphics Interface '86. pp 115-120

Calvert TW, Chapman J, Patla A (1980) The Integration of Subjective and Objective Data in the Animation of Human Movement. Computer Graphics 14(3):198-203

Camurri A, Morasso P, Tagliasco V, Zaccaria R (1986) Dance and Movement Notation. In: Morasso P, Tagliasco V (eds) Human Movement Understanding. North-Holland, pp 85-124

Special Issue of IEEE Computer Graphics and Applications (November 1982) Human Body Models and Animation

Special Issue of IEEE Computer Graphics and Applications (June 1987) Articulated Figure Animation

Chua T-S, Wong W-H, Chu K-C (1988) Design and Implementation of the Animation Language SOLAR. In: Magnenat-Thalmann N, Thalmann D (eds) Proceedings of CG International '88. Springer-Verlag, pp 15-26

Collodi C (1883) Le avventure di Pinocchio

Dami L, Fiume E, Nierstrasz O, Tsichritzis D (1988) Temporal scripts for objects. In: Tsichritzis D (ed) Active Object Environments. Technical Report, Centre Universitaire d'Informatique, University of Geneva

Ferrigno G and Pedotti A (1985) ELITE: A digital dedicated hardware system for movement analysis via real-time TV signal processing. IEEE Transactions on Biomedical Engineering BME-32(11):943-950

Ginsberg CM, Maxwell D (1983) Graphical Marionette. ACM SIGGRAPH / SIGART Workshop on Motion: Representation and Perception, pp 303-310

Magnenat-Thalmann N, Thalmann D (1983) The use of high-level 3-D graphical types in the Mira animation system. IEEE CG&A, 9-16

Magnenat-Thalmann N, Thalmann D, Fortin M (1985) Miranim: An extensible director-oriented system for the animation of realistic images. IEEE CG&A, 61-73

Maiocchi R, Pernici B (1988) Temporal data management in real-time systems: a comparative view. Internal Report n 88-046, Dipartimento di Elettronica, Politecnico di Milano, accepted for publication on IEEE TDKE

Etienne-Jules Marey (1984) Photo Poche

Miller GA (1972) English verbs of motion: a case study in semantics and lexical memory. In: Coding Processes in Human Memory. John Wiley & Sons, pp 335-372

Muybridge E (1955) The human figure in motion. Dover

Raibert MH (1986) Legged robots. CACM, 29(6):499-514

Reynolds CW (1982) Computer animation with scripts and actors. In: Proceedings ACM SIGGRAPH '82, Computer Graphics 16(3):289-296

Thalmann D (1989) Motion control: from keyframe to task-level animation. In: Proceedings of Computer Animation '89. pp 3-16

Tsotsos JK, Mylopoulos J, Covvey HD, Zucker SW (1980) A framework for visual motion understanding. IEEE Transactions on PAMI PAMI-2(6):563-573

Zeltzer D (1982) Motor control techniques for figure animation. IEEE CG&A, 53-59

Zeltzer D (1985) Towards an integrated view of 3-D computer animation. In: Graphics Interface '85. pp 230-248

APPENDIX 1. - THE MOVEMENT GRAMMAR

In specifying the grammar, we adopt the following notation:

- tokens starting with a lower case letter are non-terminal symbols of the grammar

- tokens starting with an upper case letter are terminal symbols of the grammar

action: initial_position motion final_position;

initial_position : Erect | Stooped | Kneeled | Supine | Seated | Leaned | Bent;

final_position : Erect | Stooped | Kneeled | Supine | Seated | Leaned | Bent;

motion : transition qualitative_aspects | locomotion space time | environment qualitative_aspects object position | communication;

transition : Raise | Fall | Sit | Lay | Stoop | Kneel | Bend | Lean;

qualitative_aspects : Slowly | Suddenly;

locomotion : Walk | Jump | Descend | Ascend | Hop | Run | Stop | Start;

space : direction trajectory gradient other_attributes;

direction : Forward | Backward | Left | Right;

trajectory : Straight | Zig_zag;

gradient : Horizontal | Vertical | Ascending | Descending;

other_attributes : | Height | Support;

height : High | Low;

support : Stairs | Inclined_plane;

time : speed acceleration frequency;

speed : Slow | Fast;

acceleration : Constant | Accelerating | Decelerating;

frequency : Rhythmic | Continuous;

environment : Push | Pull | Hold | Release | Lift | Put | Kick | Throw | Get | Pick | Lean | Bring | Touch | Grab | Hit;

position : relation height distance;

relation : Facing | Side | Vertical;

facing : Frontal | Behind;

side : Left | Right;

vertical : Up | Down;

distance : Close | Far;

object : weight dimension quantity shape;

weight : Heavy | Light;

quantity : One | Little | Many;

shape : Cubic | Spherical;

communication : emblems | explanation_signs | regulating_signs | ostentation_signs | adaptation_signs;

emblems : Nod | Deny | Wave_hand;

Roberto Maiocchi got his doctor in Electrical Engineering degree at Politecnico di Milano, Italy. He is currently a PhD student at the Dipartimento di Elettronica of the same school. His interests in computer art and animation raised in 1987 during a visit of one year at the University of California, San Diego, where he started his work on human figure modeling. His research interests include also the introduction of temporal reasoning capabilities in database systems. He is member of ACM, ACM SIGGRAPH, and EUROGRAPHICS. **Address**: Dipartimento di Elettronica, Politecnico di Milano, Piazza L. da Vinci 32, I-20133 Milano MI, Italy

Barbara Pernici is currently an associate professor of information systems at the University Politecnico di Milano. She started working at the Department of Electronics of the Politecnico di Milano in 1981. Her research interests include object-oriented design, information systems and office systems design and time reasoning. She has published more than 50 academic/technical papers in computer science journals and international conferences. She served as program chairman of the IFIP WG 8.4 Conference on Office Information Systems design in 1988. She is a member of ACM, of IFIP WG 8.4, and affiliate member of IEEE Computer Society. Pernici received her doctor in Electrical Engineering degree from Politecnico di Milano in 1981. **Address**: Dipartimento di Elettronica, Politecnico di Milano, Piazza L. da Vinci 32, I-20133 Milano MI, Italy; e-mail: relett07@imipoli.bitnet, bpernici@euroies.uucp

Human Free-Walking Model for a Real-Time Interactive Design of Gaits

RONAN BOULIC, NADIA MAGNENAT-THALMANN, and DANIEL THALMANN

Abstract

This paper presents a human walking model built from experimental data based on a wide range of normalized velocities. The model is structured in two levels. At a first level, global spatial and temporal characteristics (normalized length and step duration) are generated. At the second level, a set of parameterized trajectories produce both the position of the body in the space and the internal body configuration in particular the pelvis and the legs. This is performed for a standard structure and an average configuration of the human body.

The experimental context corresponding to the model is extended by allowing a continuous variation of global spatial and temporal parameters according to the motion rendition expected by the animator. The model is based on a simple kinematic approach designed to keep the intrinsic dynamic characteristics of the experimental model. Such an approach also allows a personification of the walking action in an interactive real-time context in most cases.

Keywords: animation, walk, gait, inverse kinematics, biomechanics, personification, behavior, prediction, correction

1. Introduction

Research in Computer Animation tends to be more and more oriented towards animation of complex scenes involving human beings conscious of their environment (Thalmann et al. 1988). This type of animation is multidisciplinary because it should integrate some aspects and methods specific to animation, mechanics, robotics, physiology and artificial intelligence.

In order to create naturalistic human motion, it is essential to take into account the geometric, physical and behavioral aspects. No system based on only one of these aspects can give good results.

To improve the natural aspect of motion, several authors (Isaacs and Cohen 1987; Wilhelms 1987; Girard and Maciejewski 1985; Armstrong and Green 1985; Arnaldi et al 1989) introduce dynamic laws, but generally for simple characters with a few joints because of the important CPU costs of such models.

In fact, the use of a dynamic model requires switching from a problem of specifying positional joint parameters to one of specifying applied forces and torques. This new parameter space is not easier to manipulate. The introduction of inverse dynamics for dynamically processing predefined trajectories does not solve the problem of how to find the natural trajectory for a specified task. This goal may be partially reached by using criterion optimizing methods (energy-based constraints).

Combined with other criteria integrating the physiological limitations of joints, dynamic models may be appropriate for the specification of certain movements: leg balance in walking (Bruderlin and Calvert 1989), hand motion from one location to another (Girard 1989). However, when the motion involves an interaction with the environment (e.g. contact force in a walking action) the expression of such criteria is not trivial and the problem is still open. Moreover, the integration of a personification of motion may satisfy the animator but may be incompatible from a physical point of view. Likewise, results obtained by solving equations may lead to stereotype movements for persons with the same anatomic configuration. Another drawback of dynamic models is the excessive cost in terms of CPU time which prevents the appreciation of the motion in real-time. This is a major restriction for the design of a motion, especially walking which involves expressive information of social, cultural or even behavioral nature.

In this context, we propose a method based on a mathematical parameterization coming from biomechanical experimental data. The main idea of this method is to take advantage of the intrinsic dynamics of the studied motion and extend its application context to a wider range but producing results which are realistic and interesting for the animator. From a taxonomy point of view such a method may be considered as an extension of the traditional rotoscopy method. We are interested in the human walking because of its fundamental importance which also means that numerous studies in biomechanics are available. The main directions of our method are applicable to other classes of human movements more or less complex than walking. The lack of experimental data could seem a serious drawback for these other fields of applications; however, it should be noted that biomechanics has also been involved in other classes of human movement for rehabilitation or sports. Finally, in image analysis, there are research project in automatic determination of temporal evolution of a motion - at the joint level - from a series of 2D images (THEMIS team, IRISA Rennes).

2. Human walking

By definition, walking is a form of locomotion in which the body's center of gravity moves alternately on the right side and the left side. At all times at least one foot is in contact with the floor and during a brief phase both feet are in contact with this floor.

Descriptions of biped gait, and especially human gait, may be easily found in the literature (Inman et al. 1980). In medicine, the problem has been studied for surgery (Murray et al. 1964, Saunders et al. 1953), and prosthetics (Lamoreux 1971). In robotics, much has been written concerning biomechanics for constructing artificial walking systems (Gurfinkel and Fomin 1974, Hemami and Farnsworth 1977, Miura and Shimoyama 1984; McMahon 1984). Several dance notations have been proposed: Benesh notation (Benesh 1956), Eshkol-Wachman notation (Eshkol and Wachman 1958) and Labanotation (Hutchinson 1970) and walking has been described using these notations (Badler and Smoliar 1979; Magnenat-Thalmann and Thalmann 1985).

Finally, several authors (Calvert and Chapman 1978; Zeltzer 1982; Magnenat-Thalmann and Thalmann 1987, Girard and Maciejewski 1985; Girard 1987; Bruderlin and Calvert 1989; Zeltzer 1988) have developed systems for generating computer-animated walking sequences.

As walking is a cyclic activity, we only study the portion of motion between two successive contacts of the left heel with the floor. Fig.1 shows the temporal structure of the walking cycle with the main time and duration information. Fig.2 presents the spatial structure of the same cycle.

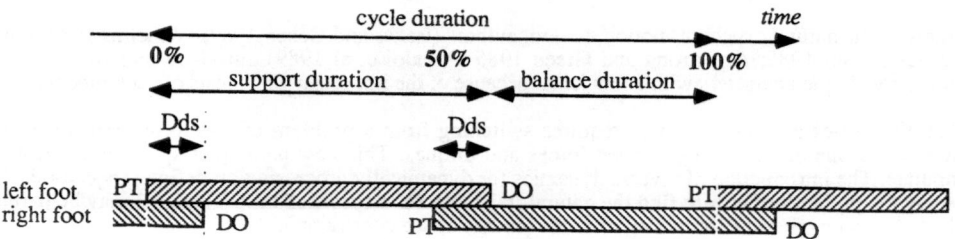

Fig. 1. Temporal structure of the walking cycle

Dc: cycle duration; PT: time when the heel touches the floor; DO: time when the toe leaves the floor; Ds: support duration (duration of contact with the floor); Db: balance duration (duration of non-contact with the floor); Dds: duration of contact of feet with the floor.

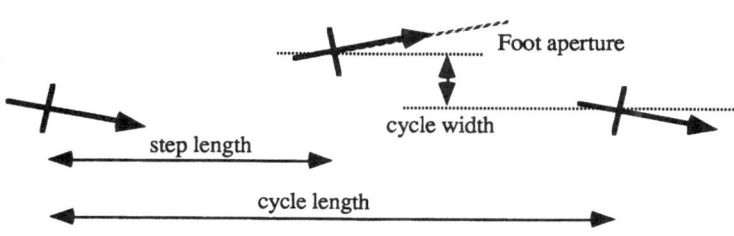

Fig. 2. Spatial structure of the walking cycle

3. The proposed model

3.1 Introduction

The proposed model is intended for producing for any point in time the values of the spatial, temporal and joint parameters of the free walking human being with average characteristics (Kreighbaum and Barthels 1985). All spatial values of the model are normalized by the fundamental characteristic of the walk: the leg length (noted T_j). This is the length between the flexing axis of the thigh and the foot sole, as shown in Fig.3. The average value is 53% of the total height of the human being (Kreighbaum and Barthels 1985).

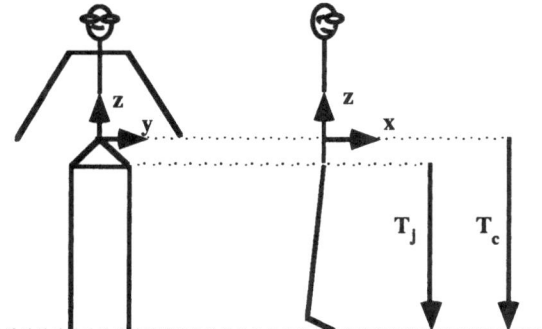

Fig. 3. Definition of the body coordinate system and the initial position

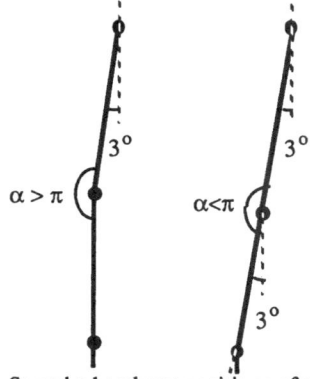

Fig. 4. Stretched and rest positions of the knee

In the following sections, we use the relative velocity, VR, defined as the average walking velocity normalized by T_j. The studies used for designing our model are based on a range of relative velocities from 0.6 to 2.3 (number of T_j/s). Outside this range, we extrapolate the walking towards an immobile attitude corresponding to a rest position of the knee as shown in Fig.4.

3.2 Spatial characteristics

The most important spatial characteristic is the length of relative cycle LcR obtained by a normalization formula from Inman et al. (1981).

$$LcR = 1.346 \sqrt{VR}$$

Two other characteristics are width of relative cycle lcR and foot open angle (in degrees) Op:

$$lcR = 0.02 \ VR + 0.05$$
$$Op = -1.4 \ VR + 8.5$$

Authors (Murray et al. 1964; Murray et al. 1966) noted a large variation in measures for both these values.

3.3 Temporal characteristics

The fundamental temporal characteristic is the cycle duration Dc, obtained by: $Dc = LcR / VR$. Murray et al. (1964) have shown that all the other temporal characteristics, the support duration Ds, the balance duration Db and the double support duration Dbs, are linearly dependent on the cycle duration Dc (see Fig.1):

$$Ds = 0.752 \ Dc - 0.143$$
$$Db = 0.248 \ Dc + 0.143$$
$$Dds = 0.252 \ Dc - 0.143$$

All trajectories will be expressed as functions of relative time defined as follows $t\% = t/Dc$.

3.4 Periodic trajectories

Trajectories which will be distinguished are those situating the body coordinate system in the world of joint trajectories internal to the body. The body coordinate system is centered at the spine origin (noted Oc); its orientation is compatible with the main axes of the body at the rest position as shown in Fig.3. The detailed expression of the trajectories is given in Appendix A.

Location of the body in the space: three translation trajectory coordinates situate the body relatively to the position it should have when moving straightforward with the velocity VR.

Vertically: the height of Oc decreases for completing the step. The amplitude of this decrease grows with VR.

Laterally: Oc oscillates laterally in order to ensure the weight transfer from one leg to the other leg. The amplitude is almost always constant.

lead/delay: For an average velocity VR, the body has in fact acceleration and deceleration phases which correspond to the advance to the new step then the stabilization on the new leg. This effect decreases when VR grows because of the smoothing effect due to the kinetic energy.

3.5 Internal joint trajectories

Forward/backward: this flexing movement of the back relatively to the pelvis is done just before each step to move the center of gravity of the body in order to help the forward motion of the leg.

left/right: the pelvis falls on the side of the balanced leg

torsion: the pelvis may rotate relative to the spine in order to perform the step more easily

These three trajectories strongly depend on the individual human being. It is also easy to build a rotation trajectory for the thorax (in opposition to the pelvis torsion) as well as trajectories for the arm motion (in phase with the opposite foot).

The truly walking trajectories are the trajectories of flexing/extension at the thigh, the knee, the ankle and the toe. These trajectories are very similar from one human being to another one on an experimental range of relative velocities. We shall model them using splines (see Appendix B).

3.6 Discussion

We have built a model which may be used at two levels:

- first at a global level in order to generate the average temporal and spatial characteristics (normalized).
- then at the trajectory level in order to describe at each time the position of the body in the space and its internal configuration.

Before going further, let us introduce the concept of virtual floor. This is the plane of the support of the body at the initial position (see Fig.3). When seen from the average location of the body coordinate system during the walk, this plane stays at an invariable height $-T_c$ according to the z_{body} axis. T_c is the origin height of the spine and its average value is about 58% of the total size of the human being (Dreyfuss 1966). It will be useful to consider and to manipulate a virtual floor coordinate system linked to the average position of the body coordinate system.

As the model comes from the synthesis of a large number of experimental data and not from solving motion equations, it is logical to obtain a rather realistic approximation which does not correspond exactly to the support constraint of the virtual floor. This problem may be overcome by modifying the leg flexing using an inverse kinematics method. This method is described in the section prediction/correction. The modification is not important relatively to the general walk motion and we may consider that the degrees of freedom of the pelvis do not intervene in this correction which decreases the dimension of the problem. Such a method allows a decisive extension of the model to fill the expressive needs of the animator.

4. Extension of the application field of the model

4.1 Spatial and temporal parameters

When strictly applied, a relative velocity, assumed to be constant, completely determines a free walking for a flat floor with a straight direction. However, it is clear that such a context is too limited for an animator who would like to recreate variable situations in space and time. Consequently, we propose to extend this strict context by the following steps:

- provide as entry points the three variables linked by the formula $VR=LcR/Dc$ with the following priorities (see Fig.5):

    - if the relative velocity is specified, it determines the two other variables
    - if only the relative cycle length varies, the cycle duration is fixed and the relative velocity is adjusted
    - if only the cycle duration varies, the relative cycle length is fixed and the relative velocity is adjusted
    - if only the relative cycle length and the cycle duration vary, the relative velocity is adjusted

It should be noted that the three last possibilities cannot be considered as a free walking; the obtained gait is a decelerated or accelerated free gait. The gait is realistic in the neighborhood of the characteristic $LcR=f_n (Dc)$ coming from the normalization formula. Otherwise it will provide a larger parameter space allowing the designer to guarantee a global spatial or temporal constraint. In particular, it will be possible to freeze any motion phase with an infinite cycle duration (in fact, we generally work with the frequency f_c expressed in cycles number/second which is zero in this case).

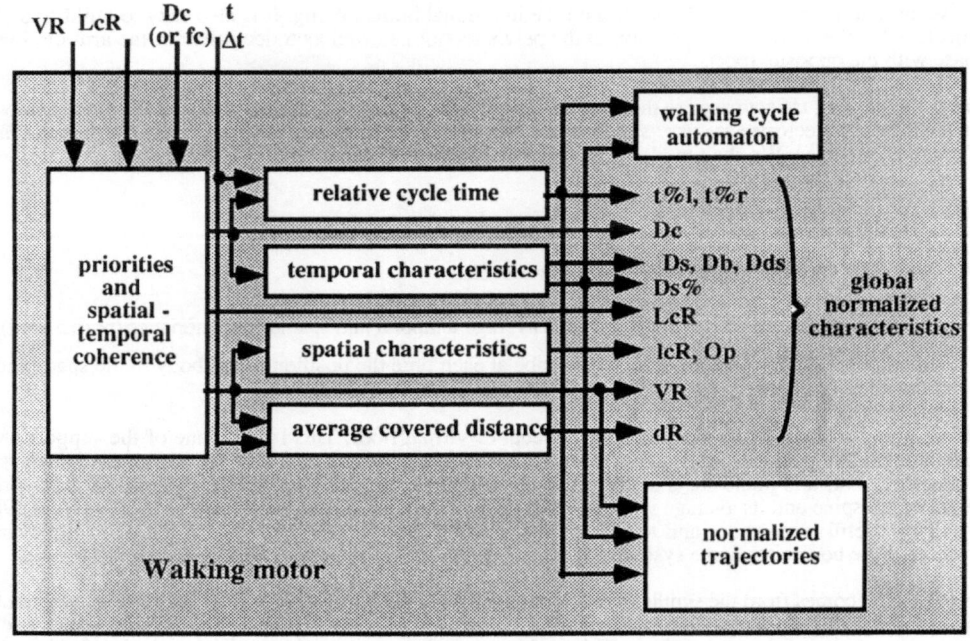

Fig. 5. Walking motor

- allow a continuous variation of the previous entry points maintaining a coherence of the walk. This allows adaptation to an environment which varies fast (e.g. displacement in a crowd)

- project the covered distance by the body at each time onto an independently defined path. VR(t), the average instantaneous relative velocity may be integrated to provide the average relative covered distance. This distance, multiplied by the T_j of the considered human being and projected on the average path, gives us the average location of the body coordinate system in the world, which means the position it would have with a zero velocity. To obtain the exact position, it is necessary to add the instantaneous vector translation dependent on VR and t%.

4.2 Personification

At the present stage, our walk motor may correspond to a wide range of qualitative needs of the animator from three point of views: the general walk function (VR), the attitude (LcR) and the animation (D_c or f_c). However the personification of the motion is intrinsically average and therefore it is necessary to introduce an extra level of individuality.

Our approach to this problem is rather simple but available independently for each instantaneous characteristic (body location and configuration):

$$\text{personified motion} = \alpha \cdot \text{reference motion} + \beta$$

A random perturbation mechanism is also proposed independently for α and β by specifying the maximal amplitude and the smoothing level of a reference noise.

All the parameters of personification should be continuously modifiable and the visual result should be synchronized on the clock model in order to correctly evaluate the design of the personified motion. The continuous variation of the spatial-temporal parameters also allows the designer to fully appreciate the characterization.

Of course, such a freedom for the animator may produce gaits which do not correspond to any free walk: this is our goal. It should be noted that the introduction of the personification does not modify the spatial and temporal coherence (t%, VR) of the initial model. The assumption of the small modifications may be invalidated by the animator's creativity. This suggests that several adaptation methods should be proposed, which will be discussed in the section on prediction/correction.

4.3 Adaptation

Behavior range may become wider by associating constraints to the walk support (foot and by extension shoes). These constraints correspond to a variation between the reality and the imaginary.

Five constraints may be introduced in the increasing order:

1. the support height stays at the virtual floor level

2. the height and the orientation of the support basis are constrained to the virtual floor

3. the support position stays fixed in the world coordinate system of the corresponding virtual floor.

4. the position and the orientation of the support basis are constrained in the world coordinate system of the corresponding virtual floor.

5. the support location is conformed to the world floor (this constraint is under research in order to coordinate walk and vision).

The application of these constraints is driven by the global characteristics of the model. In the case of a very personified gait, the spatial characteristics are generally false and make obsolete the use of the constraints. We propose to fix the value of an average personified velocity, VP, based on the value of the length of an personified cycle LcP. These two values are characterized by the length of the leg T_j and more generally by the given skeleton and its support attributes.

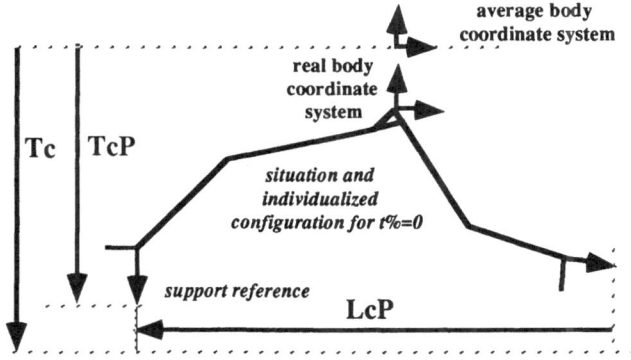

Fig. 6. Personification and adaptation

The value LcP is roughly evaluated as follows (see Fig. 6):

- current personification data are useful to derive the situation and the configuration of the human being for the time t%=0.

- LcP is then approximated by twice the distance along the displacement axis (x_{body}) between the left and right support references.

We have VP = LcP/Dc and the average covered distance dP is obtained by integrating VP(t).

Similarly, a personified height should be proposed for the coordinate system associated with the virtual floor. This value TcP is approximated by the distance along z_{body} between the body coordinate system at an average position and the support reference which starts (see Fig.6).

This primary adaptation guarantees a global spatial and temporal coherence sufficient to apply the constraints. Moreover, we provide two methodologies for following paths: either the animator does not care about the trajectory followed by the body coordinate system or he/she does not care about the coincidence of the virtual floor with a particular world floor. For us, a path is a 3D trajectory associated with a vector defining the vertical direction when it is necessary to define it. A path is private when it is followed by the average body coordinate system. In this case, the height of the virtual floor does not necessarily coincide with a reference linked to the world according to the variations of characterization (T_j, skeleton) or personification (see Fig.7). A path is public when it is followed by the virtual floor coordinate system. A support, linked to the path, is guaranteed for any human being or personification (see Fig.8).

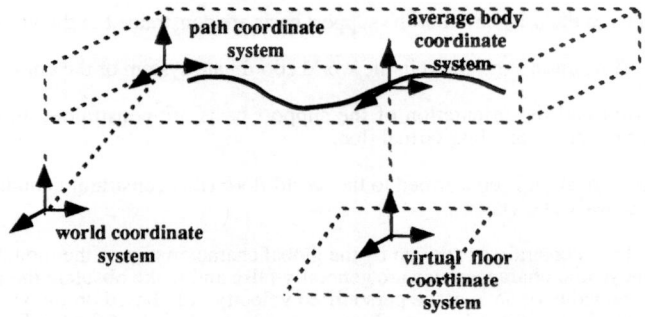

Fig. 7. Use of a private path

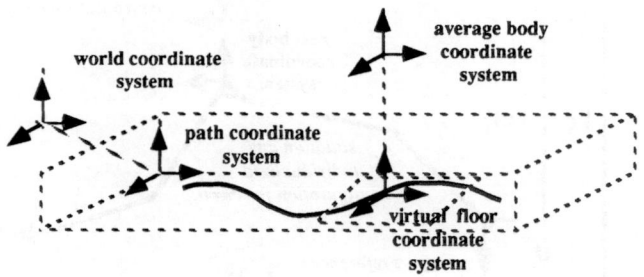

Fig. 8. Use of a public path

5. Functional diagram

The functional diagram (shown in Fig.9) is based on two blocks of prediction-correction which drive the processing of walking at the current time. It also use a module producing the current values of the parameters which are accessible by the animator. This module is strictly limited to predefined and interactive directives. It does not adapt them for a specific task like the adaptation of path velocity in order to lay the foot at specific locations. This is under research, but it should be noted that when the animator may use real-time tools, he/she may interact continuously with the system at a higher level to order a wide range of behaviors.

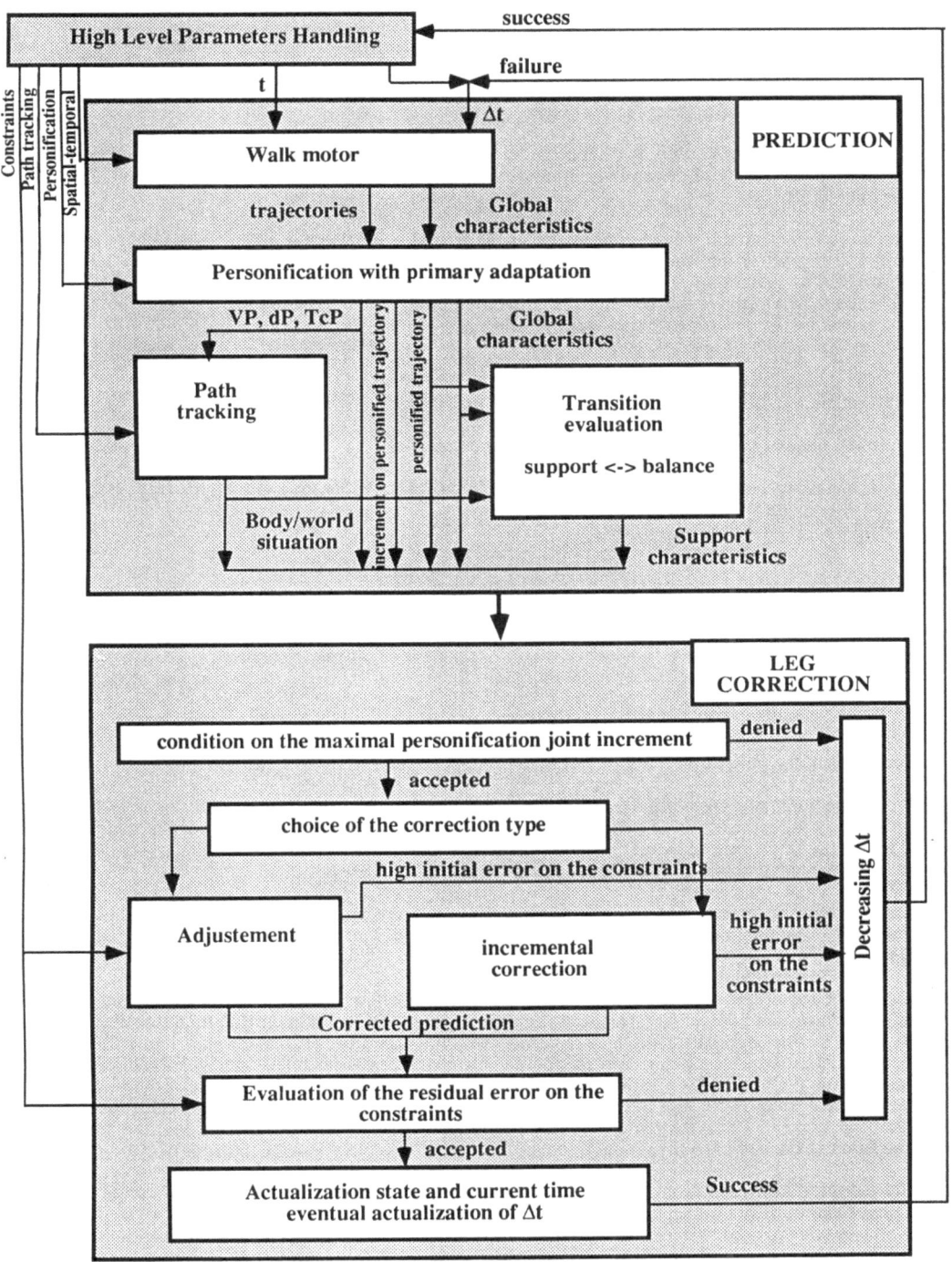

Figure 9 Functional diagram

5.1 Prediction

Prediction provides several levels of sophistication in the design – without constraints – of gaits. The animator may and should work by stepwise refinements.

For the complete case, the process is as follows:

A) The general state is known at the current time tc. This state should correspond to the specified constraints. Otherwise, a method of initial correction should modify it. The state at the time t+Δt now has to be built.

B) The walk motor guarantees the coherence of the spatial and temporal parameters. Other spatial and temporal characteristics may be updated (see 3.2 and 3.3). The average relative covered distance dR(t) is obtained by integrating VR(t). The relative cycle time t%(t) is given by integrating 1/Dc(t). It should be noted that in the restrictive case of free walking, only an analytic expression is known using the normalization formula (extended to variable values):

$$Dc(t) = 1.346.\sqrt{VR(t)}$$

It gives: $t\% = 0.495\sqrt{VR(t)^3}$

For more general cases, a numerical integration is needed.

Trajectories are synchronized using t% for the left leg (t%l), t% for the right leg (t%r) is obtained by a phase displacement of half a cycle.

$$t\%l(t) = t\%(t) \text{ module } [1]$$
$$t\%r(t) = (t\%(t)+0.5) \text{ modulo } [1]$$

Finally, the cycle state is obtained by comparison with Ds%(t) = Ds(t)/Dc(t).

For example, for the left leg:

$$t\%l(t) < Ds\%(t) \rightarrow \text{left support state}$$
$$t\%l(t) > Ds\%(t) \rightarrow \text{left balance state}$$

For the right leg, it is similar. Single and double support phases may then be distinguished.

C) Prediction integrates personified trajectories of translation and rotation of the pelvis but not of the legs. In fact, leg trajectories may be unreasonable for the algorithm of inverse kinematics which is then applied. The trajectories have an essential role to play, but not at the foreground. Their personified data have to be integrated into an abstract concept that we call "*coach* legs".

At this stage, leg prediction integrates personified trajectories at t%=0 for the so-called primary adaptation. The integration of the new velocity VP(t) provides an average personified covered distance dP(t).

D) The projection of this distance onto the desired path is immediate. The path is modelled using cardinal splines which have the advantages of passing through the control points. It is then transformed in a sequence of line segments using an adaptive sampling algorithm (Koparkar and Mudur 1983). The incremental process for making correspondence between the curvilinear abscissa with the distance dP is then trivial. We obtain the position of the body coordinate system or the position of the virtual floor coordinate system according to the selected method. The tangent to the curve provides the forward direction (x_{body}). An extra vector (normal to the forward direction) for the vertical locates the set consisting of the body and the virtual floor relative to the path.

E) The last proposed module for prediction determines the areas of potential personification support. Rather than to restrict ourselves to strictly defined phases – which impose constraints on start and end of phases that are hard to maintain – we prefer derive these values of current personification (including *coach*). This requires the specification of one support out of the four proposed: heel, base (linked to the ankle), toe and extremity (linked to the toe).

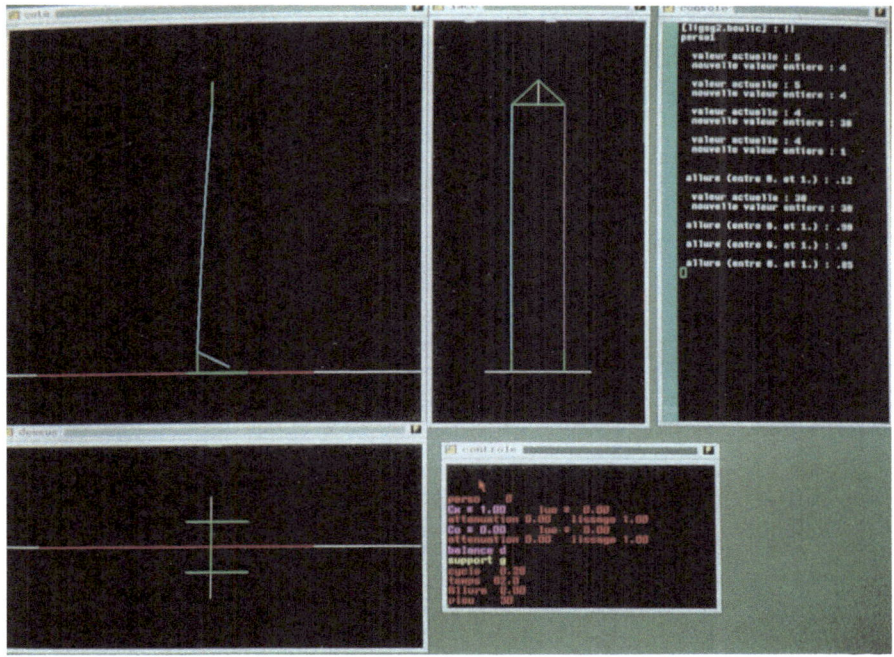

Plate 1: Equilibrium position at the rest (VR = 0).

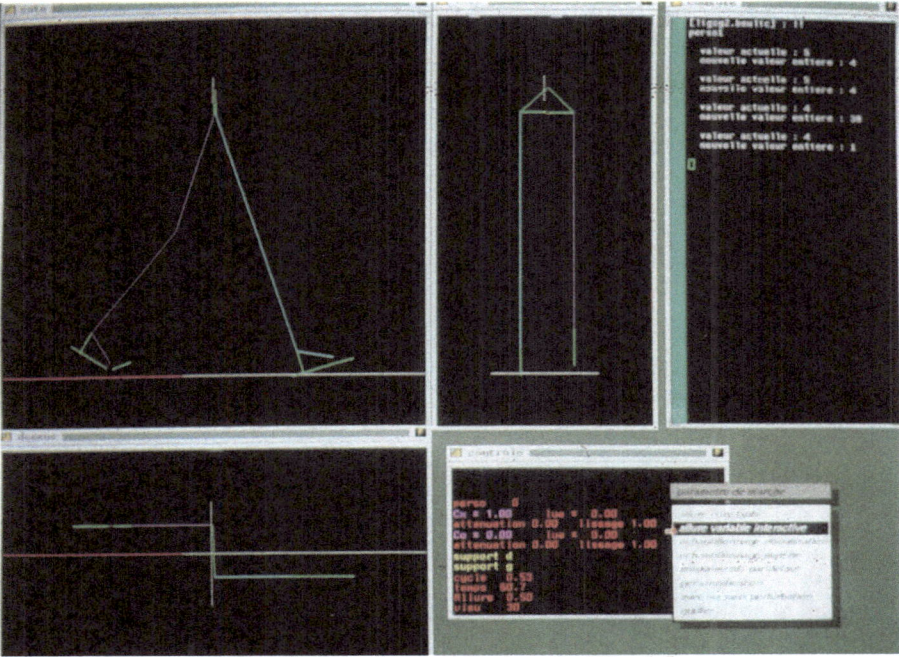

Plate 2: Beginning support phase for VR = 1.5

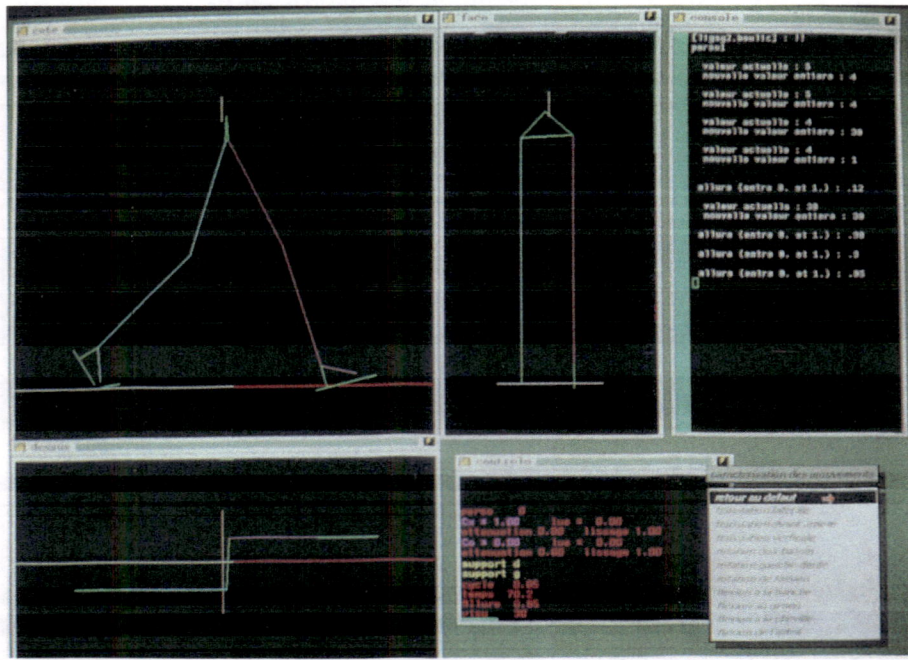

Plate 3: Beginning support phase for VR = 2.55

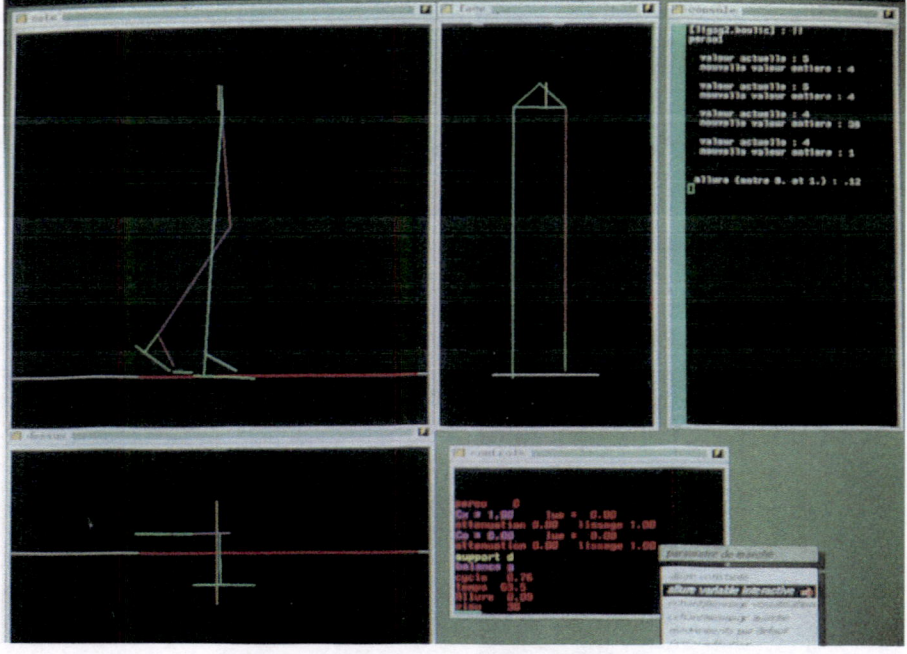

Plate 4: Middle support phase for VR = 0.27

A support request is created as soon as the reference point associated with a support passes under the personified virtual floor. These requests have a priority which is proportional to the measured divergence. We may of course decide that it is better to assign a mandatory cycle range to the support or the balance. This possibility should be used with care because it may cause totally discontinued transitions.

5.2 Correction

Paradoxically prediction is not strictly defined at the output of this block; this point will be cleared up during the selection of the correction method using inverse kinematics. We briefly summarize this technique.

Our approach to inverse kinematics

The general form of the solution provided by inverse kinematics is often used in robotics (Espiau and Boulic 1985) and Computer Animation (Girard 1989):

$$\Delta\theta = J^+\Delta x + (I-J^+J) z$$

where:

$\Delta\theta$ is the joint space solution of the inverse kinematic problem
J is the Jacobian matrix associated with the main task
J^+ is the unique pseudo inverse of J and provides the minimum norm solution to achieve the main task
Δx describes the main task to achieve in cartesian space
z describes the secondary task in joint space which is partially achieved on the null space of the main task.

This means that the second term of the solution does not affect the achievement of the main task ($\forall z$); z is chosen in order to minimize a cost function c such as $z = -\mu \nabla c$ ($\mu > 0$)

The application of this technique to walking has consisted of a strictly tracking of spatial and temporal trajectories considered as main tasks assigned to feet (or other end effectors) as defined by Girard (1989) or Zeltzer and Sims (1988). An eventual secondary task of optimization of the joint limits may complete the solution (Girard and Maciejewski 1985).

We have chosen a more qualitative specification based on the walk motor. Our main task consists of correcting the motion according to the constraints. The role of the secondary task is to retain the personification dynamic with z proportional to the coach variation.

Two types of main tasks are proposed according to the importance of the joint divergence between, on one part, the leg configuration of the current state and, on the other part, the personification (coach).

If the divergence is low: the prediction is completed by the coach legs and a simple adjustment is made.

If the divergence is important: the prediction is completed by the leg configuration of the current state. The correction integrates an extra constraint of attraction towards the coach leg.

An adaptation mechanism of time increment allows too important corrections or residual errors to be solved.

Finally, the initial correction method is an incremental correction without extra attraction constraint but with the secondary task itself. The correction loop is activated until the constraints are satisfied without temporal evolution.

6. Acknowledgments

The research was supported by le Fonds National Suisse pour la Recherche Scientifique, the Natural Sciences and Engineering Council of Canada, the FCAR foundation and the Institut National de la Recherche en Informatique et Automatique (France).

7. Conclusion

We have proposed an important extension of a walking model based on experimental data. The animator may use a wide range of stepwise refinements for the design of real-time gaits. Its major advantage is to allow a qualitative and continuous design of a gait using the dynamic feeling of an experimental model.

The implementation has been carried out in the C language using the Silicon Graphics IRIS 4D workstation. The graphic output shown in Plates 1 to 4 illustrate the personification phase.

8. References

Armstrong WW, Green MW (1985) Dynamics for Animation of Characters with Deformable Surfaces in: N.Magnenat-Thalmann, D.Thalmann (Eds) Computer-generated Images, Springer, pp.209-229.

Arnaldi B, Dumont G, Hégron G, Magnenat-Thalmann N, Thalmann D (1989) Animation Control Using Dynamics, in: State of the Art in Computer Animation, Springer, Tokyo

Badler NI, Smoliar SW (1979) Digital Representation of Human Movement, ACM Computing Surveys, March issue, pp.19-38.

Benesh R, Benesh J (1956) An Introduction to Benesh Dance Notation, A&C Black, London

Bruderlin A, Calvert TW (1989) Goal Directed, Dynamic Animation of Human Walking, Proc. SIGGRAPH '89, Computer Graphics, Vol. 23, No3

Calvert TW, Chapman J (1978) Notation of Movement with Computer Assistance, Proc. ACM Annual Conf., Vol.2, 1978, pp.731-736

Dreyfuss H (1966) The Measure of Man, 2nd edition, Withney library of design, New York.

Eshkol N, Wachmann A (1958) Movement Notation, Weidenfeld and Nicolson, London

Espiau B, Boulic R (1985) Collision Avoidance for Redundant Robots with Proximity Sensors, Proc. 3rd International Symposium of Robotic Research, Gouvieux, France, Octobre 1985

Girard M (1987) Interactive Design of 3D Computer-animated Legged Animal Motion, IEEE Computer Graphics and Applications, Vol.7, No6, pp.39-51

Girard M (1989) Constrained Optimization of Articulated Animal Movements in Computer Animation, M.I.T. Workshop on Mechanics, Control, and Animation of Articulated Figures

Girard M, Maciejewski AA (1985) Computational Modeling for Computer Generation of Legged Figures, Proc. SIGGRAPH '85, Computer Graphics, Vol. 19, No3, pp.263-270

Gurfinkel VS, Fomin SV (1974) Biomechanical Principles of Constructing Artificial Walking Systems, in: Theory and Practice of Robots and Manipulators, Vol.1, Springer, NY, pp.133-141

Hemami H, Farnsworth RL (1977) Postural and Gait Stability of a Planar Five Link Biped by Simulation, IEEE Trans. on Automatic Control, AC-22, No3, pp.452-458.

Hutchinson A (1970) Labanotation, Theatre Books, NY

Inman VT, Ralston HJ, Todd F (1981) Human Walking, Baltimore, Williams & Wilkins

Isaacs PM, Cohen MF (1987) Controlling Dynamic Simulation with Kinematic Constraints, Bahvior Functions and Inverse Dynamics, Proc. SIGGRAPH'87, Computer Graphics, Vol.21, No4, pp.215-224

Koparkar PA and Mudur SP (1983) A New Class of Algorithms for the Processing of Parametric Curves, Computer-aided Design, Vol.15, No1, pp.41-45

Kreighbaum E, Barthels KMB (1985) Biomechanics, a qualitative approach, 2nd edition, Burgess publishing Company, Minneapolis, Minn.

Lamoreux LW (1971) Kinematic Measurements in the Study of Human Walking, Bulletin of Prosthetics Research, Vol.BPR 10, No15

Magnenat-Thalmann N, Thalmann D (1987) The Direction of Synthetic Actors in the film Rendez-vous à Montréal, IEEE Computer Graphics and Applications, Vol. 7, No 12.

Magnenat-Thalmann, Thalmann D (1985) Computer Animation: Theory and Practice, Springer, Tokyo

McMahon T (1984) Mechanics of Locomotion, Intern. Journ. of Robotics Research, Vol.3, No2, pp.4-28.

Miura H, Shimoyama I (1984) Dynymic Walk of a Biped, International Journal of Robotics, Vol.3, No2, pp.60-74.

Murray MP, Drought AB, Kory RC (1964) Walking Patterns of Normal Men, Journal of Bone Joint Surgery, Vol.46A, No2, pp.335-360

Murray P, Kory RC, Clarkson BH, Sepic SB (1966) Comparison of Free and Fast Speed Walking Patterns of Normal Men, American Journal of Physical Medecine, Vol.45, No 1, pp.8-24

Saunders JB, Inman VT, Eberhart (1953) The Major Determinants in Normal and Pathological Gait, Journal of Bone Joint Surgery, Vol.35A, pp.543-558

Thalmann D, Magnenat-Thalmann N, Wyvill B, Zeltzer D, SIGGRAPH '88 Tutorial Notes on Synthetic Actors: the Impact of A.I. and Robotics on Animation.

Wilhelms J (1987) Using Dynamic Analysis for Realistic Animation of Articulated Bodies, IEEE Computer Graphics and Applications, Vol.7, No 6, pp.12-27

Zarrugh MY, Radclifh CW (1979) Computer generation of Human Gait Kinematics, Journal of Biomechanics, Vol.12, pp.99-111

Zeltzer D, Sims K (1989) A Figure Editor and Gait Controller to Task Level Animation in: Thalmann D, Magnenat-Thalmann N, Wyvill B, Zeltzer D, SIGGRAPH '88 Tutorial Notes on Synthetic Actors: the Impact of A.I. and Robotics on Animation.

Appendix A: Periodic trajectories of the body and the pelvis

Vertical translation: vertical offset from the average body position expressed in the body coordinate system

amplitude: $Av = 0.015\ VR$

expression: $-Av + Av \sin 2\pi\ (2\ t\% - 0.35)$

Lateral translation:

amplitude: for VR>0.5 $Al = -0.032$
                 for VR<0.5 $Al = -0.128\ VR^2 + 0.128\ VR$

expression: $Al \sin 2\pi\ (t\% - 0.1)$

                 a positive value expresses a displacement on the left side of the human being

Translation forward/backward:

amplitude: for VR>0.5 $Aa = -0.021$
                 for VR<0.5 $Aa = -0.084\ VR^2 + 0.084\ VR$

phase displacement: $\phi a = 0.625 - Ds\%$ with $Ds\% = Ds/D$

expression: $Aa \sin 2\pi\ (2t\% + 2\phi a)$

                 a positive value states for an advance relatively to the average position

Rotation forward/backward:

amplitude: for VR>0.5 $A1 = 2$
                 for VR<0.5 $A1 = -8\ VR^2 + 8\ VR$

expression: $-A1 + A1 \sin 2\pi\ (2\ t\% - 0.1)$

Rotation left/right:

amplitude: $A2 = 1.66\ VR$

expression:

$0 \leq t\% < 0.15$	$-A2 + A2 \cos 2\pi \, (10/3 \, t\%)$
$0.15 \leq t\% < 0.5$	$-A2 - A2 \cos 2\pi \, (10/7 \, (t\% - 0.15))$
$0.5 \leq t\% < 0.65$	$A2 - A2 \cos 2\pi \, (10/3 \, (t\% - 0.5))$
$0.65 \leq t\% < 1$	$A2 + A2 \cos 2\pi \, (10/7 \, (t\% - 0.65))$

Torsion rotation:

amplitude: $A3 = 4 \, VR$

expression: $-A3 \, \cos 2\pi \, t\%$

a negative value expresses a pelvis torsion towards the left leg

Appendix B: Periodic trajectories of the leg flexing/extension

Trajectories of flexing/extension are modelled using cubic splines passing through control points located at the extremities of the trajectories. The coordinates of these points are noted $(t\%_i, y_i)$ for the control point i. The modelling of the variations of these few points in function of VR is sufficient to rebuild the expected trajectory.

Let consider $h_1(s) = 2s^3 - 3s^2 + 1$ and $h2(s) = -2s^3 + 3s^2$ the two necessary basic Hermit splines.

A trajectory $f(t\%, VR)$ with $t\%$ between $t\%_{i-1}$ and $t\%_i$ may be for example expressed as follows:

$f(t\%, VR) = y_i + (y_i - y_{i-1}) h_1[(t\% - t\%_{i-1})/(t\%_i - t\%_{i-1})]$ where the values of $t\%_j$, y_j depend on VR.

The study of the variation of control points in function of VR is performed on the following three ranges:

	range	gaits
A	$0 \leq VR < 0.5$	starts from the immobile attitude to reach a slow gait
B	$0.5 \leq VR < 1.3$	slow gait almost constant
C	$1.3 \leq VR < \text{upper limit}$	significant evolution of the gait

B.1 Flexing at the hip

The first figure indicates the three necessary control points. The variation of their coordinates are summarized in the second figure.

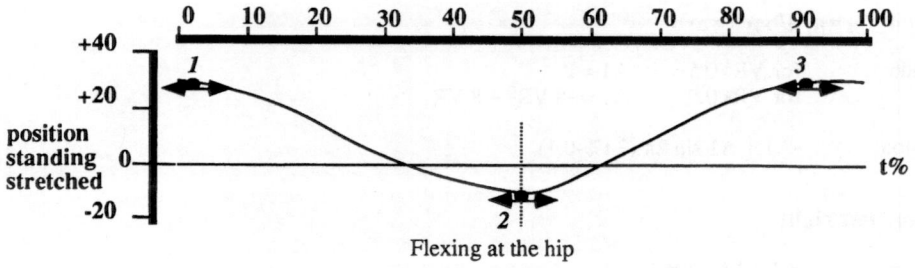

Flexing at the hip

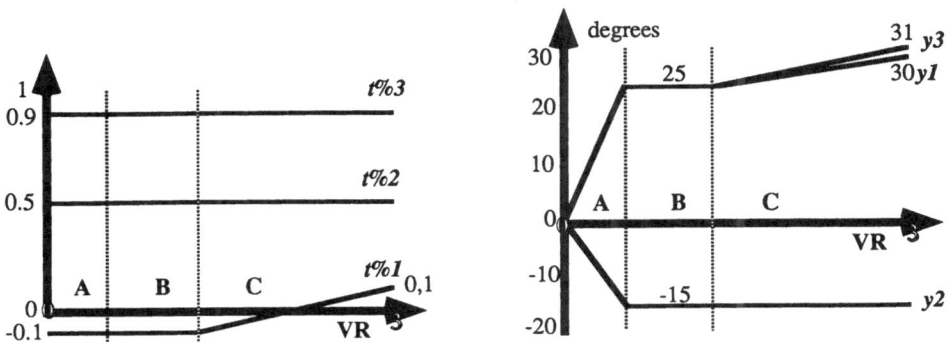

Variations of the coordinates of the control point in function of the relative velocity

B.2 Flexing at the knee

The first figure indicates the four necessary control points. The variation of their coordinates are summarized in the second figure.

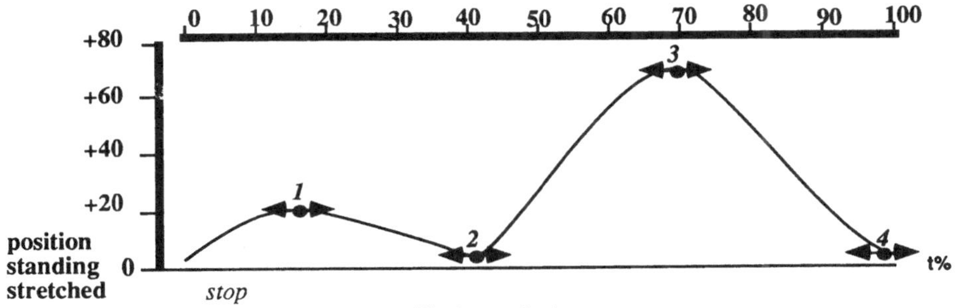

Flexing at the knee

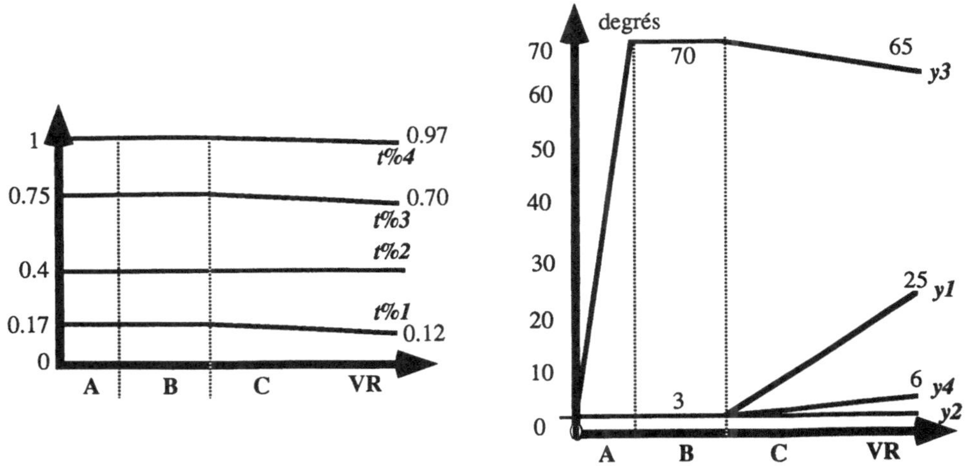

Variations of the coordinates of the control point in function of the relative velocity

B.3 Flexing at the ankle

The first figure indicates the five necessary control points. The variation of their coordinates are summarized in the second figure.

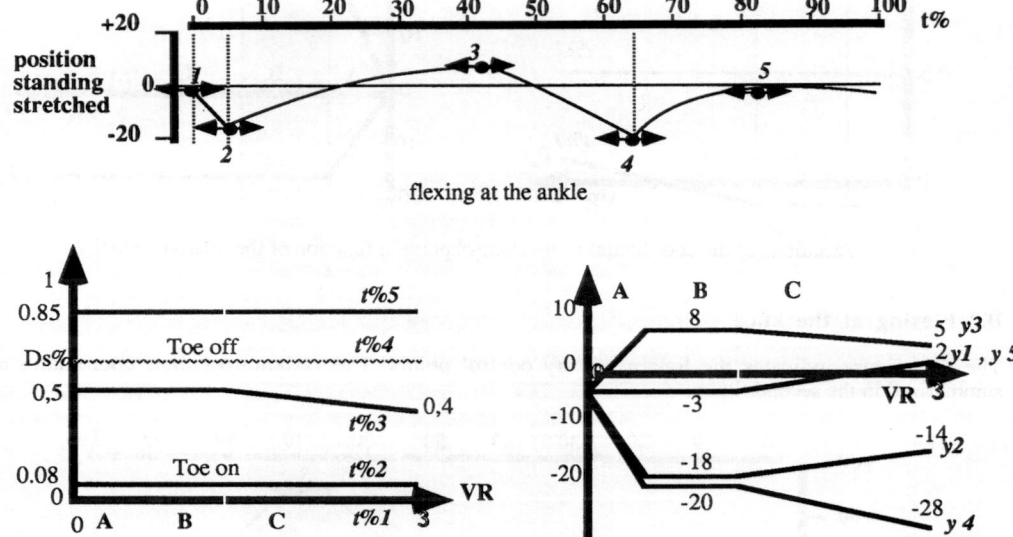

flexing at the ankle

Variations of the coordinates of the control point in function of the relative velocity

The closer a joint is to the floor, the more complex is its trajectory and the more it tends to be modified because of the variation of the floor surface. Consequently, it is useless to model the trajectory of the ankle with great accuracy.

Ronan Boulic is a research assistant in the Computer Graphics Lab at the Swiss Federal Institute of Technology in Lausanne, Switzerland. His current research interests are 3D computer animation related to perception-action control loops and real-time man-machine interaction. He received his engineer diploma from the National Institute of Applied Sciences (INSA) of Rennes in 1983 and Computer Sciences Doctorate from the University of Rennes (France) in 1986. He spent one year as a visiting research associate at the MIRALab Laboratory of the Graduate Business School of the University of Montreal.
address: EPFL-LIG CH 1015 Lausanne, Switzerland
E-mail: boulic@ligsg2.epfl.ch

Nadia Magnenat Thalmann is currently full Professor of Computer Science at the University of Geneva, Switzerland. A former member of the Council of Science and Technology of the Government of Quebec and of the Council of Science and Technology of the Canadian Broadcasting Corporation, she also has served on a variety of government advisory boards and program committees. She has received several awards, including the 1985 Communications Award from the Government of Quebec. In May 1987, she was nominated woman of the year in sciences by the Montreal community. Dr. Magnenat Thalmann received a BS in psychology, an MS in biochemistry, and a Ph.D in quantum chemistry and computer graphics from the University of Geneva. Her previous appointments include the University Laval in Quebec, the Graduate Business school of the University of Montreal in Canada. She has written and edited several books and research papers in image synthesis and computer animation and was codirector of the computer-generated films *Dream Flight*, *Eglantine*, *Rendez-vous à Montréal* and *Galaxy Sweetheart*. She served as chairperson of the Canadian Graphics Interface 85 Conference in Montreal and the CG International 88 conference.
address: MIRALab, CUI
             University of Geneva
             12 rue du Lac
             CH 1207 Geneva, Switzerland
E-mail: thalmann@uni2a.unige.ch

Daniel Thalmann is currently full Professor and Director of the Computer Graphics Laboratory at the Swiss Federal Institute of Technology in Lausanne, Switzerland. Since 1977, he was Professor at the University of Montreal and codirector of the MIRALab research laboratory. He received his diploma in nuclear physics and Ph.D in Computer Science from the University of Geneva. He is member of the editorial board of the Visual Computer and cochairs the EUROGRAPHICS Working Group on Computer Simulation and Animation. He was director of the Canadian Man-Machine Communications Society and is a member of the Computer Society of the IEEE, ACM, SIGGRAPH, and the Computer Graphics Society. Daniel Thalmann's research interests include 3D computer animation, image synthesis, and scientific visualization. He has published more than 60 papers in this areas and is coauthor of several books including: *Computer Animation: Theory and Practice* and *Image Synthesis: Theory and Practice*. He is also codirector of several computer-generated films: *Dream Flight*, *Eglantine, Rendez-vous à Montréal, Galaxy Sweetheart*.
address: Computer Graphics Lab
             Swiss federal Institute of Technology
             CH 1015 Lausanne, Switzerland
E-mail: thalmann@elma.epfl.ch

Registered 3D-Texture Imaging

Monique Nahas, Hervé Huitric, Marc Rioux, and Jacques Domey

ABSTRACT

In this paper we are presenting synthesis of faces obtained by means of a registered recording of a human face. This recording allows to get the geometrical coordinates and the corresponding intensity of each sample point at the same time. With these data organized in a 4-dimensional B-Spline surface, we are able to greatly improve the realistic quality of the reconstructed picture, coming close to a photographic result.

Keywords : Laser scanner, B-Spline, Realism, Human face and body.

1. INTRODUCTION

The synthesis of realistic characters leads to realizations quite different according to the quality to be privileged. The first models (1) (2) were more concerned with the photographic reproduction. Some quite realistic facial expressions on polygonal faces have been obtained (3). The synthetic actors, Marilyn and Humphrey, have an unquestionable resemblance with the models increased by gesture expressions and speech (4).

On another side, it is a difficult task to get the realism of the movement because it implies a complete comprehension of motion and a description of all the distorsions that go along with it such as skin or muscles deformations. Complex engineering techniques are now used for that purpose (5).

A very fine realistic appearance is still difficult to achieve mostly because the skin and hair have a very complex texture. New types of objects and most of all new textures of all kinds had to be developed.

Texture mapping is an efficient technique to improve the realism. It adds to the geometrical model an information of lighting texture (6) which underlines the microscopic structure of the surface, an information difficult to model ex nihilo. For example, the skin grain results more from a statistical distribution of lighting than from a simulated real texture obtained by shifting the calculated points. The texture mapping technique has been applied in particular to the face by John F.S. Yau and Neil D. Duffy (7). These authors start from a given polygonal model on a 3D structure registered by a laser scanner and from the acquisition of an intensity image. Our approach is very similar, except that the data basis we elaborate and use is a set of values of positions and intensity obtained simultaneously. On the other hand, this data set defines a B-Spline surface which allows quite supple deformations and animation (8). The "skin" constituted by the intensity image becomes a new space of experiments.

2. RECORDING

In order to get a registered 3D-texture of the model we use a laser scanner based on a synchronized geometry (9, 10, 11).

The optical arrangement of the 3D camera used for this experiment is shown schematically in Fig. 1. A diode laser is used for the projection and a CCD linear array provides both the position of the scattered laser spot which is giving the x,y,z coordinates of the subject surface and the texture level which is proportional to the amount of light scattered by the surface. For each scan of the CCD array we get one pixel of the range image and one pixel of the intensity image. The data rate is 20 KHz (x,y,z,t) and the resolution is 12 bits for the range image and 8 bits for the texture image. The avantage of this approach is to be able to use texture mapping techniques in order to get very realistic image of a person.

2.1 Head Recording

In order to get 360° measurements of the model's head we use a rotating table on which the model is sitting. The laser scan is adjusted vertically to coincide with the rotating axis of the rotating table and data acquisition are made while the model is rotating at a continuous speed. The model's head has been imaged in this mode of operation (see Fig. 2). The sampling along the vertical axis is of 1.2 mm and of 0.6° along the rotation. The display of Fig. 2 shows the derivative of the 3D data.

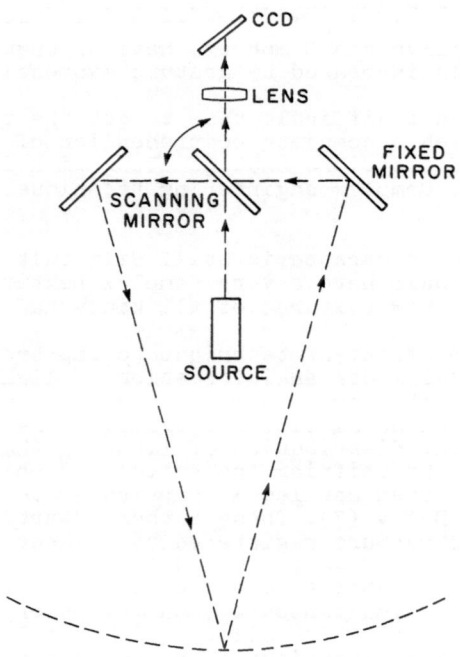

Fig. 1. Synchronized scanners ; one of the geometries which has been used for this experiment.

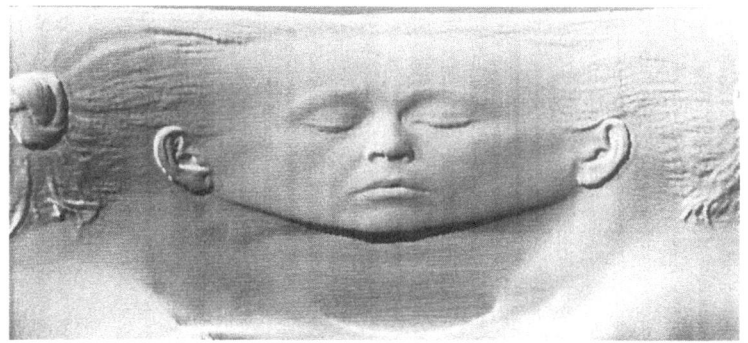

Fig. 2. Subject head recording over 360°. The derivative of the range
data is displayed.

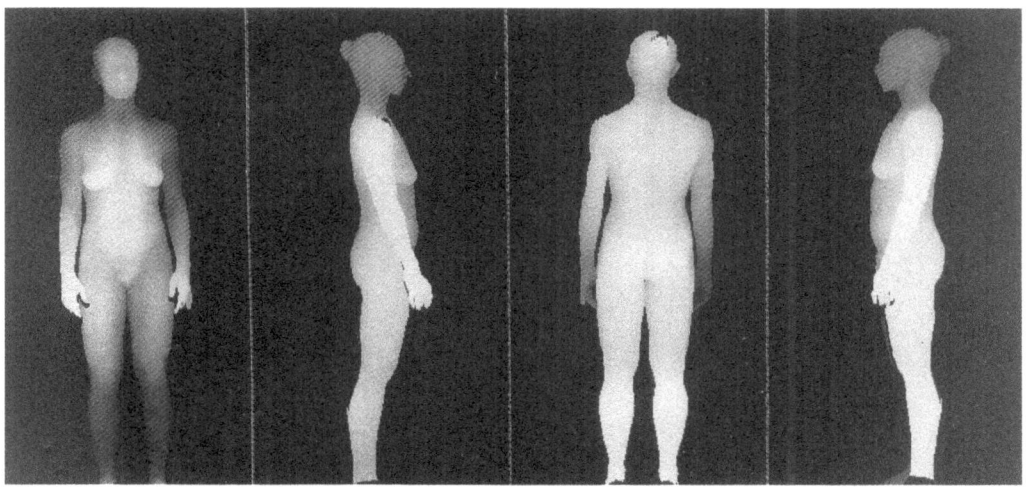

Fig. 3. Full body recording using multiple views taken at 90° intervals.
Grey levels display of the range data.

2.2 Body Recording

This mode of operating is inadequate for body measurements because of
the poor surface coverage for the arms and legs. Instead, multiple views
are used to improve surface coverage and in this mode of operating the
rotating table is fixed and a raster scan is made. A third and a fourth
raster scan are also made at 180° and 270°. The sampling along the vertical axis is 4 mm and 2 mm along the horizontal axis. Fig. 3 shows the
range data files for all the views. Here the 3D data are grey level
coded.

2.3 Face Recording

In order to synthetize and animate the model's face, a number of facial
configurations have been recorded. About 20 images are recorded in a

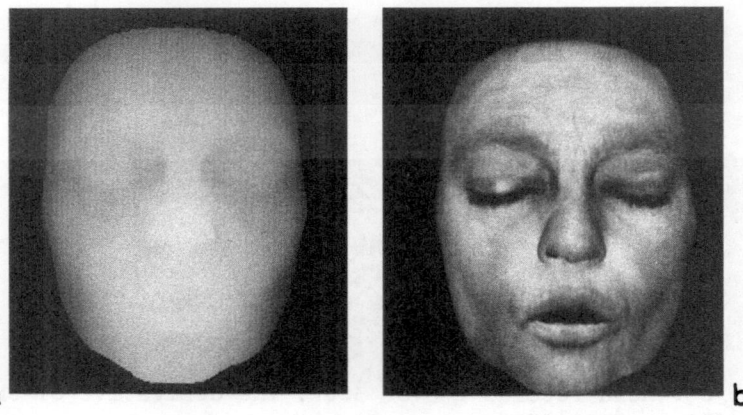

Fig. 4. Face recording. One of the recordings used to synthetize speech.
In a) we display the range data. In b) we have the registred
intensity values.

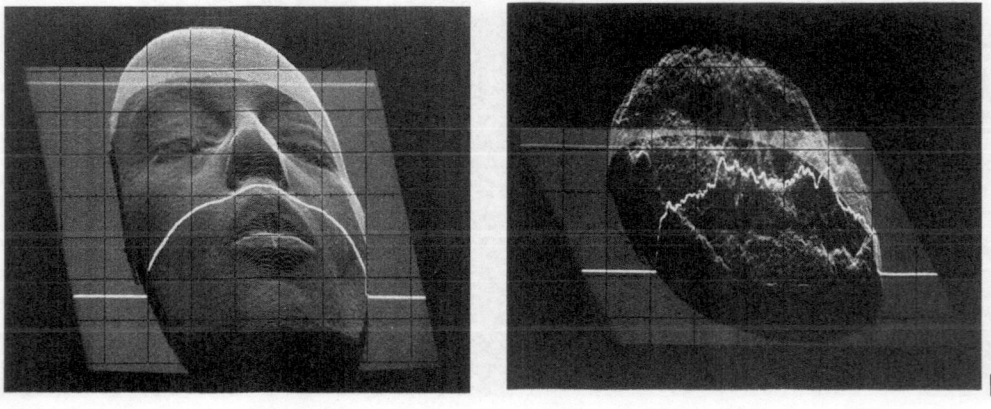

Fig. 5. Isometric views of the data displayed in Fig. 4.

raster scan mode. The sampling is 0.8 mm along the vertical and 0.6 mm
on the horizontal axis. Each face configuration corresponds to a specific phoneme and those images are superimposed onto the 360° model's
head in order to synthetize the appropriate view corresponding to the
desired phoneme. As an example, Fig. 4 shows the laser camera data for
the phoneme o . In 4a we display the 3D data in the form of a grey level coding. In 4b we have the registered texture for each 3D coordinate.

3. SYNTHETIC SKIN

It is interesting to look at both signals, such as illustrated in Fig. 5.
In 5a we display an isometric view of the 3D data. We have highlighted
one of the 256 profiles describing the entire surface of the face. In
5b we display the registered texture belonging to the same recording.
We have visualised the "skin" by generating a surface x,y,int where the
intensity int measured at the point x,y,z replaces the depth z . The

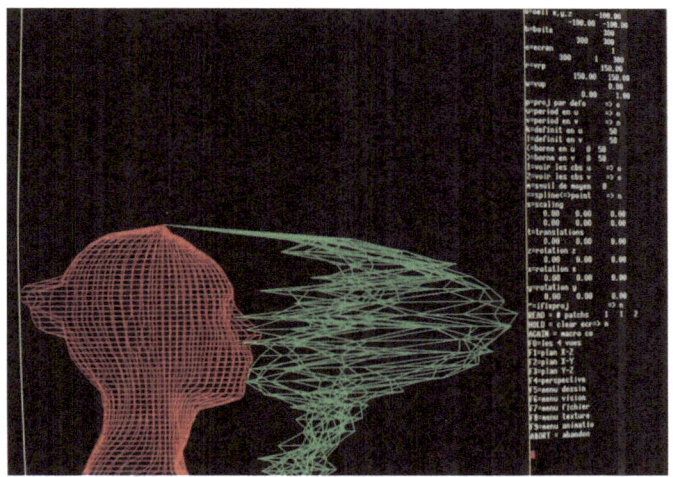

Fig. 6. The synthetic skin visualised with a surface x,y,int compared to
the surface x,y,z describing the face.

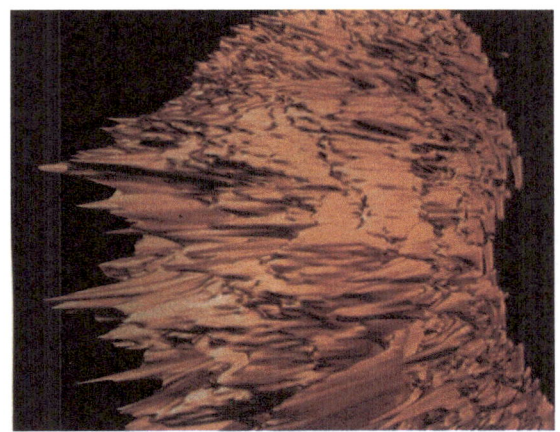

Fig. 7. Profile of the surface x,y,int
where int corresponds to the
intensity values of the skin
measured at point x,y,z.

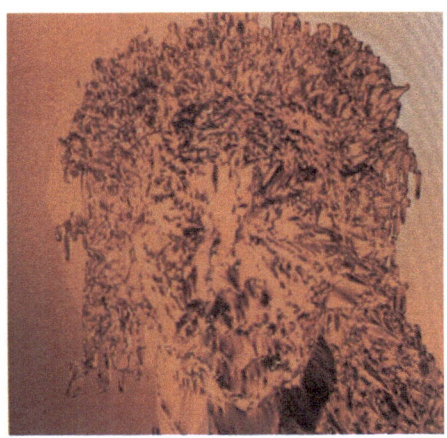

Fig. 8. Front view of the
surface x,y,int .

skin curve visible in Fig. 5 dsiplays a textured behavior which is illustrated for the surface in Fig. 6,7,8. Indeed, this texture gives the
skin grain, the hair-look and the eyesbrows reproduction which brings a
greater realism to the image.

Although we are using texture mapping directly here, we think that it
would be feasible to recreate realistic skin texture using modelisation
techniques (12, 13). Texture data obtained from laser scanning is quite
appropriate for that procedure because each pixel is measured one at a
time. This sequencial processing allows us to get surface reflectivity
variation on a point by point basis without interference by neighbour
points. In addition, the geometry of the recording as well as the shape

of the subject is known. This enables us to extract the surface reflectivity variation parameters which are describing the skin texture of a particular subject. A collection of synthetic skin could then be generated using experimental data obtained from many subjects.

Synthetic skin becomes then an independent matter of study. We can make it look younger (through polishing), make it lustreless or brighter (by increasing the contrast), or even give it a granular appearance, and try to make it look older.

4. VISUALISATION

The data of the mask or of the head in rotation have a regular matrix-structure which allow us to take them as control points of a B-Spline surface.

These points have 4 dimensions : x, y, z and the corresponding intensity. The surface calculation directly gives the interpolated intensity values of each point as well as the usual computed intensity. Rigorously, we would have to extract a value of albedo from the measured intensity and we must use this value in the intensity computation. In practice, we have simply combined the two intensities, considering the kind of combination as a new parameter of our visualisation. The following Fig. 9, 10, 11 and 12 illustrate some extreme cases of a barycentric combination : in Fig. 9, visualisation with no skin at all ; in Fig.

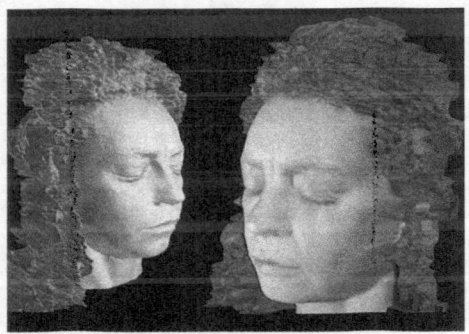

Fig. 9. Visualisation of the geometric data without the use of skin.

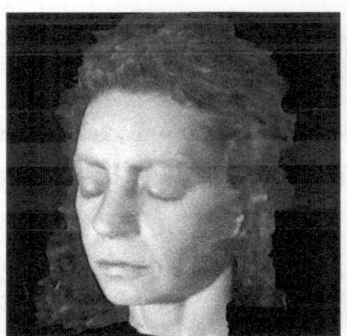
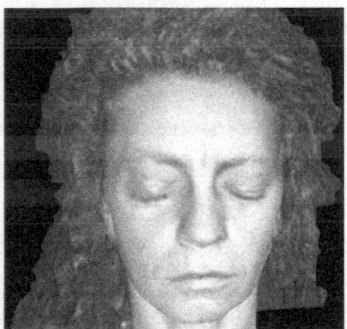

10   11

Fig. 10. 11. Visualisation of the geometric data using the skin.

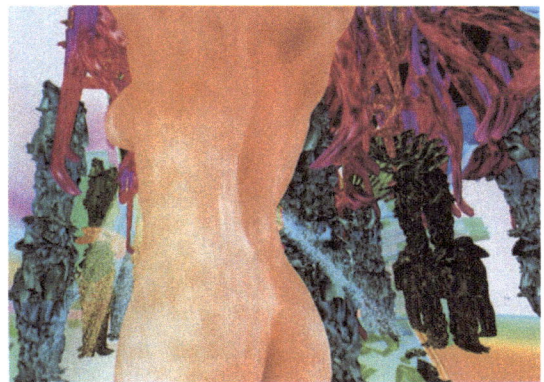

Fig. 12. Bust obtained according to registered data of geometry and intensity.

10, 11, 12, when using the measured skin intensity only. The introduction of a proportional coefficient is an artefact which allows the visualisation of the face in a given scene. It also enables the introduction of appropriate shadows when needed according to the scene represented.

5. MODELLING AND ANIMATION

In the meantime, even if the face complexion will be released by the future recording of colors, our job is to identify the different parts we want to color independently on the obtained surface. The identification of hair, eyebrows, lips, cheeks, is necessary in order to plan the experiments, for example, to make the hairdo, to put make-up on the face and to achieve facial animation such as eye-blinking or mouth movements, and so on.

5.1 Hairstyle

In the rotating image, the hair are extracted from the data basis by gathering the points of the face on one side or the other. We obtain then only one B-Spline surface for the hair and the corresponding lighting texture. We can visualise them by coloring and try to make matter effects by adding a "physical" texture and a visualisation in fibers (14), Fig. 13.

5.2 Eyes and lips

To model the eyes and lips in order to allow their animation, we have divided the face surface and its corresponding skin in 3 parts, one stopping at the middle of eyes level, the other one at the middle of the mouth level. This division is done by means of the Oslo algorithm in order to prevent any discontinuity (15). This way we get three B-Spline surfaces. Then it is easy to "open" the eyes pushing away the control points of the curves up to the limits outlined by a graph. The lips are independent surfaces using for control points those picked up on the face (Fig. 14, 15, 16, 17).

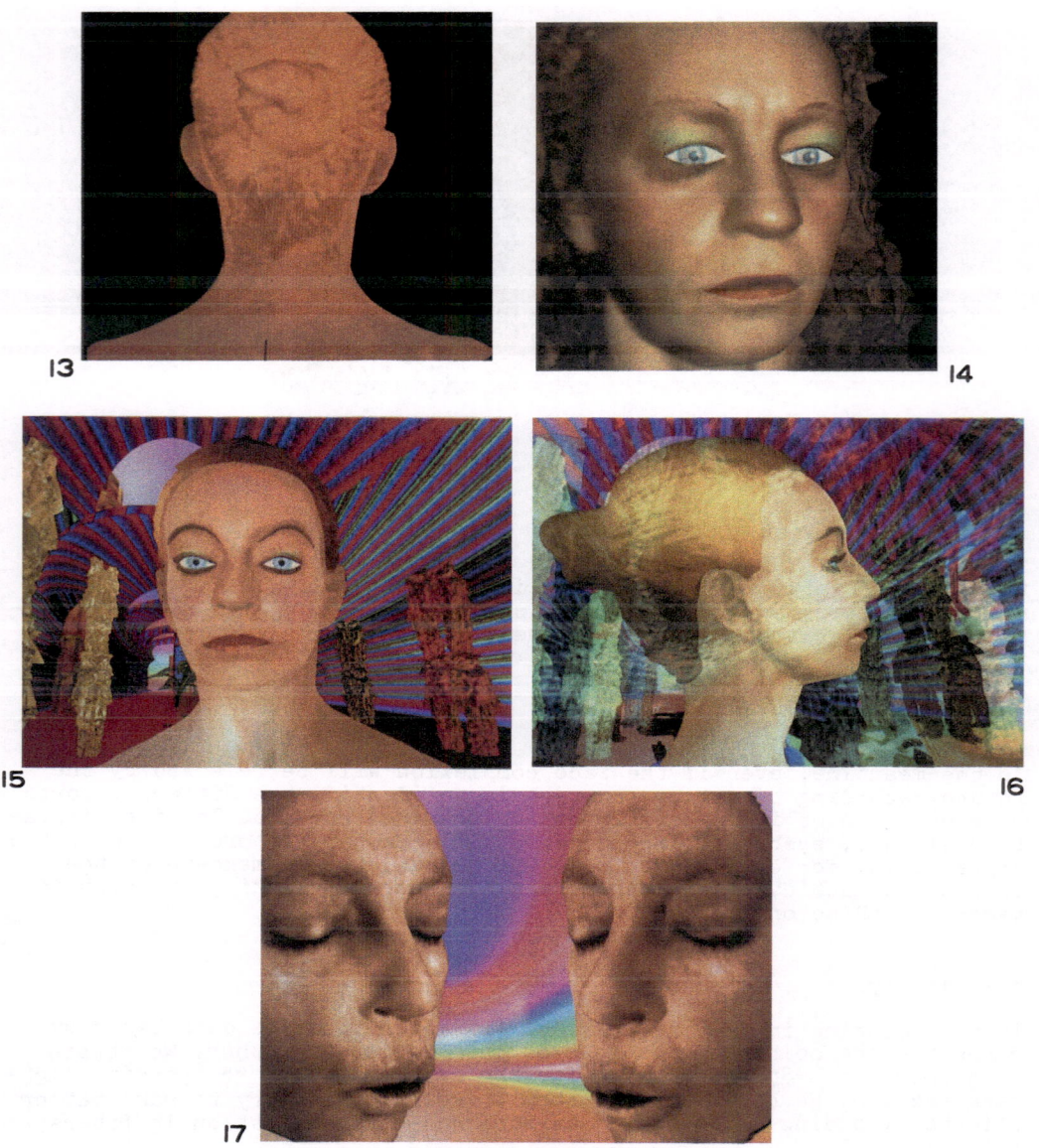

Fig. 13. Hair and skin obtained from global registered data. The line
        results from the folding of cylindric data. In order to re-
        move it we use a periodic spline.

Fig. 14. Introduction of eyes and lips.

Fig. 15. Face (scaled in x) corresponding to the recording of the head
        over 360° (Cf. Fig. 2).

Fig. 16. Profile of the head corresponding to the recording over 360°.

Fig. 17. Image from an animation of speaking faces corresponding to the
        recording shown in Fig. 4.

5.3 Animation

The technique described in Fig. 8 is applied to the lips motion and the facial expressions. Thus we need a subset of specific control points that we call attracting points. The shifting of these points is spread on a B-Spline surface producing a shifting grid for the control points of the face. We add a displacement in intensity : int, and get this way a new surface corresponding to the control points

$$(x + x, y + y, z + z, int + int) \ .$$

But even if this technique gives a coherent facial animation with wrinkles of expression, we are far from a perfect realistic animation where non predictible skin variations occur. The experiments we have realized with a face speaking every phoneme allowed us to visualise the realistic animation of a speaking face (Fig. 18). We can see how strong the expression variations are from one image to the other. We still have to develop a parametric system easy to handle which would allow us to get the variations int described above.

6. CONCLUSION

The registered recording of intensity and geometric data is a considerable help in the realization of realistic human beings. In particular, it gives the skin grain and the wrinkles which are so difficult to introduce otherwise, and more generally, it helps to get a realistic synthesis of any surface by giving the correct texture of intensity. The reconstructed figures have a very strong realism which resists to various manipulations and animations. The registered recording constitutes a very interesting material for the analysis and the generation of realistic images leading to new research developments.

7. ACKNOWLEDGEMENTS

The authors are grateful to Luc Cournoyer for his very efficient technical assistance in registration data.

8. REFERENCES

1. Parke F, (1982) Parameterized models for facial animation. IEEE C.G.A. 2(9), pp 61-68.
2. Badler N.I, (1981) Animation facial expression. Proceedings Computer Graphics, vol 15, N° 3, pp 245-252.
3. Waters K, (1987) A muscle model for animating three-dimensional facial expression. Computer Graphics, vol 21, N°4, pp 17-24.
4. Magnenat-Thalmann N, Thalmann D (1988) Rendez-vous à Montreal (film). Magnenat-Thalmann N, Primeau E, Thalmann D (1988) Abstract muscle action procedures for human face animation. Visual Computer, vol 3, pp 290-297.
5. Gourret J.P, Magnenat-Thalmann N, Thalmann D (1989) Simulation of object and human skin deformations in a grasping task. Computer Graphics, vol 23, N° 3, pp 21-30.
6. Blinn J.F, Newell M.E (1976) Texture and reflection in computer generated images. CACM, 19 (10), p 542, oct.
7. Yau J.F.S, Duffy N.D (1988) A texture mapping approach to 3D facial image synthesis. Computer Graphics Forum, 7 pp 129-134. (Eurographics (U.K.) Conference, Sussex, April 6-8, 1988).
8. Huitric H, Nahas M (1985) B-Spline surfaces : a tool for computer painting. IEEE Computer Graphics and Applications, pp 39-47.

9. Rioux M (1984) Laser range finder based on synchronized scanners. Appl. Opt., 23 (21), pp 3877-3844.
10. Rioux M, Bechthold G, Taylor D, Duggan M (1987) Design of a large depth of view 3D camera for robot vision. Opt. Eng., 26 (12), pp 1245-1250.
11. Rioux M, Cournoyer L (1988) The NRCC 3-dimensional image data files. CNRC 29077, June.
12. Boulanger P, Gagalowicz A, Rioux M, Integration of synthetic surface relief texture to range images. To be published in Computer Vision Graphics and Image Processing.
13. Gagalowicz A, DeMa S (1985) Sequential synthesis of natural textures. Computer Vision Graphics and Image Processing, 30, pp 289-315.
14. Nahas M, Huitric H, Saintourens M (1988) Animation of a B-Spline figure. Visual Computer, 3, pp 272-276, Springer-Verlag.
15. Cohen E, Lyche T, Riesenfeld R (1980) Discrete B-Splines and subdivision techniques in computer-aided design and computer graphics. Computer Graphics and Image Processing, 14 (2) October, pp 87-111.

Hervé Huitric is a professor in computer art and computer graphics at the University of Paris VIII. He received a doctorate in aesthetics and an MS in computer science from the University of Paris VIII. He also attended the Beaux Arts de Paris.

Hervé Huitric's address is LUAP, Tour 33-43, E2, Université Paris VII, 2 Place Jussieu, 75251 Paris Cedex 05, France.

Monique Nahas is a professor in computer graphics and physics at the University of Paris VII. She earned a doctorate in theoretical physics at the University of Orsay, Paris Sud, and has worked in computer art since 1971.

Monique Nahas' address is LUAP, Tour 33-43, E2, Université Paris VII, 2 Place Jussieu, 75251 Paris Cedex 05, France.

Jacques Domey is Head of the Photonics and Sensors Section of the Division of Electrical Engineering at the National Research Council of Canada in Ottawa. He holds a B.A.Sc. from Ecole Polytechnique de Montréal and M.S. degree from the Institute of Optics of the University of Rochester. His research activities have been, in the past 12 years, in the field of optical sensors for industrial automation. His current activities are in 3D machine vision sensors. He is a member of the Association of Professional Engineers of Ontario and of the International Society for Optical Engineering (SPIE).

Jacques Domey's address is National Research Council Division of Electrical Engineering, Photonics and Sensors Section, Building M-50, Montreal Road, Ottawa, Ontario, KIA ORS, Canada.

Marc Rioux is a Research Officer in the Electrical Engineering Division of the National Research Council of Canada. His present interests are in optical inspection techniques and, in particular, three-dimensional sensing for machine vision and optical dimensional inspection. He received his Bachelor's degree in Engineering Physics in 1971 and a Master's degree in Physics in 1976, both from Laval University. He worked five years on TEA CO_2 laser development and applications, two years in infrared holography and joined the National Research Council of Canada in 1978, to work on optical sensor research. His current activities are related to 3-D machine vision and the development of 3-D measurement techniques.

Marc Rioux's address is National Research Council, Division of Electrical Engineering, Photonics and Sensors Section, Building M-50, Montreal Road, Ottawa, Ontario, KIA ORS, Canada.

Artificial Intelligence, Behavior, and Motion Control

Part III

Artificial Intelligence, Behavior, and Motion Control

Behavioral Animation Using an Interactive Network

JANE WILHELMS

ABSTRACT

Behavioral, or *stimulus-response*, control for computer animation refers to motion generation through the use of rules defining how objects react to their environment. This automatic approach removes the onus of detailed motion specification from the animator, and is particularly good for cases when the generalities but not the details of the desired motion are known. An important issue in behavioral control is the user-interface by which the rules are specified. This paper describes an interactive network approach for defining these rules. Objects are given sensors and effectors (motors), and the user interactively designs a mapping between them using nodes and connections.

KEYWORDS: Graphics, Animation, Behavioral, Control, Interactive.

· 1. INTRODUCTION

Behavioral, or stimulus-response, animation is one of a number of automated approaches to motion control which have appeared in recent years. These approaches can help to remove (when desired) the burden of explicit motion specification from the animator. Some of these approaches operate on a rather low-level, in terms of the motion of single degrees of freedom or a few joints. These approaches include inverse kinematics (Badler 1987, Forsey 1988, Girard 1985, Korein 1982), automatic constraint satisfaction (Barzel 1988, Terzopoulos 1987, Witkin 1987), Witkin 1988), physical simulation (dynamics) (Brotman 1988, Isaacs 1987, Wilhelms 1987), and collision detection and response (Baraff 1989, Hahn 1988, Moore 1988). The question of higher-level motion control has also been pursued. Two prominent approaches that have arisen are hierarchical control systems (Bruderlin 1989, Chadwick 1989, Girard 1985, Zeltzer 1982), which are concerned mainly with locomotion of articulated bodies, and behavioral or stimulus-response control (Reynolds 1987, Wilhelms 1987), which deal more with defining the paths of objects within an environment. This paper describes a means of interactively controlling a behavioral animation system.

Behavioral animation was introduced first by Reynolds (Reynolds 1985, Reynolds 1987), whose model involved assigning objects procedurally defined behaviors which could be used to automatically generate their motion. This was used very successfully to generate the motion of bird flocks and fish schools. The objects' motion was determined by their desire to avoid collisions, to imitate the motion of neighboring birds, and to stay near the center of the flock. Their senses detected how much these desires were being satisfied, and this information was weighted, according to the importance of these desires, to produce new motion.

This elegant and very natural approach to high-level motion control was most appealing. An obvious important issue in its use is the means by which the animator defines and alters the behavior interactively. The approach used here was inspired partly by the book *Vehicles* by Valentino Braitenberg (Braitenberg 1984), which advances the idea that relatively simple mappings between sensors and effectors can produce motion that, while difficult to predict exactly, effectively gives an impression of emotions and thoughtful behavior on the part of the objects. The approach of allowing the user to interactively specify these simple mappings to define behaviors was used in developing the system *Notion* described here.

The biological model for this scenario, of course, predated any abstraction made about it by humans: such a network can be seen as a simple brain. In animals, stimulus-response networks work effectively by massive duplication of simple elements (Camhi 1984). The close relationship between biological neuronal circuits and the simple logical relations that came to lie at the heart of digital computers was recognized in the 1940's by McCulloch and Pitts. They discussed the "logical calculus of ideas immanent in nervous activity" (McCulloch 1943), and recognized that neurons exhibited the fundamental logical relations *and, or* and *not*. Though neurons and their connections are more complex and less "digital" than logic gates, they have in common with computers the use of massive networks to process information. Similar ideas are fundamental to the neural nets used in artificial intelligence and machine learning (Rumelhart 1986).

In brief, the approach taken here establishes connections between procedurally defined and parameterized *sensors* and *effectors* associated with animated objects. Sensors detect the qualities and proximity of other objects. Effectors are most commonly motors but could also alter object color or other qualities. Using an interactive interface, sensors and effectors can be connected together with *nodes* to form a network. *Connections* pass signals of variable strength from sensors to effectors; nodes control the mapping of signals. Nodes may be simple *transfer functions* that invert, emphasize, or apply thresholds to the signal, or may involve more sophisticated procedural operations which alter that mapping in more complex ways, sometimes using previous experience or stochastic methods.

Initial results suggest that this method can be used to produce interesting and automatic motion whose general characteristics are under the control of the user. Though it has not been implemented, a natural extension of these networks would be to develop them into a neural net (Rumelhart 1986) to explore learned behaviors.

2. OVERVIEW OF THE SYSTEM

Stimulus-response networks are associated with each of the animated objects. The objects need *sensors* that detect the stimuli of their environment, and *effectors* (motors) to propel them about. There must be *connections* established between sensors and effectors to produce a response. The nature of the response is also determined by *nodes* that alter the signals passing along the connections. Objects can be given *qualities* that allow other objects to recognize and react to them individually. Objects are initialized to have fixed sensors and effectors with no connections, and behaviors are designed by the user interactively connecting these either directly or through nodes, and by altering parameters. Animated objects also possess the usual geometric and visual properties (such as position, orientation, topology, geometry, and color) necessary for ordinary kinematic animation.

2.1. The Sensors

Sensors detect specific characteristics of objects in the environment. They each have a location and orientation on the body which affects how strongly they are stimulated. Because the relative strengths of the sensors localizes the signals, it is simplest if sensors for a particular quality are symmetrically arranged. Sensors also have a number of parameters which control how the stimulus is interpreted and passed on through the output connections. Parameters proved very important for developing desired behaviors. Standard parameters include:

Maximum and Minimum Range: Defines the distance over which the sensor is active.

Maximum and Minimum Scale: Scale the incoming signal according to distance, allowing the sensivity to vary depending how close the object is to the origin of the signal.

Angular Range: The field of view, in degrees, about the present object heading within which the sensor can detect. Some senses (such as vision) are more sensitive to orientation than others (such as smell or hearing).

Sensitivity: Either *dominant*, where only the most powerful stimulus in the environment is recognized, or *average*, where the signal is the average of all those in range.

There are two main types of sensors. *Distance* sensors (and *proximity* sensors, which are their inverse) detect the distance to other objects. They are particularly useful for collision avoidance maneuvers. *Quality* sensors detect characteristic qualities that are properties of other objects. Objects may have zero or more recognizable qualities, each of which has a scalar value indicating how strongly it is present. An example is the color of the object. Quality sensors have an added *filter* parameter which affects how sensitive they are to a particular quality.

Philosophically, the network model was planned to pass scalar sensor values and allow the nodes to resolve location from them. However, the implemented objects typically had two sensors in two dimensions and three in three, which make it impossible to determine a unique stimulus location from scalar sensor values alone (unless the angular range was limited). If another sensor were added, a unique location can be found (VanGelder 1988), but at the cost of further complexity in the network. As a simple (not very aesthetically satisfying) solution, sensors now pass a scalar output indicating how strongly they are stimulated and a vector output indicating the direction of the stimulus.

Perhaps a better future approach would be to abandon the low-level biological paradigm and use only a single sensor per quality. The sensor could interpret the signals coming from the entire environment and pass a simple signal to the further nodes. This, in a sense, extends the sensors to include part of the brain's function. This approach would also simplify the network.

2.2. The Effectors

Effectors are jet motors attached to a fixed location on the body. Potentially, effectors could take other forms, such as color or shape changes. Motor effectors act as a force pushing on the object (or pulling on it if the value is negative). The effector's position and orientation on the body defines the point of application of the force and the force direction. The current value of the effector represents the magnitude of the force being applied, which is the sum of the scalar values input to the effector scaled by a parameter. Effectors also have a parameter that limits the total force it can apply.

In the real world, a force applied to a rigid body, such as these simulated objects, produces a linear acceleration; it may also produce an angular acceleration if applied away from the body's center of mass, because it also acts as a torque. Physically correct dynamics (Wilhelms 1988), in which the acceleration is proportional to force and objects will continue to move at constant speed once started unless slowed by friction or other forces, is not used here.

Rather, the motion dynamics assume that the force is directly proportional to velocity, which inherently produces friction and causes objects to stop when not acted upon by other forces. (This does retain the ability to produce angular motion due to propulsive forces acting upon different parts of the body, which would be hard to imitate merely using kinematics.)

The equations used to generate motion are

$$\frac{\mathbf{F}}{m} = \mathbf{v}$$

$$\mathbf{J}^{-1} \cdot \tau = \omega$$

$$\tau = \mathbf{p} \times \mathbf{F}$$

where

$\mathbf{F}$ = 3D force vector in the local frame
τ = 3D torque vector ""
$\mathbf{p}$ = 3D point of application of force ""
m = mass
$\mathbf{J}$ = 3x3 inertial tensor matrix relative to the local frame
(moments of inertia on diagonal and products of inertia on off-diagonals)

Simple Euler integration is used to find new positions. Euler integration is notorious for accumulating errors (the "evil Euler method"), but adequate for present purposes.

$$\mathbf{p}_{t+1} = \mathbf{p}_t + \mathbf{v}_t \times \delta t$$

$$\theta_{t+1} = \theta_t + \omega_t \times \delta t$$

where $\mathbf{p}$ and θ are the position and orientation of the body at times t and $t+1$, and δt is the time step.

More information on simple ways to calculate these quantities can be found in Wilhelms (Wilhelms 1988), or in any introductory physics or mechanics text.

2.3. Connections and Nodes

A connection takes the value from the output of a sensor or a node and sends it to the input of one or more nodes or effectors. The connections implemented are slightly more complex, in that they can scale the signal and add to it as it passes. Sensors can have zero or more outputs but have no input connections. Effectors can have zero or more inputs but have no output connections.

Inclusion of nodes between sensors and effectors allows more complex mappings. Nodes can have both multiple input connections and multiple output connections. Each node type is associated with a procedure that calculates the output signal based upon its input. Parameters for nodes allow the user to more carefully control how the mapping takes place.

2.3.1. Transfer Function Nodes

The simplest, standard node type is a *transfer function*, which takes the sum of the input values and produces a single output value based upon a user-defined function. The user defines the function as points on a cartesian coordinate system (see Figure 1). Transfer functions can be monotonic (steadily increasing) or non-monotonic functions, involving complex changes in tangent and thresholds. Transfer functions that produce a constant value independent of input, when attached to an effector, will keep the motor running continuously. Transfer functions most closely resemble the low-level nodes described by Braitenberg (Braitenberg 1984), but are not very appropriate for controlling animation. For example, consider a transfer function node to cause objects to avoid one another based upon their distance. The sensor nearest the object will send a stronger signal to the effector on that side of the body than the farther sensor will send to the opposite effector. This will cause the objects to veer away, but how quickly they turn will depend upon the differential push on the motors which will vary with distance. Furthermore, forward speed will also be affect by distance in ways that may not confirm to the users wishes. Transfer functions are quite good for very regular, "mind-less" behaviors. Therefore, more sophisticated, parameterized nodes were developed.

2.3.2. Love and Hate Nodes

Two very useful nodes are *love* and *hate*, which cause movement toward or away from incoming stimuli. For these nodes, inputs and outputs are ordered and one-to-one, so that each input (from a particular sensor) will pass to an associated effector. Potentially, a different value is be sent to each output connection, depending upon the input from all known sensors, allowing better control over turning.

Parameters for these nodes include: *range* of stimuli to which they are sensitive; *forward scale factor* to control how much to push on all motors to produce forward motion; *revolute scale factor* to control how much more to push on one motor to cause turning; and *angular threshold* which specifies how many degrees the object's orientation may diverge from the goal direction before an attempt is made to correct. If the threshold is set to zero, even the slightest divergence causes a corrective turn, and motion may appear jittery. On the other hand, if the threshold is set high, the object will follow a zig-zag path toward (or away from) the goal.

2.3.3. Avoid Nodes

Another very useful node is *avoid*, which acts much like hate nodes but passes output values that go up exponentially as objects approach. The sensory input for avoid nodes is assumed to be distance.

2.3.4. Arbitrate Nodes

A final important node is *arbitrate*. It was soon found that the importance of signals must be weighted for reasonable motion. For example, if an object is strongly attracted to a goal some distance ahead, but also trying to avoid an obstacle in the way, the signal to go forward to the goal should be turned off to prevent a collision from occurring. Parameters for the arbitrate node indicate how signals should be passed through. Typically, the present of an avoid signal takes precedence over all other signals.

2.3.5. Other Node Types

The previous five node types were found most useful for general behaviors. Miscellaneous other nodes have been implemented. Some are simple, such as *and*, *or*, and *not* nodes. Network values are real, so these nodes respond as if a zero input is false, and any non-zero input is true. A *random* node is available that occasionally produces a positive signal and can make motion less smooth as well as break up cycles which sometimes happen when stable patterns are found. A *history* node alters its mapping according to the kind of signals it has already received. If it scales the signal up, it mimics a kind of habit formation, where the node reacts quicker to familiar signals; if it scales down, it mimics accommodation, where the node becomes less sensitive to its input.

2.4. Collision Response

Avoid nodes attempt to avoid a collision with the nearest object within range. When many objects are close, this strategy may fail and collisions can occur. A rather simplistic form of collision response has been implemented. When it is noted that forward motion will cause interpenetration, the object's velocity in the direction of the collision is removed (for inelastic collisions) or scaled by a value greater than zero and less than one and reversed (for elastic collisions). More realistic methods for collision response have been discussed elsewhere (Moore 1988).

3. ESTABLISHING BEHAVIORS: THE NOTION SOFTWARE

Notion is an interactive, multiple-window, behavioral animation system that runs on Silicon Graphics IRISes. *Notion* provides three permanent windows, as well as several temporary ones. The three permanent windows are:

1) the *graphics* window, which shows the objects in the scene (see Figures 3 and 4);

2) the *animation control* window, which accepts user input concerning the animation state, e.g., starting and stopping, running under behavioral or keyframe control, size of time steps and present time, and display characteristics; and

3) the *active object* window, which shows characteristics and values of the present active object picked by the user; some of the active object fields can also be interactively edited by the user.

Behaviorally generated animation can be stored as keyframes for replay. Motion may be three-dimensional, or clamped to a two-dimensional plane.

In the graphics window, objects are drawn according to their geometric descriptions, and icons representing sensors and effectors appear automatically. Lines extending from the sensor/effector icons indicate graphically the intensity of stimulus and effect. It is possible to leave a trail along the objects's prior path to more clearly represent their motion. Multiple input choices, including keyboard, sliders, and (for orientation) a virtual sphere (Chen1988) are available in temporary windows and can be used to alter the values in the window fields and the positions of graphical objects. A temporary window can be called upon to show the current network for the active object (see Figure 2). By default, sense icons appear along a leftward column of the network window, effector icons similarly along the right. The user can move these icons about and add nodes and connections between them. Picking a transfer function node calls up another temporary window (Figure 1) which indicates the current transfer function for the node. Transfer functions are defined by adding, deleting, and moving points about on a cartesian grid. The network window and the transfer function windows zoom, pan, and scroll to show all sections clearly.

Behavioral animation is achieved by setting up the appropriate network and transfer functions, placing objects of interest under behavioral control, and setting animation control to *go*. Networks are synchronized, in the sense that there is an internal clock which, each time step, calculates new values. The sensors are set once at the beginning, then the nodes are pulsed until their data stabilizes (up to a maximum number of pulses), and then the effector values are calculated. Thus, a network consisting of a sensor, two nodes in sequence, and an effector will require two time steps for stimulus of the sensor to reach the effector and cause a response. The user can set the actual motion (and display) time step to be any integral multiple of the network time step, as it may be desirable to give the network time to settle before producing new motion values for display.

4. SAMPLE BEHAVIOR PATTERNS

4.1. Path Finding in Two Dimensions

Figure 2 shows the network for objects that are attracted to blue cubes but desire to avoid collisions. Figure 3 shows the motion produced by this network. Considerable variation in the actual paths taken can be produced by changing parameters associated with sensors, nodes, and effectors. For example, changing the range over which the avoidance reaction occurs will prevent the objects from moving between the eight obstacles and force them to take the long way around to the goal white cube at the upper right.

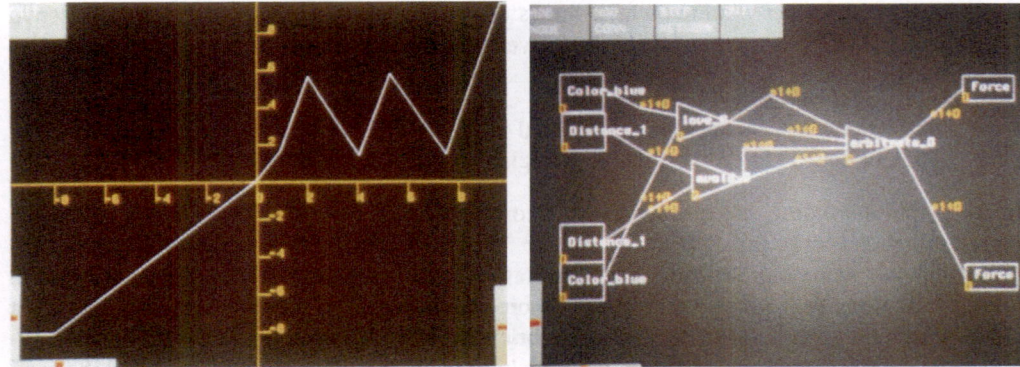

Figure 1. Transfer Functions

Figure 2. The Network Window

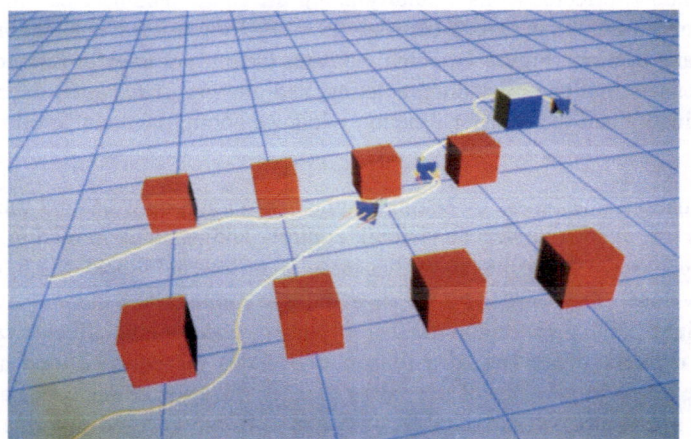

Figure 3. The Graphics Window

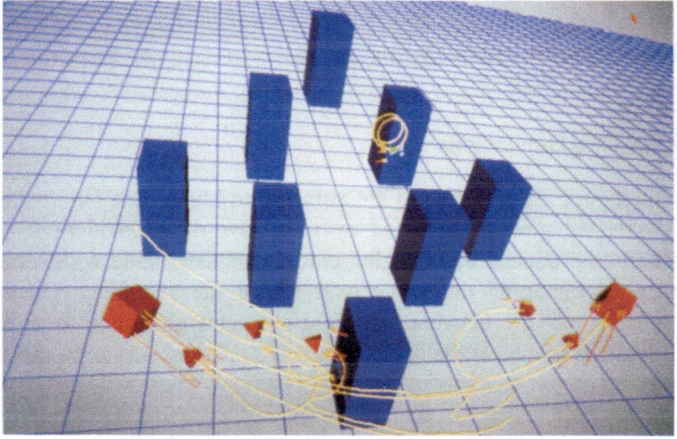

Figure 4. Three-Dimensional Motion

4.2. Attraction and Avoidance in Three Dimensions

Figure 4 shows a similar attraction/avoidance behavior in three dimensions. The tall blocks are obstacles that do not move. The two cubes are attractors that cycle the cubes due to constant forces being applied to their effectors using transfer function nodes. The tetrahedrons are objects with senses. The tetrahedron that cycles in the center of the obstacles is attracted to everything except other tetrahedrons. The other tetrahedrons are attracted only to the moving cubes.

5. DISCUSSION AND CONCLUSIONS

A network approach can be useful for quickly developing behavioral animations. It is particularly useful when many objects must be animated using simple behavioral rules. The purpose of this system was to devise a useful tool for animating and exploring behavior, rather than to exactly simulate biological circuits. Very early it became clear that sensors and nodes should be high-level and parameterized, in order to simplify the user's task of building networks. This involves a conceptual move away from low-level Braitenberg vehicles and similar connectionist systems such as McCullough-Pitts neurons (McCulloch 1943), logic circuits, and neural nets (Rumelhart 1986).

Behavioral animation is not expected to be the answer to all problems of specifying animation, any more than are any of the many other techniques such as key-positioning, hierarchical control, inverse kinematics, or dynamics. The ideal animation system should contain all of these tools. Behavioral control might be best used for generating group behaviors, or finding paths through an environment. Once a possible pattern is devised, other techniques could be brought in to refine the motion. Behavioral control is one tool among many to aid the animator in bringing his or her own vision to life.

ACKNOWLEDGEMENTS: The author wishes to thank Robert Skinner, for much of the implementation of the system, with some assistance from Matthew Moore. This work was supported by an NSF Grant #CCR-8606519. Many thanks also go to Silicon Graphics Inc. and Digital Equipment Corporation for their generous donations of equipment.

An earlier version of this paper appeared in the Proceedings of Graphics Interface 1989.

References

Badler1987.
> Norman I. Badler, Kamran Manoochehri, and Graham Walters, ''Articulated Figure Positioning by Multiple Constraints,'' *IEEE Computer Graphics and Applications*, vol. 7, no. 6, pp. 28-38, June, 1987.

Baraff1989.
> David Baraff, ''Analytical Methods for Dynamic Simulation of Non-Penetrating Rigid Bodies,'' *SIGGRAPH '89 Conference Proceedings*, vol. 23, no. 3 , pp. 223-232, July, 1989.

Barzel1988.
Ronen Barzel and Alan H. Barr, "A Modeling System Based on Dynamic Constraints," *SIGGRAPH '88 Conference Proceedings*, vol. 22, no. 4, pp. 179-188, August, 1988.

Braitenberg1984.
Valentino Braitenberg, *Vehicles, Experiments in Synthetic Psychology,* The MIT Press, Cambridge, Massachusetts, 1984.

Brotman1988.
Lynne Shapiro Brotman and Arun N. Netravali, "Motion Interpolation by Optimal Control," *SIGGRAPH '88 Conference Proceedings*, vol. 22, no. 4, pp. 309-315, August, 1988.

Bruderlin1989.
Armin Bruderlin and Thomas W. Calvert, "Goal-Directed, Dynamic Animation of Human Walking," *SIGGRAPH '89 Conference Proceedings*, vol. 23, no. 3, pp. 233-242, July, 1989.

Camhi1984.
Jeffrey M. Camhi, *Neuroethology: Nerve Cells and the Natural Behavior of Animals,* Sinauer Associates Inc., Sunderland, Massachusetts, 1984.

Chadwick1989.
John E. Chadwick, David R. Haumann, and Richard E. Parent, "Layered Construction for Deformable Animated Characters," *SIGGRAPH '89 Conference Proceedings*, vol. 23, no. 3 , pp. 243-252, July, 1989.

Chen1988.
Michael Chen, S. Joy Mountford, and Abigail Sellen, "A Study in Interactive 3-D Rotation Using 2-D Control Devices," *SIGGRAPH '88 Conference Proceedings*, vol. 22, no. 4, pp. 121-130, August, 1988.

Forsey1988.
David Forsey and Jane Wilhelms, "Manikin: Dynamic Analysis for Articulated Body Manipulation," *Graphics Interface '88*, June, 1988. to appear.

Gelder1988.
Allen Van Gelder, 1988. Personal Communication.

Girard1985.
Michael Girard and Antony A. Maciejewski, "Computational Modeling for the Computer Animation of Legged Figures," *SIGGRAPH '85 Conference Proceedings*, vol. 19, pp. 263-270, July, 1985.

Hahn1988.
James K. Hahn, "Realistic Animation of Rigid Bodies," *SIGGRAPH '88 Conference Proceedings*, vol. 22, no. 4, pp. 299-208, August, 1988.

Isaacs1987.
Paul M. Isaacs and Michael F. Cohen, "Controlling Dynamic Simulation with Kinematic Constraints," *SIGGRAPH '87 Conference Proceedings*, July, 1987.

Korein1982.
James U. Korein and Norman I. Badler, "Techniques for Generating the Goal-Directed Motion of Articulated Structures," *IEEE Computer Graphics and Applications*, vol. 2, no. 9, pp. 71-81, November, 1982.

McCulloch1943.
W. S. McCulloch and W. H. Pitts, "A Logical Calculus of Ideas Immanent in Nervous Activity," *Bulletin of Mathematical Biophysics*, vol. 5, pp. 115-133, 1943.

Moore1988.
Matthew Moore and Jane Wilhelms, "Collision Detection and Response for Computer Animation," *SIGGRAPH '88 Conference Proceedings*, vol. 22, no. 4, pp. 289-298, August, 1988.

Reynolds1985.
Craig W. Reynolds, "Description and Control of Time and Dynamics in Computer Animation," *SIGGRAPH '85 Tutorial Notes: Advanced Computer Animation*, pp. 289-296, July, 1985.

Reynolds1987.
Craig W. Reynolds, "Flocks, Herds, and Schools: A Distributed Behavioral Model," *SIGGRAPH '87 Conference Proceedings*, vol. 21, pp. 25-34, Association for Computing Machinery, July, 1987.

Rumelhart1986.
David Rumelhart, James McClelland, and the PDP Research Group, *Parallel Distributed Processing, Volumes 1 & 2*, The MIT Press, Cambridge, MA, 1986.

Terzopoulos1987.
Demetri Terzopoulos, John Platt, Alan H. Barr, and Kurt Fleischer, "Elastically Deformable Models," *SIGGRAPH '87 Conference Proceedings*, July, 1987.

Wilhelms1987.
Jane Wilhelms, "Using Dynamic Analysis for Animation of Articulated Bodies," *IEEE Computer Graphics and Applications*, vol. 7, no. 6, June, 1987.

Wilhelms1987.
Jane Wilhelms, "Towards Automatic Motion Control," *IEEE Computer Graphics and Animation April, 1987*, vol. 7, no. 4, pp. 11-22, April, 1987.

Wilhelms1988.
Jane Wilhelms, "Dynamics for Computer Graphics: A Tutorial," *Computing Systems*, pp. 63-93, USENIX Association, Winter, 1988. also UCSC Computer and Info. Sci., Tech. Report UCSC-CRL-87-5

Witkin1987.
Andrew Witkin, Kurt Fleischer, and Alan H. Barr, "Energy Constraints on Parameterized Models," *SIGGRAPH '87 Conference Proceedings*, (Anaheim, CA, July, 1987).

Witkin1988.
Andrew Witkin and Michael Kass, "Spacetime Constraints," *SIGGRAPH '88 Conference Proceedings*, vol. 22, no. 4, pp. 159-168, (Atlanta, GA, August, 1988).

Zeltzer1982.
David Zeltzer, "Motor Control Techniques for Figure Animation," *IEEE Computer Graphics and Applications*, vol. 2, no. 9, pp. 53-60, November, 1982.

 Jane Wilhelms has been an assssistant professor with the Computer and Information Sciences Board at the University of California, Santa Cruz, since 1985. Her research interests include computer animation (particularly that of articulated bodies), physical simulation, and scientific visualization. She received a BA in zoology from the University of Wisconsin, Madison, an MA in biology from Stanford University, and an MS and PhD in computer science from the University of California, Berkeley. She is a member of IEEE and ACM, and a member of the Editorial Board of Computer Graphics and Applications.

Address: UCSC Computer and Information Sciences, Applied Sciences Building, Santa Cruz, CA 95064, U.S.A.

Animating Microworlds from Scripts and Relational Constraints

GARY RIDSDALE and TOM CALVERT

ABSTRACT

This paper discusses a method for producing computer-generated microworlds populated by synthetic actors, using an expert system to interpret a script from known and inferred relational constraints. To generate an animated scene, the interactive user specifies a simplified script and a set of relational constraint rules. From these, the movements of the figures are generated automatically. The relationship between this work and that of other projects in figure animation is characterized, and the mechanism of the expert system is demonstrated with the aid of an example.

Keywords: microworlds, virtual environments, actors, relational constraints, figure animation

1. INTRODUCTION

Computer-animated films of human figures are typically specified as a sequence of key positions for each animated figure, together with an interpolation function that links these positions. While this method can yield impressive results in the hands of a professional animator(Bergeron, 1985; Pixar Corp., 1986; Symbolics Graphics Division, 1987), the process is labor intensive and has a steep learning curve. For a user who wishes to produce a short film involving human figures but who lacks experience in figure animation, key frame methods are prohibitively difficult.

More significantly, there is growing interest in the use of computer animation for generating simulated or "virtual worlds"(Brett, 1989; Brooks, 1989; Fisher, 1989; Sturman, 1989; Zeltzer, 1985) whose figures interact directly with the user as he or she "explores" the imaginary environment. Clearly, an animation technique that requires precise pre-planning of all of the actions and interactions of the figures would not work here, since there would be nothing to explore. Instead, *task-level* animation may be used to replace the key frames with *goals*, and the interpolation functions with *constraints*. By altering the goals and constraints and the environment that they function in, the user is able to influence the behavior of the figures *indirectly*. This paper describes a task-level animation system that employs an expert system. Using inference rules and property inheritance, the system defines the relationships between the observer, the figures and the scene. Since these relationships are used to constrain the behavior of the figures as they try to achieve their goals, we call them *relational constraints*. Thus a "virtual environment" (Fisher, 1989) or "microworld"(Sturman, 1989; Zeltzer, 1985) is created consisting of the user, the figures in the scene, and their environment.

The user's role is split into two: the writer of the script which defines the goals and scene-specific constraints for each figure in the scene, and the "observer" who may interact with the scene as a participant. Since the current LISP-based implementation does not run in real time, the observer's involvement in the scene is presently limited to making adjustments to the strengths of the relational constraints at the beginning of a sequence, and to observing the results. With a faster implementation, the aim is to make the observer a full-fledged actor in the scene.

Even as it is, our system promises to be quicker (albeit less flexible) than using key frames, particularly when a large number of figures are involved. In fact, scenes involving dozens or even hundreds of figures can be created with little extra work on the part of the user. So, for example, an animated matte painting depicting a crowd scene could be created for use as a movie background.

Creating a functioning microworld should involve a minimum of specification on the part of the user. Still, in most interesting scenes the figures do have specific jobs to do and actions to perform if the theme of the scene is to be in keeping with the intentions of the script.

Our current system assumes that the user will supply two positions, a "start" and a "goal" for each figure. The start and arrival *times* may also be supplied explicitly, or they may be left as free variables. The intervening frames are then computed automatically as the expert system attempts to maintain the relational constraints that have been established for the figures, including their relationship to the observer. This requires a means to flexibly encode this knowledge in a form that is easily understood by both humans and computers, and rule-invoking daemons organized into a property-inheritance network appear to fit the requirements. A working prototype system is described after other, related research is reviewed.

2. RELATED RESEARCH

Most computer animation systems developed over the past decade employed a forward kinematic approach using parametric key frame interpolation(Badler, 1978; Calvert, 1980; Calvert, 1982; Dooley, 1982; Herbison-Evans, 1978; Kochanek, 1982; Kroyer, 1986; Steketee, 1985; Sturman, 1984). In these implementations, a sequence of positions of each of the independent elements in the scene is specified directly by the animator and is interpolated mathematically.

For complex jointed motion, inverse kinematic animation methods(Girard, 1985; Korein, 1982), originally derived from robotics research(Lee, 1982; Paul, 1981), provide increased expressive power by permitting the user to express the desired motion of, for example, a figure's hand or foot, directly in the coordinates of the task, such as "step right here" or "push the red button". Where the number of degrees of freedom is small, fixed constraints on joint angle range and on the structure of the linkage may reduce the solution space to a unique result. In complex scenes, however, heuristic methods may be needed to pare down the solution space.

Task-level animation goes one step further by allowing the user to specify the goal of the action rather than the action itself. In one of the first papers on task-level animation of human figures, Zeltzer(Zeltzer, 1982) described the use of multiple layers of control, arranged in a hierarchy which successively refined the figure's task until low-level "motor control units" could take over to move the limbs. Later Girard(Girard, 1987) described an inverse-kinematic mechanism which could model the complex gait patterns of multi-legged animals, while Badler(Badler, 1986) focused on reaching tasks. Magnenat-Thalmann(Magnenat-Thalmann, 1987) described the creation of a procedurally-animated film involving a pair of complex and realistic figures. None of these directly addressed the issue of figure relationships as a part of the specifications, although it would probably fit in at Zeltzer's "Task Manager" level (Fig. 1).

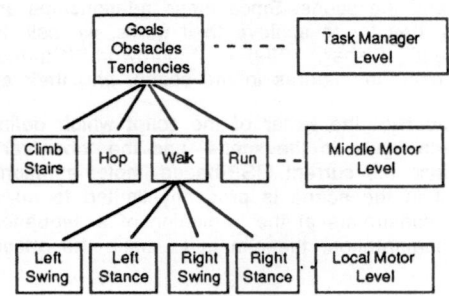

Fig.1. Zelter's Hierarchy

Reynolds(Reynolds, 1987) made what was possibly the first major break with key frame and inverse-kinematic methods in the context of figure animation. (Also, see Kahn(Kahn, 1979) for an important early attempt at relating goals and intentions to animated action from an AI viewpoint). Reynolds was attempting to construct what amounted to a microworld populated by fish and birds that swim and fly in realistic flocks. Reynolds' system modeled each figure as an "actor" possessing both self-knowledge and an awareness of the other figures. The result(Symbolics Graphics Division, 1987) convincingly demonstrated the power of such an actor-centered approach, since, by varying only a small number of parameters, many different and convincing sequences could be quickly generated. Any one of these sequences would have been prohibitively time-consuming to animate using interpolated key frame methods. Also, since the action of the computer-animated characters was not precisely specified, Reynolds' "boids" were true virtual creatures. With sufficient computing power, the observer could have joined the flock himself. Essential differences between Reynolds' approach and ours are described later.

Earlier work by the authors(Ridsdale, 1986; Ridsdale, 1987) proposed a design for an animation system for human figures that move within an environment constrained both by physical obstacles and by behavioral constraints imposed by social and theatrical considerations. The system that resulted from this design, described below, is capable of quickly generating actions for a set of several figures that interact with the environment and with each other in complex ways. Once the relational constraints of the figures have been determined by the expert system, robotics techniques are used to deal with collision avoidance and to generate the walking gait for each figure in the scene. As demonstrated by Kahn and Reynolds, an AI-based animation system allows the user to automatically generate many different and interesting variations on the scene action by altering a small number of parameters. Further, these parameters can be directly related to concepts that are meaningful to the user, such as which objects in the scene do each figure tend to avoid, to what extent one figure likes or dislikes another, and which figure takes precedence in the event of a conflict. For an inexperienced animator, these relationships are more intuitively related to the script than are interpolation functions, and they are critical for creating an interactive microworld populated with human figures.

An important difference between Reynolds' approach and ours can be explained by comparing them to two classic approaches in numeric simulation. In the first, or "initial value" formulation, the inputs to the problem solver are the starting state of the system, and the set of constraint functions that will be used to determine the outcome at a series of future times. Most classical simulation methods employ this formulation, as is similar to that used by Reynolds. In the second, or "boundary value" formulation, several boundary states of the system are specified beforehand, and the constraint functions are used to determine a sequence of in-between states consistent with all boundary values. We chose this formulation since we feel that it closely models the theatrical concept of a "scene" where one boundary is the start of the scripted scene ("curtain rises") and the other boundary is the end of the scripted scene ("curtain falls"). Further, each scripted scene may be divided into any number of (possibly overlapping) sub-scenes.

Research in dynamic animation provides another analogy. In forward dynamics formulations(Armstrong, 1986; Wilhelms, 1986), the user inputs set of forces acting on an articulated figure and the resulting accelerations are used to predict what will happen in the future. Whereas in inverse dynamics formulations(Brotman, 1988; Isaacs, 1987; Witkin, 1987; Witkin, 1988) a set of boundary events (positions, speeds, or accelerations) are specified at key intervals, and a set of forces compatible with (that is, possibly *causing*) those boundary events is calculated. Those forces may then be used to determine the remaining (unconstrained) motion of the figures. Similarly, in our task animation system, the user specifies a set of boundary events in time and space for each figure, and the expert system finds a set of behaviorals consistent with those events. These constraints then determine how the action between the boundary events will appear.

3. REPRESENTING ANIMATED FIGURES AS ACTORS

We believe that a figure animation system that treats animated figures as motivated actors, rather than as mere geometric forms, can provide increased expressive power to the designer of a microworld. After all, It is generally the behavior of these figures, and our expectations of them, that defines what a scene is all about. Further, if the behavior of the figures is influenced by, but not limited to, the events in the script, this will facilitate the creation of interesting environments by permitting the user to explore behavioral variations interactively.

As mentioned previously, our system employs an expert system to organize and interpret the relational constraints. The expert system consists of a *knowledge base* describing the model entities (in this case, figures, sets, and the audience) and their relationships, together with an *inference engine*, which is a mechanism for automatic reasoning. Our system is written in Common Lisp running on a Hewlett-Packard 350SRX workstation, using the FROBS(Muehle, 1987) ("Frames and Objects") package to encapsulate the knowledge base in manageable chunks. FROBS is a set of object-oriented extensions to Common Lisp which incorporate frame-like (Minsky, 1975) reasoning capabilities.

Each actor in the scene is represented by a FROBS structure, which communicates with other FROBS by message passing. For example, if the script called for a figure to walk from one location to another, the figure first sends a message to each of the static "actors" in the scene (the furniture and walls) to obtain their locations. This triggers the inference engine to find a constraint-compliant path using a modified VGraph algorithm(Brooks, 1983; Lozano-Pérez, 1983). Messages then go out to all other figures to inquire what their planned paths are. If any potential conflicts arise, the figures involved undertake negotiations to resolve them. A property-inheritance network allows the user to define "stock types" from which new types of figures can be synthesized. Each node in the network defines a set of "parent" classes, a set of "child" classes, and a set of constraint rules that affect only the children and their descendants.

"Cabin Fever"
Scene 1

The setting:

>   A ski cabin. At center stage is a low table. To the left of the table is a white chair. To the right of the table is a wood stove, supplying the only heat in the room. The room is cold. Upstage of the table is bar. There are exits at both of the downstage corners of the set.

The cast:
- Lemmon, a drunk.
- Red, owner of the cabin and Lemmon's boss.
- Pinky, a nervous type.
- Lime and Blue, neighbours.
- Blanche, Pinky's wife.

The action:
- As the curtain rises:
  Pinky is standing center stage at the left, facing the stove. Red is standing next to Pinky, downstage. Lemmon is at the bar, drinking a beer. Pinky and Red are shivering. Blanche is sitting in the white chair. Blue is standing at the upstage right corner, and Lime is standing at the downstage right corner.
- Red says to Lemmon, "Don't drink it all. Leave some for me."
- Lemmon looks at him nervously and begins to guzzle his beer.
- Blanche begins to harangue Pinky about his appearance.
- Red strolls toward the bar.
- As Red approaches the bar, Lemmon suddenly puts down his drink and exits to the left of the stage as Pinky exits to the right.
- Suddenly, Blanche stops speaking then cries out in anguish.

Fig. 2: Original Script of Scene

```
newscript ("Cabin Fever"){
    + locations =
        SkiCabin: {location and dimensions of Ski Cabin}
    + view =
        * from downstage-right
    + properties =
        * Bar: {location and dimensions of Bar}
        * Table: {location and dimensions of Table}
        * Stove: {location and dimensions of Stove}
        * ExitRight: {location of ExitRight}
        * ExitLeft: {location of ExitLeft}
    + characters =
        * principals:
            Pinky: {size and initial location of magenta figure}
            Red: {size and initial location of red figure}
            Blanche: {size and initial location of white figure}
            Lemmon: {size and initial location of yellow figure}
        * extras:
            Blue: {size and initial location of turquoise figure}
            Lime: {size and initial location of green figure}
    + relationships:
        * Pinky defers-to Lemmon with-strength 1
        * Pinky defers-to Lime with-strength 1
        * cold-people are-attracted-to source-of-heat
        * hot-people are-repelled-by source-of-heat
        * stove is-a source-of-heat
        * cries-out is-a dramatic-event
    + action:
        * in SkiCabin:
        * when (curtainrise)
            Pinky is-a cold-people, and
            Red is-a cold-people
        * when (curtainrise) Blanche starts-to speak-to Pinky
        * when(curtainrise + 20 sec) Red walks-to Bar
        * when( (Red at bar) - 2 secs)
            Lemmon walks-to ExitLeft
        * Pinky walks-to ExitRight
        * when (Pinky at ExitRight ) Blanche cries-out
        * end scene
}endscript
```

Fig. 3: Translated Script

4. AN EXAMPLE SCENE

Figure 2 shows the original script. Figure 3 is a hand translation into a form that the parser can understand, effectively filtering out relationships and actions that the expert system cannot currently deal with. (Please note that the names of the figures were chosen to make them easily recognizable on the accompanying video tape: "Lemmon" is yellow, "Red is red, "Pinky" is magenta, "Lime" is green, "Blue" is turquoise blue and "Blanche" is seated in a white chair.).

Figure 4 shows the layout of the set and the paths that the principal figures would take if the relational constraints are turned off: they would walk straight from one boundary event to the next. See also Photo 1.

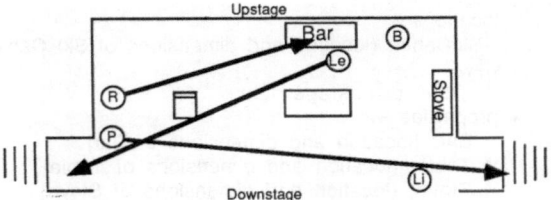

Fig. 4: Layout and Path Boundaries

5. Analysis

5.1: Script Interpretation

The first part of the script consists of a set of declarations. Here the locations, stage properties and figures are described. Two classes of characters are currently understood, "principal" and "extra". Characters designated as "extra", such as "Lime", are those that the system is free to move around, while principal characters such as "Red" must comply with the boundary events taken from the script. The "relationships" section defines the relational constraints peculiar to this script. For example, the relationship "defers-to" determines which figure takes precedence in the event of an unresolvable conflict. "Attracted-to" and "repelled-by" have the obvious meaning. Each relationship has a weighting ("with-strength") that can be adjusted interactively. Here the reference in the original script to Lemmon and Pinky shivering becomes an identification of them as being members of the class "cold-people", attracted to sources of heat such as the stove. Other, more general relational constructs such as non-intersection are defined in a global library.

The "action" section sets up the boundary events for each figure. The first of these occurs when Blanche begins to speak. According to the rules of good theatrical direction(Allensworth, 1982; Brown, 1936), no figure should come between the observer and the figure who is currently speaking. Thus, when Red walks from his starting position to the bar, he is *constrained* to pass behind Blanche despite the fact that he could have taken a shorter path had he passed in front of her.

Figure 5 shows Red's revised path behind Blanche. Figure 5 also shows Pinky and Red detouring behind Blanche. See Photo 2. And, since Pinky and Red are "cold-people" and since cold-people are said to be attracted to a source of heat, their paths also detour to be closer to the stove. See Photo 3 and Photo 4.

At the last line of the script translation, Catherine ends her first speech and cries out. Since a cry is defined as a dramatic event, the extras are brought into play to draw attention to it just before it occurs (the entire script is read and analyzed before any action is generated). This is called "focus" and can be considered to be a form of anticipation. To achieve this, the extras Lime and Blue position themselves in a straight line, like an arrow that points toward the Blanche.

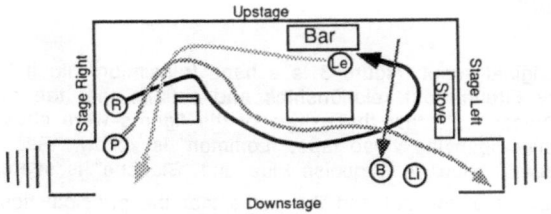

Fig. 5: Resulting Paths

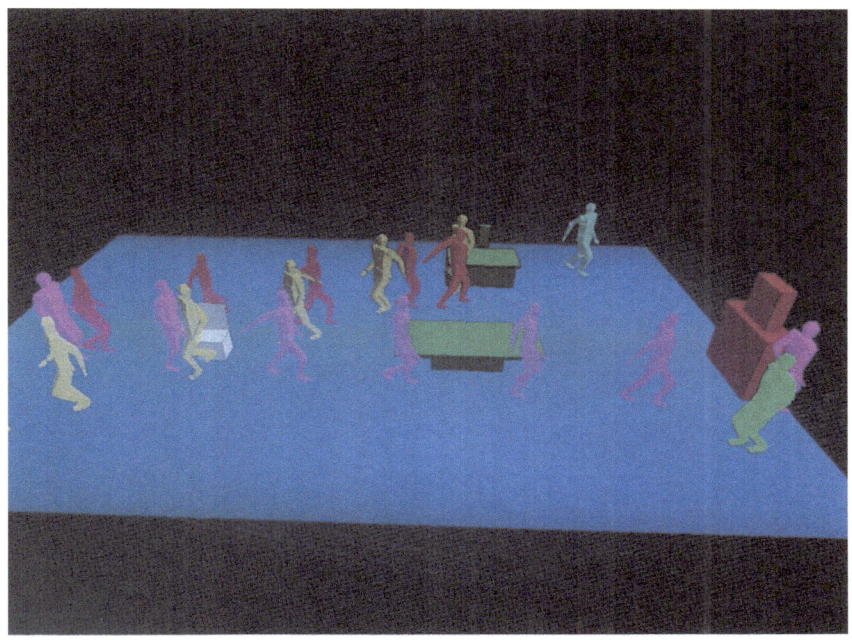

Photo 1: Multiple Exposure of Figures Moving without Relational Constaints

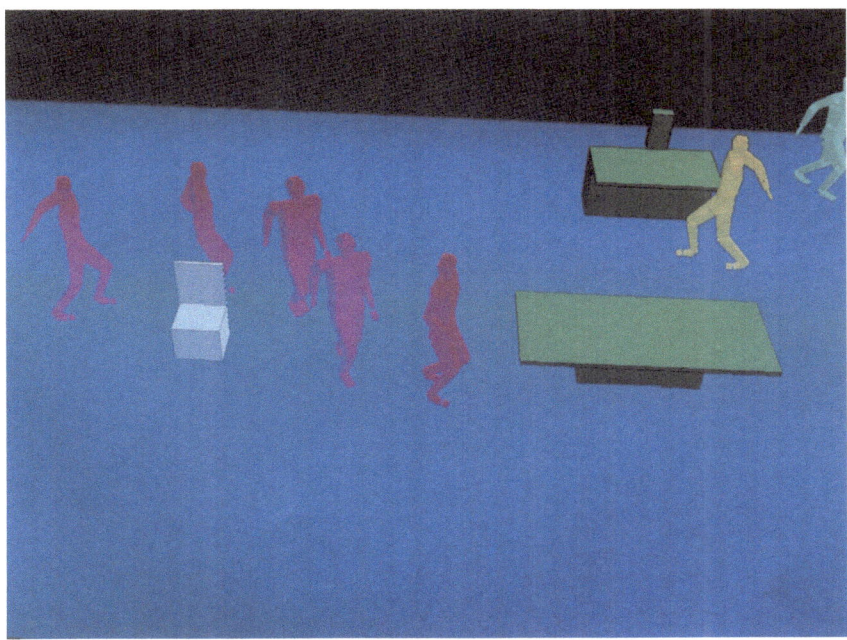

Photo 2: Red Character Constrained by Relationship to Audience and to Character in White Chair

Photo 3: Red Character Moving Under the Influence of Non-Contact and Coldness Relationships

Photo 4: Paths of Pink and Yellow Characters under Relational Constraints

Figures 6 and 7 shows how easily variations on a given scene can be generated merely by altering a few parameters. Figure 6 is the same scene as Figure 5, but with the viewpoint rotated 180 degrees.

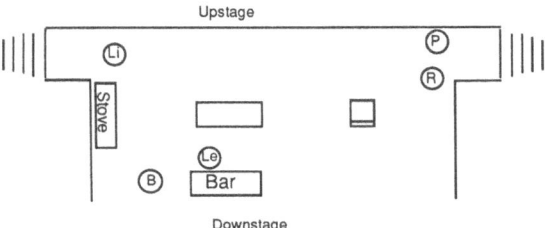

Fig. 6: Scene Inverted

Figure 7 shows the result, with Red re-classified as a "cold-person" and Lemmon as a "hot person". Note that Pinky, Lemmon and Red still correctly go behind Blanche, while Lemmon detours to be closer to the fire.

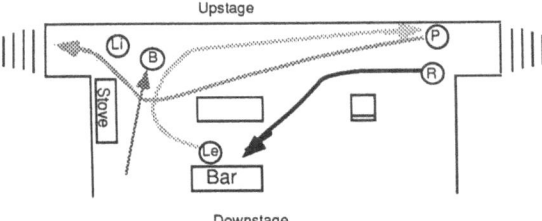

Fig. 7: Result of Inversion

With optimized code and a faster processor, we expect to be able to move the observer freely, and to have changes like this made in real time. Also, with relational constraints defined between the characters and the observer, the observer will be able to participate in the scene.

5.2: Generating the Locomotion

Once paths consistent with the stated and implicit constraints have been determined, inverse kinematics are used to actually generate the locomotion. Given each figure's path, known velocities along the path, leg length, and gait, a "foot-step" structure is produced, which, rather like a dance-school diagram, specifies where and when the figure is to place its feet for each step. An inverse kinematic method then uses the foot-step structure to generate the locomotion of each figure data associated with the different gait characteristics known to the expert system.

6. CONCLUSIONS

Our system works out the initial animation automatically in about five minutes on an HP 350SRX workstation, and wire-frame rendering requires approximate one second per frame. Most simple revisions, such as those described, can be executed in less than a minute. And although the current LISP-based implementation is clearly too slow for real-time interaction, we are confident that this can be solved by going to a faster processor (the HP350 is a 2-MIPS machine) and by re-implementing critical loops in "C". Further, larger scenes involving dozens or even hundreds of figures are completely feasible, even though they would seldom even be attempted using conventional computer animation techniques.

A number of limitations in the current version of the program make it unsuitable for producing a complete animated feature. First, the rendering of the figures is restricted to boxy robot-like forms. However, for use in generating an interactive microworld, boxy forms are probably acceptable.

Second, dynamic simulation is missing since inverse dynamics cannot currently be implemented in real time. However, we are investigating the use of connectionist methods(Barhen, 1989; Jordan, 1988) to approximate the complex dynamic functions of motion in real time.

Apart from these problems, and the fact that the knowledge base is still rather simple, we feel that the current system is a useful tool for exploring microworld construction. We wish to thank the National Science Foundation, Hewlett-Packard Corporation, the University of Utah and Simon Fraser University for their support of this project.

REFERENCES

Allensworth C (1982) The Complete Play Production Handbook (Rev. Ed.). Harper and Row, Inc., 1982.

Armstrong W, Green M, Lake R (1986) Near Real-Time Control of Human Figure Models. Proceedings Graphics Interface-86 Conference, pp 147-151.

Badler N (1986) Animating Human Figures: Perspectives and Directions. Proceedings Graphics Interface Conference, pp 115-120.

Badler N, Bajcsy R (1978) Three-Dimension Representations for Computer Graphics and Computer Vision. Computer Graphics, Vol. 2:(1), pp 153-160.

Barhen J, Gulati S, Zak M (1989) Neural Learning of Constrained Nonlinear Transformations. I.E.E.E. Computer, Vol. 22:(6), pp 67-76.

Bergeron P, LaChapelle P (1985) Tony de Peltrie. Film, SIGGRAPH-85 Film Show, San Francisco, 1985.

Brett C, Pieper S, Zeltzer D (1989) Putting it All Together: An Integrated Package for Viewing and Editing 3D Microworlds. In Zeltzer D (Ed.), Implementing and Interacting with Real-Time MicroWorlds, SIGGRAPH-89 Course 29, Boston Mass., pp 5-1 to 5-15.

Brooks F P (1989) Walkthrough - A Dynamic Graphics System for Simulating Virtual Buildings. In Zeltzer D (Ed.), Implementing and Interacting with Real-Time MicroWorlds, SIGGRAPH-89 Course 29, Boston Mass., pp 3-1 to 3-11.

Brooks R A (1983) Solving the Find-Path Problem by Good Representation of Free Space. IEEE Transactions on Systems, Man and Cybernetics, Vol. 13:(3), pp 190-196.

Brotman L (1988) Motion Interpolation by Optimal Control. Computer Graphics, Vol. 22:(4), pp 309-315.

Brown G, Garwood A (1936) General Principles of Play Direction. Samuel French Ltd., 1936.

Calvert T, Chapman J, Patla A (1980) The Integration of Subjective and Objective Data in the Animation of Human Movement. Computer Graphics, Vol. 14:(3), pp 198-203.

Calvert T, Chapman J, Patla A (1982) Aspects of the Kinematic Simulation of Human Movement. I.E.E.E. Computer Graphics and Applications, Vol. 2:(9), pp 41-50.

Dooley M (1982) Anthropometric Modelling Programs: A Survey. I.E.E.E. Computer Graphics and Applications, Vol. 2:(9), pp 17-25.

Fisher S S (1989) Virtual Environments, Personal Simulation and Telepresence. In Zeltzer D (Ed.), Implementing and Interacting with Real-Time MicroWorlds, SIGGRAPH-89 Course 29, Boston Mass., pp 3-1 to 3-11.

Girard M (1987) Interactive Design of 3-D Computer-Animated Legged Animal Motion. IEEE Computer Graphics and Applications, Vol. 7:(6), pp 39-51.

Girard M, Maciejewski A (1985) Computational Modeling for the Computer Animation of Legged Figures. Computer Graphics, Vol. 19:(3), pp 263-270.

Herbison-Evans D (1978) NUDES2:A Numerical Utility Displaying Ellipsoid Solids. Computer Graphics, Vol. 12:(3), pp 354-356.

Isaacs P, Cohen M (1987) Controlling dynamic simulation with kinematic constraints, behavior functions, and inverse dynamics. Computer Graphics, Vol. 21:(4), pp 215-224.

Jordan M I (1988) Supervised Learning and Systems with Excess Degrees of Freedom. Technical Report No. 88-27, COINS, University of Massachusetts at Amherst.

Kahn K (1979) Creation of Computer Animation from Story Descriptions. Ph.D. Thesis, Computer Science, M.I.T.

Kochanek D, Bartels R, Booth K (1982) A Computer System for Smooth Keyframe Animation. M.Sc. Thesis, Computer Science, University of Waterloo.

Korein J, Badler N (1982) Techniques for Generating Goal-Directed Motion of Articulated Structures. I.E.E.E. Computer Graphics and Applications, Vol. 2:(9).

Kroyer B (1986) Animating with a Hierarchy. SIGGRAPH-86 Course Notes on Advanced Animation, Dallas, pp 266-288.

Lee C S (1982) Robot Arm Kinematics, Dynamics and Control. I.E.E.E. Transactions on Computers, Vol. 15:(2).

Lozano-Pérez (1983) Spatial Planning:A Configuration Space Approach. IEEE Transactions on Computers, Vol. 32:(2), pp 108-117.

Magnenat-Thalmann N, D.Thalmann (1987) The Direction of Synthetic Actors in the Film "Rendezvous à Montréal". I.E.E.E. Computer Graphics and Applications, Vol. 12, pp 9-19.

Minsky M (1975) A Framework for Representing Knowledge. The Psychology of Computer Vision, McGraw Hill, pp 211-277.

Muehle E (1987) FROBS: A Merger of Two Knowledge Representation Paradigms. M.Sc. Thesis, University of Utah.

Paul R (1981) Robot Manipulators: Mathematics, Programming and Control. MIT Press, 1981.

Pixar Corp. (1986) Luxo Jr. Film, SIGGRAPH-86 Film Show, Dallas, 1986.

Reynolds C (1987) Flocks, Herds and Schools: A Distributed Behavior Model. Computer Graphics, Vol. 21:(4), pp 25-34.

Ridsdale G, Calvert T (1986) The Interactive Specification of Human Animation. Proceedings Graphics Interface-86 Conference, Vancouver, pp 121-130.

Ridsdale G J, Calvert T W (1987) The Director's Apprentice. Technical Report No. TR-87-2, Computer Science, Simon Fraser University.

Steketee S, Badler N (1985) Parametric Keyframe Interpolation Incorporating Kinetic Adjustment and Phrasing Control. Computer Graphics, Vol. 19:(3), pp 255-263.

Sturman D (1984) Interactive Key Frame Animation of 3-D Articulated Models. Proceedings Graphics Interface Conference, pp 35-40.

Sturman D J, Zeltzer D, Pieper S (1989) Hands-on Interaction With Virtual Environment. In Zeltzer D (Ed.), Implementing and Interacting with Real-Time MicroWorlds, SIGGRAPH-89 Course 29, Boston Mass., pp 5-1 to 5-15.

Symbolics Graphics Division (1987) Stanley and Stella: Breaking the Ice. Film, Symbolics Corporation Graphics Division, 1987.

Wilhelms J (1986) Virya – A Motion Control Editor for Kinematic and Dynamic Animation. Proceedings Graphics Interface-86 Conference, Vancouver, pp 141-146.

Witkin A, Fleischer K, Barr A (1987) Energy Constraints on Parameterized Models. Computer Graphics, Vol. 21:(4), pp 225-229.

Witkin A, Kass M (1988) Spacetime Constraints. Computer Graphics, Vol. 22:(4), pp 159-168.

Zeltzer D (1982) Motor Control Techniques for Figure Animation. IEEE Computer Graphics and Applications, Vol. 2:(9), pp 53-59.

Zeltzer D (1985) Towards an integrated view of 3-D computer animation. The Visual Computer, Vol. 1:(4), pp 249-259.

Gary Ridsdale is currently an assistant professor of Computer Science at the University of Utah. Prior to this, he was a research assistant in Professor Tom Calvert's lab at Simon Fraser University. His research interests include virtual worlds, computer animation and physically-based modeling. Prof. Ridsdale obtained his B.Sc. from the University of British Columbia, his M.Sc. from Queen's University, and his Ph.D. from Simon Fraser University.

Address: Computer Science Department, 3190 Merrill Bldg., University of Utah, Salt Lake City Utah USA 84112. E-mail address: ridsdale@cs.utah.edu

Tom Calvert is Vice President of Research at Simon Fraser University and is also a full professor in the School of Computing Science. His research interests include computer animation, computerized support for choreographic planning, and robotics. He obtained his Ph.D. from Carnegie-Mellon University.

Address: School of Computing Science, Simon Fraser University, Burnaby, Canada, V5A 1S6.

GEMSA: Computer-Aided Movement Generation for Scene Animation

NABIL CHÉRIF

ABSTARCT.

This paper presents a first approach to a computer-aided movement generation for scene animation on the basis of a written text. Animated scenes are composed of animated (humanoid) characters performing actions in a fixed or mobile objects environment. The aim to be achieved is the animation of synthesized images. Symbolic processing languages Prolog and Lisp are used, in addition to numeric processing languages and systems.

Keywords: computer animation, artificial intelligence, plan generation.

1. INTRODUCTION.

Computer-aided animation and movement control systems can be simply classified in two categories: low level and high level. **Low level** control requires an explicit description of each character's movements, the trajectory of each object to be animated, and interaction between animated objects and environment (background within which the animated objects move). In contrast, with a **high level** control system, the user describes the movement in more abstract terms, allowing the system to find the appropriate low level description. The major difficulty in creating a high level control system lies in the conversion of general descriptions into low level primitive actions.

The purpose of many behavioral-simulation systems (that of a robot, for example) is the use of the highest level of natural languages to specify commands in a very simple way. A command such as "go open the door" is certainly more natural and direct than an explicit description of each movement and trajectory required to perform the action. However, this simplicity for the animator presupposes the existence of a hidden, complex system, based on artificial intelligence techniques such as robotics, language analysis, and so on ... The input animation script does not need to spell out all the details of each movement (trajectory, acceleration, etc ...), since this job is left to the system, which makes decisions using data from knowledge bases about the character's skeleton and environment, integrated with the input scenario.

Let us imagine that, from the text of "Little Red Riding Hood" story input on the computer keyboard, we could watch the characters gradually act out the well-known fairy tale on the screen in a series of animated synthesized images .

Now let us imagine an automated system whitch could generate animation from three types of descriptions: environment, objects to be animated, and a set of behavioral rules.

Finally, let us complete this system with some low level tools allowing the animator to make some changes in order to give him full control of the desired animation. Without these tools, the system would be undesirable, since the animator would not have complete and precise control over the resulting animation.

The objective of this paper is to propose as a first approach an architecture of such a system associating symbolic processing and numeric processing techniques.

2. SYSTEM ARCHITECTURE.

Before defininig the system architecture, let us recall that the general context of this study is the **generation of animated scenes from a script written in natural language,** which at the outset seems to be very ambitious. Numerous difficulties exist, but we think that some sub-problems can be resolved by using a combination of symbolic and numeric processing techniques, thus relieving the animator of many fastidious tasks and allowing him to concentrate on his true role: **creation**. Therefore, the purpose is not to design a completely **automatic** tool for animating films on the basis of a text (which would be very complicated, not to mention the risk that the results might be *déjà vu*), but rather to furnish the animator with a Computer-Aided Movements Generation for Animated Scenes (GEMSA). This system should, in addition, offer possibilities for interaction, enabling the creator to personalize his or her work.

To define the scenario, the animator will use a rather abstract story description, often called: "**scene level**" story description. For example, the text of "Alice of Wonderland" can be considered a "scene level" story description. Some specialists describe systems which use this kind of formulation as "**goal-oriented**" or "**Task-Level**" systems (Korein 1982, Zeltzer 1981, Zeltzer 1985).

Considering the scope of the subject, we found it necessary at the outset to narrow our aim, without losing sight of the initial goal. To do so, we tried to answer the following questions:
- **what kind of objects** are movement models designed for?
- **what types of movements** are to be modeled, and how?
- where should we introduce **symbolic processing** techniques (techniques of artificial intelligence)?

Regarding the first point, we preferred to consider the movements of "figurative" objects, rather than of objects of simple geometric forms (sphere, cylinder, etc ...) as was done by Michael Kahn in his Ph.D. dissertation (Kahn 1979). Our choice finally was an **articulated, rigid body** such as the **human skeleton**. Of course, the environment surrounding the human skeleton contains objects of any geometric form. In making this ambitious choice, we wanted to contribute to the field of computer-aided animation and also to open a new application field for symbolic processing specialists. Until now, this field has been reserved to numeric processing associated with graphic interfaces.

As to the second point, and according to the first point as discussed above, we needed a technique for modeling the movements of the human body. The movements that a human skeleton can perform are innumerable, and among the most common (walking, running, jumping, falling, dancing, ...), we chose **walking**. By walking, we mean a variety of walks such as the walk of a burglar (on tiptoes), the walk of an elderly person, the walk of a young man, the walk of a woman with or without high heels, etc ...

Not having found a satisfactory existing model of the human body walking, we developed our own model, establishing as a strong constraint that parameters had to enable the generation of exaggerated movements, even to the extent of movements impossible for the normal human body to perform.

This model is based on kinematics. The causes of movements, that is, force and torque effects (physics causes) (Armstrong 1985, Wilhelms 1985) on the body's mass were not taken into consideration.

Additionally, in order to allow bodies to interact with objects in the environment, such as chairs, we defined movements such as sitting, rising, and opening a door, including transitions between different types of movements (accelerating, stopping, etc ...).

Concerning the last point, the use of symbolic processing techniques, derived from artificial intelligence techniques, is useful for certain phases, such as the understanding of natural language, the plan generation for moving characters in an environment that includes obstacles, the knowledge representation, the choice of reasoning methods, etc ...

To sum up, the GEMSA system is an **articulated skeleton behavior simulator (of the humanoid type) in interaction with an environment**. This simulation is guided by a **goal-oriented** abstract formulation. An environment is a set of objects with which a skeleton interacts to perform actions. This environment can be a house composed of walls, rooms, corridors, stairs, tables, chairs, etc ...
The main purpose of the interaction with the environment are:
- collision avoidance in the specification of a skeleton path;
- the use of some environment objects by a skeleton in order to accomplish a given purpose (as the use of a chair to replace a light bulb).

As shown in fig. 1, the GEMSA system has three components:
- **knowledge bases**;
- a **user interface**;
- a **behavior controller** (the kernel).

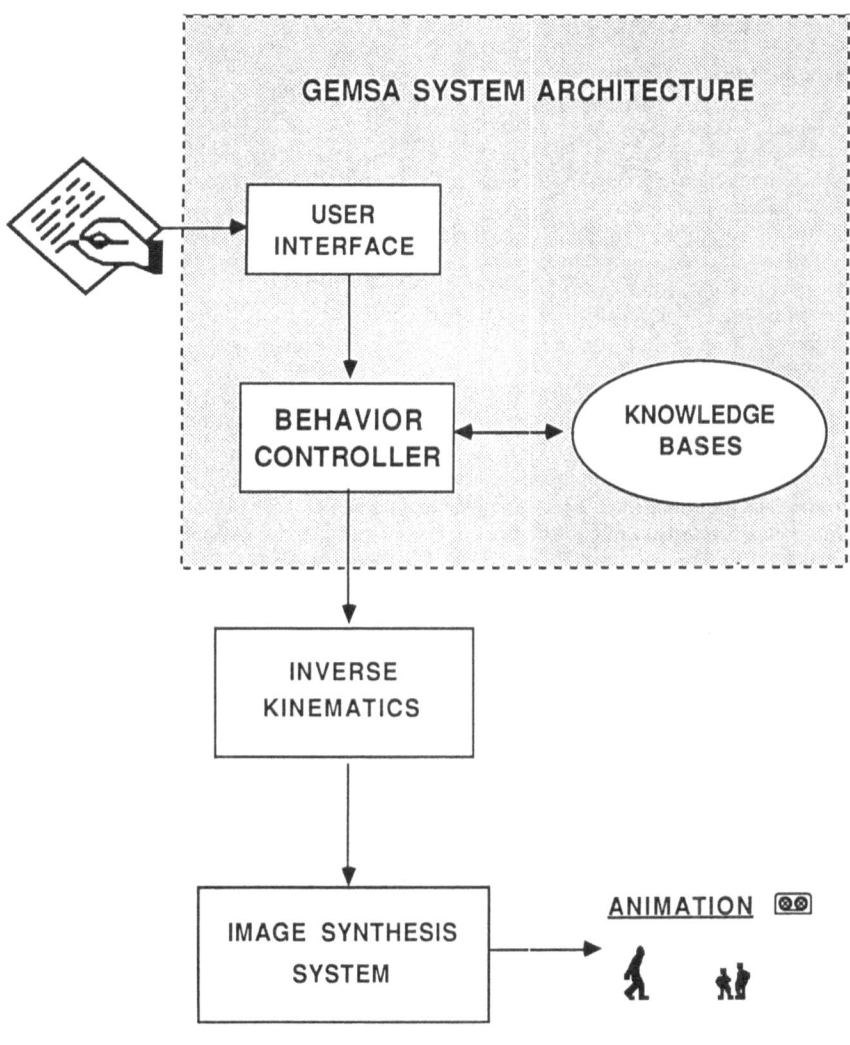

GEMSA SYSTEM ARCHITECTURE

USER INTERFACE

BEHAVIOR CONTROLLER

KNOWLEDGE BASES

INVERSE KINEMATICS

IMAGE SYNTHESIS SYSTEM

ANIMATION

Fig. 1.

To generate a final image sequence, the GEMSA system is coupled with a module using the **inverse kinematics** technique (Girard 1985), which is integrated with an **image synthesis** software to output and record images.

All the knowledge bases in the GEMSA system are **centralized**. Only the kernel has the "**consulting and decision-making power**". A skeleton is therefore considered as a "pawn" without sensory organs, manipulated by the behavior controller, which is the system's kernel.

2.1 Knowledge bases.

In order to generate animated sequences, the GEMSA system needs several types of information, which are stored in different knowledge bases:
- objects;
- scripts and action plans;
- movement models;
- cinematographic rules.

2.1.1 Objects.

By objects, we mean both animated objects (an articulated skeleton, for example) and inanimate objects (environment elements).
In addition to information about their geometrical aspects (position, dimensions, etc ...), other more symbolic information will be associated with each object such as its type (chair, door, humanoid, ...) and its characteristics (weight, color, type of clothing for a humanoid, etc ...).
These data will be used at all levels of movement generation, from the analysis of input story down to the image synthesis.

Some environment objects can be considered as **resources** that can be shared between several different skeletons. But this is not always the case, for example, a chair can only be used by one skeleton at a time.

To represent objects of the same type within an environment, the GEMSA system can use the **class** and **inheritance** notions introduced by object-oriented languages. The object knowledge base therefore enables a **hierarchical representation** of environment objects. For example, a chair can inherit the properties of a stool plus the "orientation" property. In turn, a stool can inherit the obstacle properties.

When a character's action in the script involve an object o, the character/object interaction obeys the following rules:
- to perform the required action, does the character possess specific interaction rules for the object class O, of which o is a particular instance?
- the behavior controller must inquire about important characteristic details of the instance o;
- modifications made to object o generated by the postconditions resulting from the action performed by the character must be taken in account .

Animated objects are distinguished from inanimate objects by their behavioral diversity (see paragraphs 2.1.2 and 2.1.3).

2.1.2 Scripts and Action Plans.

By scripts, we mean **knowledge representation models** concerning **typical situations and events**. This notion of scripts was introduced by Schank and Abelson for "understanding" stories (Schank 1977). Given a story, Shank's system SAM (Script Applier Mechanism) finds a relevant script and matches the individual events of the story against the patterns in the script. In the process, events in the script not explicitly mentioned in the story are filled in.

A script is a standardized sequence of events describing a stereotyped human activity, for example, "going to a restaurant". The input phrase "John goes to a restaurant for dinner" can be translated into a sequence of actions: find a restaurant, order a meal, eat, pay the bill, leave. This sequence of actions is drawn from the script "going to a restaurant" after selection of this script from the input sentence; this is the **script expansion phase**. The actions appearing in a script are described in terms of **attributes** and **constraints** related to the values of these attributes. Default values can be specified, with the effect of assigning values to attributes which have not been instantiated by the input sentence.

This feature enables the animator to write scenarios without having to specify parameters that do not seem significant.

As regards scenario formulation, the GEMSA system kernel enables the animator to coordinate input sentences with the script events previously stored in the script knowledge base. When a script from the knowledge base is selected (**instantiated**) by the input story description, the story actors take their respective roles in the instantiated script. In order for an action in the instantiated script to be executed, the preceding actions must be successfully achieved. Otherwise, the impediments must be resolved; a new action can be generated in order to make the actor evolve in the story. Two mechanisms are required for application of this method:
- **recognition** and **triggering** of a script mentioned in the input story;
- finding the steps and **parameters** omitted in the input story.

Script expansion is carried down to the most elementary actions; thus, in the previously mentioned script, the action, "order a meal", is itself described by a script in the knowledge base, and will be further translated into a sequence of smaller actions, and so on ...

As with the environment knowledge base, the notion of **hierarchical abstraction** is likewise present for the system's **dynamic knowledge** (scripts).

Complementary to these scripts, which can be characterized as "symbolic", "geometric" scripts must be added; they represent the trajectory sequence to make a skeleton go from point A to point Z, avoiding certain obstacles or following imposed paths. For example, the action "find a restaurant" will be translated into the sequence: walk from point A to point B, walk from point B to point C, and so on, until a restaurant is found at point X. This sequence is generated from the **graph of the streets** in a given town.

The function enabling the generation of "geometric" scripts will be called **action plan generation** so as to employ the terminology currently used in robotics. This sequence, once generated, is executed by an **action plan executor**.

The **planning** is a development process of an action sequence in order to accomplish a given purpose. An action plan is an **ordered sequence** of actions to accomplish certain purposes before beginning other actions. Each purpose in a plan can be replaced by a more detailed subplan in order to accomplish this purpose. A complete plan is therefore a **linear sequence** of **executable operators** that can be performed by the plan executor.

The fact that the generated actions are not executed immediately enables the movement controller to reconsider its latest decisions. This is called **non-monotonous reasoning**.

2.1.3 Movement Models.

The third knowledge base of the GEMSA system contains the set of all the elementary movements performable by a skeleton. This knowledge is used as an input data by the **action plan executor**.

The process adopted for the design of GEMSA was to develop, first, a description model of elementary movements, applied to the human walk, then to use this model to define sequences putting a skeleton in an environment of buildings and furnished interiors. To achieve this model, we were inspired by research carried out at the turn of the century, for purely medical purposes, concerning a dynamic analysis of the human walk (Hardt 1980, Inman 1981).

This model gives us some articulation trajectories of the human skeleton while walking, according to a certain number of parameters.

Without going into the details, it can be said that this model enables the following actions to be performed:
- initiation of an animation sequence: *"begin sequence"*;
- skeleton posture definition in a standing position: *"standing position"*;
- positioning of the skeleton at a given point and in a given direction: *"position in space"*;
- walking speed definition: *"starting speed"*;
- initiation of walking: *"start walking"* (transition between the standing position and the walking cycle);
- accomplish n steps: *"walk"* ;
- end of walk:*"stop walking"* (transition between the walking cycle and the standing position);
- acceleration and deceleration while walking: *"acc/dec"* (modification of speed while walking);
- skeleton rotation: *"pivot"* (changing walking direction);
- end of current animation sequence: *"end sequence"*.

Of course, some of these actions can be combined, for example, walking with gradual acceleration or deceleration while also changing direction.

The model for movement description was designed in such a way as to enable other movement specification relatively easily, such as running, jumping, or falling, for example, on the basis of knowledge from a rotoscopy technique. Another useful feature of this model is the movement **parameterization**. So, for walking, the height, length, and rhythm of steps can be adjusted at will, which lets us create **exaggerations**, or even generate movements that would be impossible for a normal human being!

Finally, an essential characteristic of this model is that each basic movement is described in terms of coordinates relative to an observable point in the body, which makes it possible to combine any kind of movements and trajectories very easily.

2.1.4 Cinematographic rules.

The cinematographic rules make possible the realization of a final composition of good quality by avoiding scene direction errors and by facilitating the creator's work by computing camera placement, focus, field of vision, centering, etc ...

These rules are used by the system to deduce changes in viewpoint with respect to the current context.

One can, for example, express the change in camera position when the main character leaves the field of vision. Or again, for a particular sequence, one can express that the camera should be positioned on one of the character's head to show "what he sees".

It should be noted that some parameters (camera position, focus, field of vision, etc ...), derived from the scene direction characteristics and using the cinematographic rules, are associated with "elementary graphic" commands. These parameters make possible the final computation of what will be seen on the video screen.

2.2 Behavior controller.

The kernel, or supervising module, is an essential part of GEMSA as a "behavior controller." Its first major role is the generation of animated sequences from scenarios translated by the user interface. To do this, it carries out:
- **expansion** of "symbolic" scripts;
- **generation** and **execution** of action plans down to "elementary graphic" commands feeding the inverse kinematics module.

The kernel accesses all of the knowledge bases to generate appropriate sequences.

The second major role of the kernel, in association with the user interface, is that of a **development environment**. In fact, the known information in the knowledge bases is not static over the system life, but instead, some **enrichment** is necessary, in terms of either new scripts, new elementary movements, or new environment elements.

Let us take the example, "John goes to a restaurant for dinner", and imagine that the action "order a meal" is not yet described by a script; when this happens, the kernel sends a request to the user asking for the creation of a new script to enable it to continue generation of the movements. Updating the knowledge bases is then carried out by the kernel.

Here an essential characteristic of the system appears: **interaction** with the user. This interaction is necessary at certain levels, but not just anywhere. For example, "introduce a touch of humor" would be difficult to describe by a high level language. Likewise, retouching a movement directly on the video tape seems unachievable.

In addition to the information in the knowledge bases already defined, the system needs information on the **current status** of the skeleton (position, posture, etc ...) or its **current context**. Specifying, for example, that the skeleton is located within a furnished room makes it possible to enhance the system knowledge. The system can thus deduce the presence of a door through which it can make the skeleton exit from the room. Thus, for the command, "leave the room,", it will not be necessary to designate the placement of the door explicitly, since the movement controller should be able to find the answer by asking such questions as:
- where is the skeleton?
- what must the skeleton do if not in a walking position?
- where is the door?
- are there obstacles between the skeleton and the door?
- what is the best path to take?
- how should the skeleton walk? (choice of parameters for walking)
- and so on ...

An important notion taken into account by the kernel is **character/object interaction,** that is the character's behavior towards an object. This notion enables the behavior controller to understand the usefulness of the various objects in the environment for all the actions the animator might describe in the input scenario. Concerning the fact that the animator might wish to have the character go from one room to another, the behavior controller is expected to know that from one room to another, it is necessary to **use** a door. This is a character/door interaction.
The system must possess information about the operation of the object "door." In other words, the system needs to know what action types an object can be involved in, and in what ways it can be used.

To accomplish a given action, the behavior controller can use **secondary objects,** without their having to be explicitly mentioned in the input scenario. For example, the use of a key to open a door. The script knowledge base makes this deduction possible.

A simple example illustrates clearly the problem of a **movement chain**: asking a skeleton to go to a given location while it is seated. The system must be intelligent enough to know that before giving the basic command *"walk"*, it must first modify the skeleton's posture in such a way as to place it in a standing position, then make it face in the direction of its destination. The behavior controller thus chains a sequence of several different movements in order to accomplish the requested action.

As regards planning, the GEMSA system treats the problem at different levels. This separation enables the behavior controller to avoid going into the details until it has resolved more general problems. This process is described as levels of **hierarchical abstraction**. For example, once the behavior controller knows which rooms are to be crossed and which doors are to be used, then it goes on to the second phase of planning, which is the obstacle detection.

The problem of detecting and avoiding obstacles is solved by the creation of a **visibility graph** (Lozano-Pérez 1979) for each room in the environment. The present version of the GEMSA system does not allow

mobile obstacles to be taken into account. Therefore, the visibility graphs are created once and for all on the animator's demand. Once created, the visibility graphs are explored in different searching strategies, with a choice:
- according to the shortest or longest distance;
- with the minimum number of phases (number of direction changes in walking);
- in passing by a given point;
- in passing round a given obstacle;
- in approaching, at each phase, as near as possible to the final destination;
- and so on ...

At present, the GEMSA system does not allow the generation of more than one action plan at a time. Therefore, the animator cannot have two skeletons in the scenario. The animation corresponding to the input scenario, "Skeletons S1 and S2 meet in the room" is impossible to generate!

It is also important to introduce **several skeletons** in the same scene. These skeletons can be considered as mobile obstacles for each other. However, these are a special type of mobile obstacles. Because of this, they must be treated in a special way. The behavior controller must provide each skeleton with an action plan, so that their paths do not induce collisions. The behavior controller must take into account the goals of all skeletons before providing them with action plans. The **ordering** of the basic commands provided by the behavior controller for all skeletons becomes important; this is the problem of **multiple agents** that is encountered in plan generators. New strategies of paths across the two graphs of the system (rooms/doors and visibility) must be integrated. It is obvious that **time** becomes an important parameter for solving this problem. The planning strategy must be **non-linear**, that is, integrating the notions of parallel actions and relations between these actions. Here, therefore, we again run into the problem of the **temporal plan generators**.

2.3 GEMSA User Interface.

First, the user interface is the privileged means of communication with the rest of the system, whether it be the kernel, the knowledge bases, the image synthesis system, etc ...

The communication language must be adapted to each type of problem so that the animator can use the system without any computer scientist's help; close to "natural language" for the animated scene creation and the knowledge enrichment with scripts, and this language becomes graphic when it deals with the definition of environment elements or new movement models.

The communication is based on an adequate hardware set-up (bit-map screen, mouse, keyboard, tablet, etc ...), in association with a software composed of integrated interpretation modules.

3. CONCLUSION.

At present, the GEMSA system includes some mechanisms allowing the generation of synthesized images on the basis of a text written in formal language. The model for specifying elementary movements has demonstrated that it was relatively easy to describe a great variety of movements. We have created a script interpreter and a navigation system for an environment composed of obstacles (room or town). The implementation language is Lislog-c (Lepape 1987), which enables us to use the languages Prolog, Lisp, and Object within the same programming environment. Lisp serves as a numeric computation language and as a support language, while Prolog is used for the development of interfaces, the script interpreter, and the navigation system.

The first results, obtained in the form of a video film composed of synthesized images, are very encouraging for subsequent research, even though the path to follow in order to generate a ninety-minute film starring the great Arletty in the classic *"Les Enfants du Paradis"* (in color this time) is strewn with snares!

ACKNOWLEDGEMENTS.

I would like to thank S. Bourgault (Centre National d'Etudes des Télécommunications), J.F. Colonna (Lactamme Laboratory of Ecole polytechnique, Paris), A. Nicolas, D. Boreinsten, and L. Alt (Thomson Digital Image) for their co-operation, and the persons who helped in translation and revision of this paper.

REFERENCES.

Armstrong W. W., Green M. W. (1985)
    The Dynamics of Articuled Rigid Bodies for the Purpose of Animation
    Visual Computer, Special Issue on Computer Animation, 1(4): 231-240.
Girard M., Maciejewski A. A. (1985)
    Computational Modeling for the Computer Animation of Legged Figures
    Proc. ACM Siggraph'85:263-269.
Hardt T., Mann R. W. (1980)
    A Five Body - Three Dimensional Dynamic Analysis of Walking
    J. Biomechanics, Vol. 13:455-457
Inman V. T., Ralston H. J., F. Todd (1981)
    Human Walking
    Williams and Wilkins ed.
Kahn K. M. (January 1979)
    Creation of Computer Animation from Story Descriptions
    PhD dissertation at MIT (Massachusetts Institute of Technology).
Korein J. U., Badler N. I. (1982)
    Techniques for Generating the Goal-Directed Motion of Articuled Structures
    IEEE CG&A 2(9):71-81.
Lepape J. P., Bourgault S., Ranson D. (1987)
    LISLOG-C: Une première étape vers l'expression généralisée des contraintes en programmation
                en logique.
    Proc. Séminaire de Programmation en Logique de Trégastel, France, SPLT: 59-75.
Lozano-Pérez T., Wesley M. A. (1979)
    An Algorithm for Planning Collision-Free Paths Among Polyhedral Obstacles
    Comm. of the ACM, 22(10):560-570.
Schank R., Abelson R. (1977)
    Scripts, Plans, Goals, and Understanding
    Lawrence Erlbaum Associates, Publishers, Hillsdale, New Jersey.
Wilhelms J., Barsky B. A. (1987)
    Using Dynamic Analysis for Realistic Animation of Articuled Bodies
    IEEE CG&A June:12-27.
Zeltzer D. (1981)
    Goal-Directed Movement Simulation
    Proc. Canadian Man-Computer Communications Society, CMCCS:271-280.
Zeltzer D. (1985)
    Towards an Integrated View of 3D Computer Animation
    Visual Computer, 1(4):249-259.

128

Nabil Chérif is a researcher at Thomson Digital Image and seconded to the France Télécom Research Center (Centre National d'Etudes des Télécommunications). Chérif is currently preparing a Ph. D. on Artificial Intelligence and Computer Animation at Paris XI University.
The author's address is:
C.N.E.T. (LAA/SLC/PLA)
B.P. 40
22301 Lannion (France).

Part IV
Models, Systems, and Languages

Modeling and Animation of Garment Wrinkle Formation Processes

Tosiyasu L. Kunii and Hironobu Gotoda

ABSTRACT

Modeling of soft objects, such as garments, is becoming more and more important in computer graphics and animation. Since many complex factors are involved in a deformation process of a soft object, analyzing and modeling it are difficult. Although several works have been reported recently in this area, the approaches that have been taken are either purely kinetic or purely geometric, and thus fail to capture the essential elements of the behavior of a soft object, such as the interaction between kinetic properties and geometric properties.

This paper presents new modeling primitives for garments and their wrinkles as a class of soft objects. Our modeling primitives incorporate both the kinetic and geometric properties in the following way: local analysis by kinetics and global analysis by differential geometry. We show that the local structures around the characteristic points introduced here can describe the shape of garment wrinkles, and also show that the movement of these points and the change in local structures can represent the deformation process of the wrinkles. Animation of the wrinkle formation process is performed by specifying and manipulating these points.

Keywords: garment wrinkle formation process, soft object, computer animation, singularity theory, differential topology

1. INTRODUCTION

1.1 Modeling of Soft Objects

Modeling of *soft* objects has long been outside the scope of computer graphics and animation (Wyvill et al. 1986). It is mainly because soft objects are very hard to be handled, and partially because soft objects have been regarded to be less important in engineering. Even in a simple shape change of a soft object, many factors, usually interacting with each other, totally form the process of deformation, and give an impression of *softness*. In the case of hard or rigid objects, shape change occurs on a comparatively small scale and only a few factors, such as Young's modulus, Poisson's ratio, and Lamé's constant, are sufficient to mostly determine the deformation process. Such difference between soft and hard objects seems to have directed many researches to the modeling of hard objects and kept the domain of *softness* unexplored.

To describe the difficulty in modeling the shape change of a soft object in more detail, we take cloth as an example of soft objects. Cloth is an object composed of many threads in various woven patterns. Physical properties of cloth depend both on the physical properties of threads and on the patterns in which they are woven. The threads are also composed of smaller units, called fibers. Their physical properties can be determined by the properties of fibers and the ways they are bundled. Friction, anisotropy, and viscoelasticity inherent in such complex structures make cloth completely different from a thin metallic film. It seems that performing simulation of cloth by taking into account all these factors is almost impossible.

Although modeling of soft objects is very important especially in computer animation, it was not until recently that the problem has become fully addressed. One of the earliest works attempting to model soft objects was done by Barr(1984). His method is purely geometric in the sense that no physical constraints appears in his model: Jacobians are employed to deform a solid object locally and globally. Other works such as in Terzopoulos(1987, 1988) are, on the other hand, purely kinetic. A set of differential equations derived from physical laws play a central role there. Since a differential equation is no more than a local description of an object, numerical simulation is necessary to find out the global structure. Since purely kinetic models provide no schemes to geometrically interpret the results of simulation, the resulting shape can be chaotic and can vary drastically according to the change of parameter values. Unfortunately, a large choice of parameter values is possible. There are also other works (Weil 1986; Platt and Barr 1988), but all of them can be classified into the above two categories: purely kinetic or purely geometric. Furthermore, all of them address the problem by presenting generalized metallic film models which can hardly be considered adequate for modeling soft objects.

Modeling represents a simplified understanding of complex phenomena. Our understanding of soft objects is quite different from those that have been already reported. We take the viewpoint that active interaction between kinetic and geometric properties is an essential element of "softness". To observe such an interaction, we first employ a woven thread model, not a metallic film model, to numerically simulate its behavior. Our next step is to analyze the geometric properties of the result. From the repetition of these steps, some characteristics of soft objects can be extracted.

1.2   Surface Reconstruction Techniques

Before we state our method more specifically, we first look into several surface representations and reconstruction techniques, and consider their applicability to the modeling of soft objects. This will be helpful in clarifying our fundamental idea of modeling soft objects.

There are two main categories of surface reconstruction techniques: points based methods and contours based methods. The points based methods reconstruct a surface from a set of sample points (or control points) which are scattered in the 3-dimensional space. The spline surface and the Bézier surface are examples of this category. The number of points required depends on the complexity of the surface. Tangent or curvature discontinuities may occur if an insufficient number of sample points are used. The contours based methods, on the other hand, use a stack of cross sectional contours for reconstruction (Christiansen 1978). Connections between series of contours are determined by some principles, for example minimal distance neighbors, and the surface is represented as a collection of triangular patches. The number of cross sections required depends on the complexity of the surface. Irregularities may arise if an insufficient number of cross sectional contours are used (Shinagawa et al. 1989).

The methods of both categories are general in the sense that any kind of (orientable, of course) surfaces can be represented. However they have the following drawbacks when they are applied to the modeling of soft objects:

- Since these methods are primarily intended to reconstruct a surface in an exact way, they tend to require too much data for reconstruction. This is a great disadvantage when animation of the surface is required. (Note that in the case of a rigid surface, the motion of the surface is completely specified by an Affine transformation which can be efficiently handled by hardware usually equipped in graphics machines. In the case of a soft surface, the situation is not at all so simple.)

- These methods can deal with not only soft surfaces but also hard surfaces. This means that users have to prepare by themselves their own schemes for representing "softness".

If the "softness" itself can be modeled by some geometric properties of the shape, we will be able to take advantage of that fact. Our approach outlined in the next section is an attempt to extract such geometric properties as a model of soft objects.

1.3   Singularity Based Modeling

As a class of soft objects for us to model, we take the case of garment wrinkles, and investigate their characteristic behavior. By limiting the class of objects in this way, we can expect to get more distinctive properties of "softness".

Our solution for extracting geometric properties of garment wrinkles is to employ a mathematical method, known as singularity theory, for shape analysis. This method, which was recently found to be useful also in medical applications (Kergosien 1989), provides a mathematical foundation to deal with qualitative changes of a system. If a qualitative change occurred at some point in time, then the very moment had a greater meaning than the other moments. The theory shows what kind of changes occurred at that moment and how important (or rare) such moment was.

To put it more concretely, we look at a wrinkle formation process from various directions and observe the qualitative shape change of the contour lines of the wrinkle. If a shape change occurs at some direction, we analyze the type of the change. Since such change does not occur so often, we can classify a set of possible directions into general and special ones. From the theory, it can be shown that the special directions correspond to a point on the wrinkle surface, and thus we get several special points on the wrinkle which are more important than the others. Such points can become the characteristic points of a wrinkle. Note that since the number of characteristic points is small they are suitable as the primitives of modeling.

The rest of the paper is organized as follows: chapter 2 describes the mathematical models of surfaces, the methods of numerical simulation, and the analysis of the simulation; chapter 3 presents the primitives of modeling garment wrinkles and chapter 4 shows the animation of the wrinkle formation processes; chapter 5 concludes this paper.

2. CHARACTERISTIC POINTS OF SURFACES

2.1 Mathematical Description of Surfaces

In mathematics, two different ways are provided to study a given surface: local and global. Locally, a surface can be described in terms of curvature. Although local descriptions themselves contain certain implicit global information, they are not usually well recognized until they are explicitly globalized. For example, a surface with everywhere positive curvature represents a completely distinct figure from a surface with everywhere negative curvature, but it is not so simple to tell the difference if we examine the surfaces only locally. Also a surface which has two regions, one with positive curvature and the other with negative curvature together with a boundary of null curvature separating these two regions, is certainly different from a surface with everywhere positive curvature, but it is difficult to distinguish them when we compare them locally at the positive curvature regions. Thus when we talk about a distinctive property of a given surface, it is not the local structure of the surface but the global structure.

Singularity theory, which has been developed by Morse, Whitney, Thom and others, provides a method for globalization: a passage from local descriptions to global structures (Thom 1972). It first studies a surface locally and then examines its meaning (particularly, a sign) from a global viewpoint. More specifically, a series of projections of a given surface are taken and analyzed. Figure 2.1 shows three typical types of projections. In the framework of singularity theory we are interested in contour lines only. The theory shows that the signs depicted in figure 2.1 are the only stable patterns in general, and the other types of signs are unstable, i.e., if we take a projection from a slightly different direction, the pattern is decomposed into some combinations of the signs in figure 2.1. The basic idea of singularity theory is that one can distinguish general types of signs which are stable from special types of signs which are unstable. If no *a priori* knowledge is assumed on the surface to be analyzed and if a projection is taken in an arbitrary direction, then the sign to be observed is almost always one of those in figure 2.1. The other types of signs are too rare to be observed. However, if the surface does have a special structure, one can expect that the rare types of signs are observed.

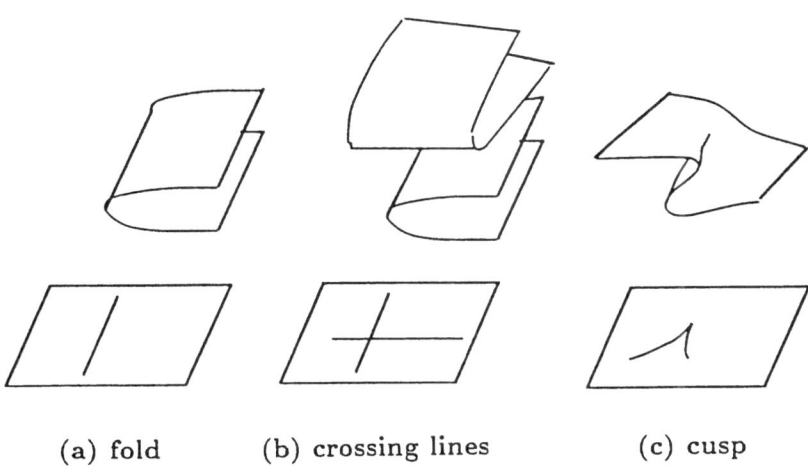

(a) fold   (b) crossing lines   (c) cusp

Fig. 2.1 Typical Signs

Although the kind of signs which were observable and the "rareness" of these signs were extensively studied and classified by 1960's, it was not until recently that the relationship between the signs and the local structures of a surface was determined. What was remarkable in Kergosien's work (1981) was that the signs were shown to be related to the concepts of the classical differential geometry such as curvature and geodesics. By using his theory, local and global structures can be explored simultaneously. In section 2.3, we apply the method to analyze the shape of garment wrinkles.

2.2 Kinetic Analysis

Since garment wrinkles are formed by some physical constraints, studying the physical properties of a garment is necessary. Although the physical constraints are completely described by a set of differential equations and the local structures of wrinkles may be deduced from these equations, their global structures cannot be immediately known by studying only the behavior of these equations. Numerical simulation gives us an effective way when the theoretical analysis is too difficult.

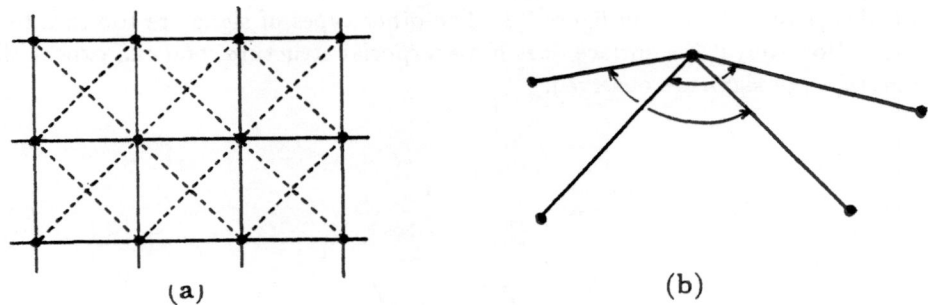

(a)   (b)

Fig. 2.2 Physical Model: metric energy (a)

and curvature energy (b)

Before performing simulation, a physical model that represents outstanding properties of a garment should be prepared. Figure 2.2 briefly explains our physical model. Our model can be described as a collection of a finite number of lines that correspond to the threads in a real garment and a finite number of nodes that correspond to the crossings of these threads. In figure 2.2, each line works as a spring that reacts to the change of the length of the line, and each arc also works as a spring that reacts to the change of the angle of the arc. Here we note that the dotted lines, which seem to have no physical counterparts, also work as springs. These lines are necessary to distinguish the different configurations as shown in figure 2.3. If no dotted line works as a spring, the configurations (a) and (b) may have the same local energy, although in reality, it will not happen and (a) will have less local energy than (b). Such difference comes from the complex structures each pair of threads form at their crossing point. Thus the dotted lines do not directly correspond to physical objects, but represent some factors in thread interactions to form varieties of the weave patterns.

We call that the energy stored at the places represented in solid or dotted lines *metric energy* and call the energy stored at the places represented in arcs *curvature energy*. The interaction between the metric and curvature energy is one characteristic phenomenon which will not be observed in the deformation process of rigid objects where the metric will not change so much in comparison with the curvature. In our simulation, parameters are carefully chosen not to suppress either one of the two types of energy.

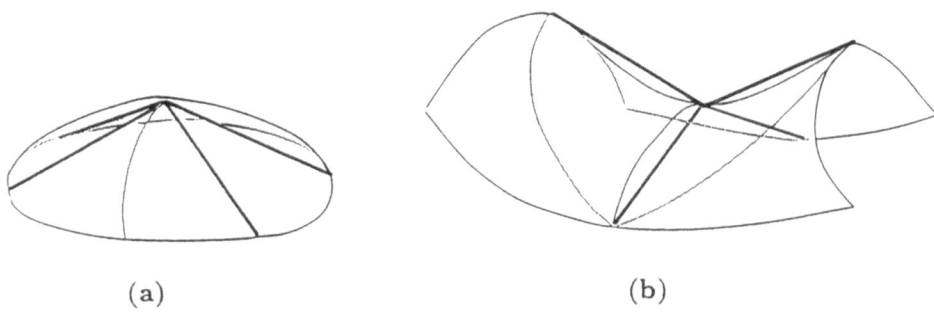

(a)   (b)

Fig. 2.3 Local Energy at a Peak Point (a)

and a Saddle Point (b)

What is most interesting in the shape of garment wrinkles is *branching* and *creation/disappearance*. *Branching* is the phenomenon that one wrinkle splits into two wrinkles, and *disappearance* is the phenomenon that one wrinkle vanishes. To observe these phenomena, a piece of cloth is prepared and deformed by picking up two sides and gradually moving the two ends inwards. The changes on the boundary are propagated into the interior region by using the following procedure:

(1) select one node randomly

(2) move the node in an arbitrary direction by small distance

(3) compute the local energy at the node

(4) If the energy has increased, then recover the previous configuration.

By the minimal energy principle, this procedure, although brute force, can correctly compute the shape of garment wrinkles. A part of the results is shown in figure 2.4 in the next section.

2.3 Characteristic Points of Garment Wrinkles

The results obtained by simulation is analyzed as follows. To apply the method of singularity theory, a series of projections in the horizontal directions are taken as the first step. The next step is to compare the signs of these projections with the signs which are theoretically known. Theoretically, the signs that will appear in these projections are, almost always, the following ones: cusps, folds, or crossing lines. As shown in figure 2.4, however, there are special instances where the other types of signs emerge. This figure shows a situation where a cusp and a fold approach to each other (a), then merge (b), and finally depart from each other (c). Note that the (a) and (c) show different configurations: the lines that form a cusp and a fold are exchanged in the process of merging. The merged state (b) can be classified as the $p + +c$ singularity (Arnold 1986; Kergosien 1981) which determines the behavior of branching.

Also, in the case of creation/disappearance, the same $p + +c$ singularity is shown to be responsible for determining the behavior. (Branching and disappearance are dual with each other. A point on a surface can be a branching point when it is looked from one side, and can be a disappearing point when it is looked from the other side.) Since these singularities are very rare, the behavior of the points corresponding to these singularities will become far more greater constraints than the behavior of the other points. Such points can be the characteristic points of garment wrinkles. By specifying the local structures around the characteristic points, more realistic garment wrinkle images can be synthesized.

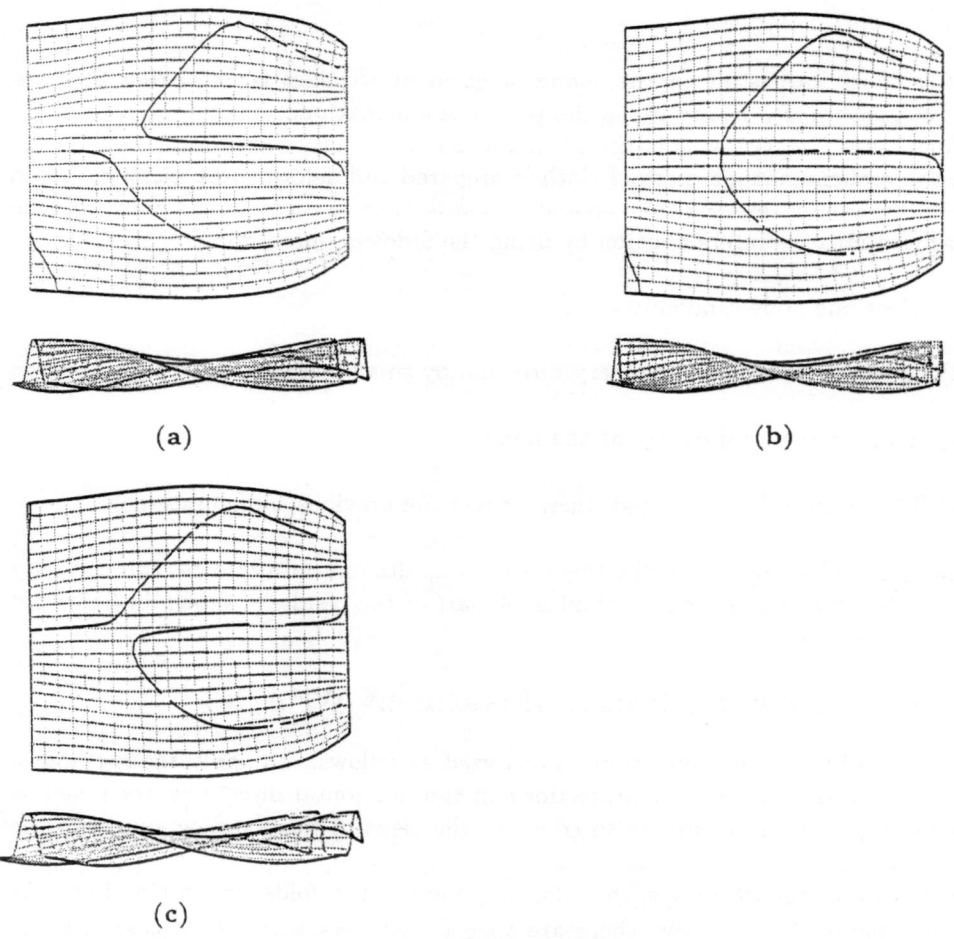

(a)

(b)

(c)

Fig. 2.4 (a),(c): Fold and Cusp

(b): $P + +C$ Singularity

3. MODELING OF WRINKLES

3.1 Modeling Primitives of Garment Wrinkles

As is explained in the previous chapter, the local structures around the character-istic points remarkably influence the global structures of garment wrinkles. Since the number of characteristic points are small (one for each branching or creation/ disappearance), we can achieve great data compression if the shape of wrinkles can be represented by a collection of characteristic points and the local structures around them. In the following, we present modeling primitives of wrinkles and the method to reconstruct the shape from the primitives.

The two most basic sets of modeling primitives are the positions and the types (branching or creation/disappearance) of characteristic points. These sets of primi-tives alone, however, are not sufficient to reconstruct the original shape in a satisfac-tory way. Other primitives are necessary to specify the local structures around the characteristic points more precisely. There is a trade-off between the simplicity of the modeling primitives and the exactness of representation. We have several choices.

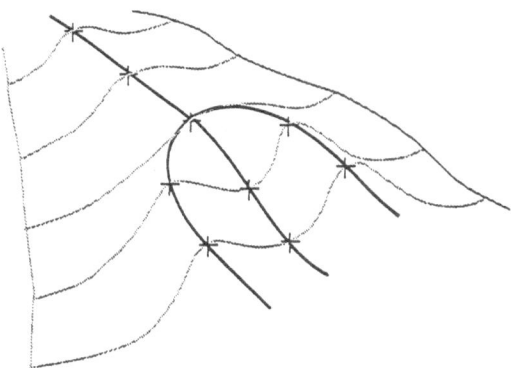

Fig. 3.1 Cross Sectional Reconstruction

Our choice is to add the contour lines that are associated with the special singular configurations (see figure 2.4) as another set of modeling primitives. This enables us to restrict the number of possible wrinkle shapes to be reconstructed. Later in chapter 4, we will see that the contour lines serve as markers in the formation process of wrinkles. For specifying the contour lines, we choose some sample points and interpolate the values between those points by a special kind of spline function, called "spline in tension" (Schweikert 1966). This function is known to be adequate in representing the effect of tension which is applied to the both ends of a curve. Other choices are of course possible, but our method can produce a reasonably good appearance without requiring so much computation.

In summary, the modeling primitives of garment wrinkles are

- the positions of characteristic points,

- the types of characteristic points, and

- the sample points for approximation of contour line curves.

To reconstruct a surface from these primitives, first the contour lines are formed by interpolating the values between the given sample points. These lines will be the backbones of the surface. Next the surface is generated cross sectionally as indicated in figure 3.1. Here again the "spline in tension" is used to approximate the cross-sectional curves. Ideally the total energy contained in the surface is minimized. By using spline functions, the minimal energy principle is satisfied to some extent, but not always completely.

3.2 Strategies of Surface Generation

The primitives presented above can suitably represent the shape change around branching or creation/disappearance points. The next step is to reconstruct a surface entirely including the multiple characteristic points connected with each other.

Generally, more than one wrinkles will appear on one garment cloth, and become connected with each other or diminish at their ends. In order to totally describe such situations, topological data are necessary to represent the connections and endings. From the observation of the garment wrinkles in the real world, one can soon experimentally find that the topology can be represented by a graph, connected or disconnected, that has only two types of nodes, i.e., of degree 3 and of degree 1. Our modeling primitives allow us to handle both of these two types: the nodes of degree 3 by "branching" and the nodes of degree 1 by "creation/disappearance".

However, there remains a slight problem when two wrinkles are too close to each other. In this situation the reconstruction method may produce wrinkles whose outskirts overlap.

To resolve this problem, the surface generation procedure could be modified to take into account of the total arrangement of the wrinkles at all times, i.e., checking every possibility of overlapping and reconstructing the surface as a whole. However, this is not the best solution. By observing the real garment wrinkles more precisely, if interference occurs between a pair of neighboring wrinkles, they are, in most cases, topologically connected with each other through at most two intermediate branching nodes. This fact greatly saves the time and amount of computation without damaging the quality of the wrinkle appearance.

The surface reconstruction procedure with the above resolution strategy is used to generate the animation of the formation process of wrinkles. The strategy seems to work reasonably well unless two wrinkles get too close to each other.

4. ANIMATION OF GARMENT WRINKLES

4.1 Formation Process of Garment Wrinkles

In the previous chapters, we have shown that the garment wrinkles are characterized by a set of characteristic points and the local structures around them. The formation process of garment wrinkles can be described as the movement of the characteristic points and as the structural change around these points. If the movement and the structural change are also characterized by some rules, more efficient data compression becomes possible. Such compression is important in performing animation.

From the observation of natural phenomena, wrinkles seem to be stable, i.e., they will not be easily extinguished once they are formed. The positions of the characteristic points will certainly move and the depth of the wrinkles will change further more drastically. The next step should be to observe the phenomenon in full detail through simulation. However, in contrast to the analysis done in chapter 2, the task is not as simple as it first looks. Because of the following reasons, we should be careful in interpreting the result of simulation:

- We do not have so much control over the formation process. Although there are many possible formation processes, we cannot simulate all of them.

- If the energy is lost due to the frictions between threads or due to the non-linear nature of the threads, the process becomes irreversible. This means that the shape of wrinkles should depend on the history of the formation process and that the nature of hysteresis needs to be studied.

Thus from a limited number of simulation, it is difficult to extract characteristic features which are generally applicable. Our preliminary simulation, however, seems to indicate that some common rules exist which govern the process of wrinkle formation. In the following, we briefly outline the rules.

Figure 4.1 shows a series of wrinkle formation steps. The contour lines which are responsible for representing the local structures around the characteristic points get sharper as the wrinkle formation proceeds. The positions of the characteristic points move away from the sharpened contour lines as if they were pushed by such sharp change of the contour lines. This can be the result of the interaction between the metric and curvature energy explained in section 2.2 (we owe for the theoretical proof).

From now on, we hypothesize that the shape change as stated above occurs in general. When we animate the process of garment wrinkle formation, specifying both the positions and behavior of the characteristic points may become a great overhead; we prefer to specify as few parameters as possible. In the next section, several assumptions are proposed to decrease the number of parameters. Animation is also made on those assumptions.

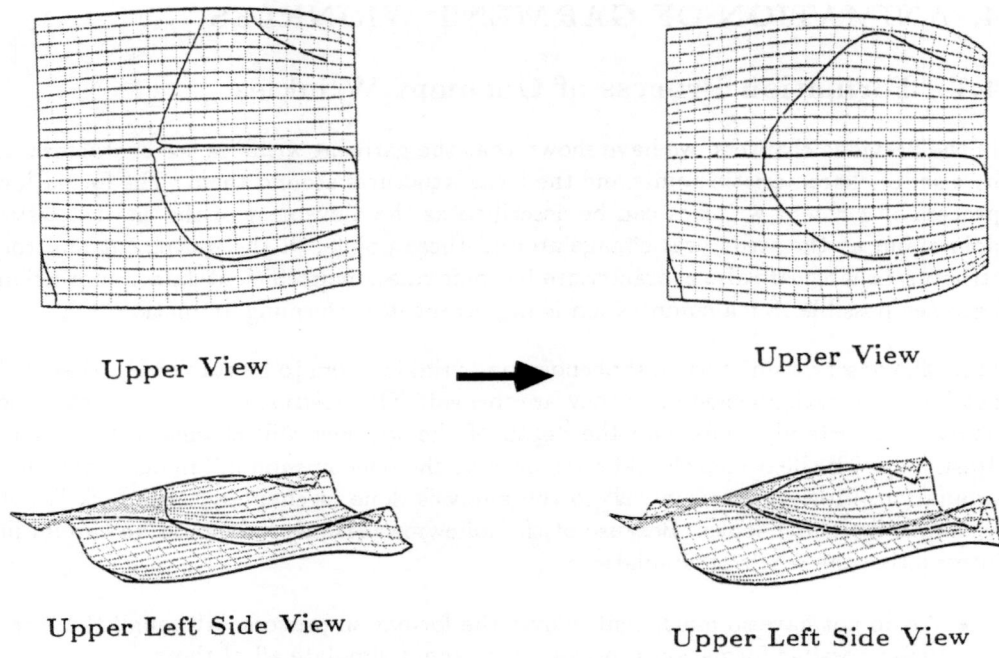

Upper View   Upper View

Upper Left Side View   Upper Left Side View

Fig. 4.1 Wrinkle Formation Process

4.2   Animation of Formation Processes

As an example, we take the wrinkles formed around the arm of a jacket. The first basic parameter here is the angle between the human forearm and upper arm at the elbow. The more the arm is bent, the deeper the wrinkles becomes. In order to animate such phenomenon, we assume the following:

- The points that are initially characteristic will remain so during the process of wrinkle formation;

- The contour lines will get sharper during the process;   and

- The wrinkles will become deeper during the process.

Based on these assumptions, animation is conducted by using the modeling primitives of wrinkles. Now, the initial configuration of characteristic points needs to be added to the angle at the elbow as the second parameter of this animation. Figure 4.2 shows two animation sequences of wrinkle formation. The difference in the two cases lies in the initial configuration data. Case (a) has 7 branching points and 19 ending points. Case (b) has 9 branching points and 27 ending points. Also, (b) uses smoother splines than (a). The results are relatively good for such a small number of parameters.

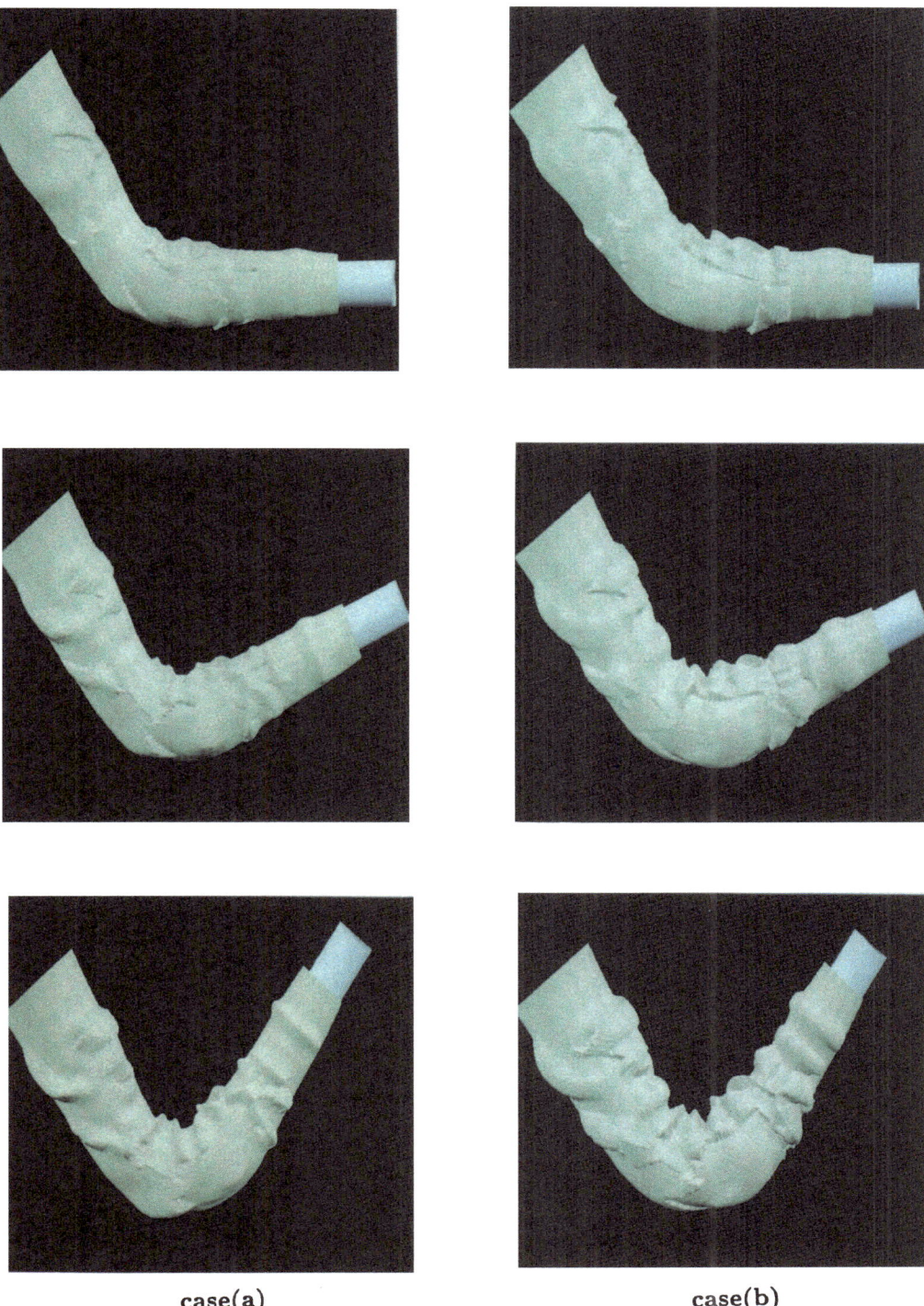

case(a)   case(b)

Fig. 4.2 Animation of Wrinkle Formation Processes

4.3 Clarifying the Problems in Deriving the Initial Configurations by Simulation

Although the assumptions in the previous section greatly simplify the task of animation, the initial configuration data of wrinkles are still required as the parameter values. This requirement, at first sight, seems to be unnecessary if the initial configuration can be gained by numerical simulation. However, for the following reasons, getting the initial configuration by simulation is not practical.

First, cloth is usually inhomogeneous according to the material, the wearing process, and the history of its use. In fact, if we repeat bending and stretching the arm, it can be observed that wrinkles tend to be formed at the places where they existed before. Since the process of deformation is irreversible, the past history strongly influences the current state. In a short term simulation, such history cannot be correctly incorporated. Since the initial configuration can be considered to correspond to the inhomogeneity of cloth, requiring it as a part of the physical properties is not unreasonable.

Second, the simulation will be time consuming because a system that contains both small and large scale factors is hard to handle. While a wrinkle has its own structure such as the characteristic points (a small scale factor), the problem to be answered is the total arrangement of the wrinkles (a large scale factor). To correctly solve such a system, we have to decompose it into the smallest unit, a polymer molecule, which means to handle a very large amount of data at a time.

Third, it is theoretically difficult to predict an emergence of a new wrinkle. An emergence of a wrinkle is a qualitative shape change involving the creation of new characteristic points and establishment of new connections to the other wrinkles. Singularity theory can deal with such changes and there are several works that address the problem in the case of an elastic object. So called *Euler buckling* phenomenon (Chillingworth 1975; Zeeman 1977), in which a metallic beam bends drastically at some moment when increasing force is applied at its ends, can be explained in the framework of this theory. In the case of a 2 dimensional plate, however, the type and mechanism of the shape change have not been sufficiently understood yet.

The problem we are looking at is still an open research area. The initial configuration data are, therefore, necessary for efficient execution of the animation. As our understanding on the nature of singularity to create drastic cloth shape changes advances, we intend to develop a different approach.

5. CONCLUDING REMARKS

Modeling of soft objects is getting popular in computer graphics and animation. This paper took a garment wrinkle as a class of soft objects, and attempted to model its static and dynamic structures.

First the static structures of garment wrinkles were examined. We presented modeling primitives which could sufficiently represent the static structures of wrinkles. Since the primitives were extracted from the geometrical analysis of the results of kinetic simulation, they successfully integrated both the kinetic and the geometric characteristics in a unified manner.

Then the dynamic structures were studied. Although analysis of dynamic structures was far more difficult than that of static structures, we could come up with a simple model with several assumptions for efficient execution of animation. The result of the animation showed the applicability of the dynamic model.

The modeling procedure we described in the case of garment wrinkles, is expected to apply to the modeling of the other soft objects. The combination of kinetic simulation and mathematical analysis of the results by singularity theory will become a powerful tool to explore the world of "softness".

The future directions of our research include mathematical analysis of the dynamic structures of the wrinkles, representation of the initial wrinkle formation process by singularity theory, and intergration of the animation systems and the database systems to find the further effective use of pattern information.

ACKNOWLEDGMENTS

We would like to thank Dr. Yannick L. Kergosien for his valuable comments at the early stage of this research. Thanks are also extended to International Information Science Foundation for support to invite Dr. Kergosien to Kunii Laboratory.

REFERENCES

Arnold VI (1986) *Catastrophe Theory*. 2nd ed., Springer, Berlin Heidelberg, New York, Tokyo

Bar AH (1984) The Global and Local Deformations of Solid Primitives. *ACM Computer Graphics*, 18 (3), pp.21–29

Chillingworth D (1975) The Catastrophe of a Buckling Beam. In *Dynamical Systems –Warwick*. Lecture Notes in Mathematics 468 (A. Manning, ed.), pp.86–91. Springer, Berlin and New York

Christiansen HN and Sederberg TW (1978) Conversion of Complex Contour Line Definition into Polygonal Element Mosaics. In *Proc. ACM SIGGRAPH'78*, pp.178–192

Kergosien YL (1981) Topologie Différentielle. *Comptes Rendus*, 291, série I, pp.929–932

Kergosien YL (1989) Topological Methods for the Analysis of Medical Images. In *Preliminary Proceedings of VISUDA '89*

Platt JC and Barr AH (1988) Constraint Methods for Flexible Models. *ACM Computer Graphics*, 22 (4), pp.279–288

Schweikert DG (1966) An Interpolation Curve Using a Spline in Tension. *J. Math. and Physics*, 45, pp.312–317

Shinagawa Y, Kunii TL, Nomura Y, Okuno T, and Hara M (1989) Reconstructing Smooth Surfaces from a Series of Contour Lines Using a Homotopy. In *New Advances in Computer Graphics.* (R. A. Earnshaw and B. Wyvill eds.), Springer, New York, Berlin, Heidelberg, Tokyo, pp.147–161

Terzopoulos D, Platt JC, Barr AH, and Fleisher K (1987) Elastically Deformable Models. *ACM Computer Graphics*, 21 (4), pp.205–214

Terzopoulos D and Fleisher K (1988) Deformable Models. *The Visual Computer*, 4, pp.306–311

Thom R (1972) *Stabilité Structurelle et Morphogénèse.* Benjamin, New York

Weil J (1986) The Synthesis of Cloth Objects. *ACM Computer Graphics*, 20 (4), pp.49–54

Wyvill G, McPheeters C, and Wyvill B (1986) Data Structure for Soft Objects. *The Visual Computer*, 2, pp.227–242

Zeeman EC (1977) *Catastrophe Theory : Selected Papers (1972–1977).* Addison Wesley, Reading, Mass.

Tosiyasu L. Kunii is currently Professor and Chairman of Information and Computer Science, the University of Tokyo. At the University of Tokyo, he started his work in raster computer graphics in 1968 which was let to the Tokyo Raster Technology Project. His research interests include computer graphics, database systems, and software engineering. He authored and edited more than 30 computer science books, and published more than 100 refereed academic/technical papers in computer science and applications areas.

Dr. Kunii is Honorary President and Founder of the Computer Graphics Society, Editor-in-Chief of The Visual Computer: An International Journal of Computer Graphics, and on the Editorial Board of IEEE Transactions on Knowledge and Data Engineering and IEEE Computer Graphics and Applications. He is on the IFIP Modeling and Simulation Working Group, the IFIP Data Base Working Group and the IFIP Computer Graphics Working Group. He organized and was chairing the Technical Committee on Software Engineering of the Information Processing Society of Japan from 1976 to 1981. He also organized and was President of the Japan Computer Graphics Association(JCGA) from 1981 to 1983. He served as General Chairman of the 3rd International Conference on Very Large Data Bases(VLDB) in 1977, Program Chairman of InterGraphics in 1983, Organizing Committee Chairman and Program Chairman of Computer Graphics Tokyo in 1984, Program Chairman of Computer Graphics Tokyo in 1985 and 1986, Organizing Committee Chairperson and Program Chairperson of CG International '87, Program Co-Chairman of IEEE COMPSAC '87, and Honorary Committee Chairperson of CG International '88. He served as Organizing Committee Chairperson and Program Chairperson of IFIP TC-2/WG 2.6 Working Conference on Visual Database Systems in 1989 and Program Chairperson of IFIP TC-5/WG 5.10 Working Conference on Modeling in Computer Graphics in 1991.

He received the B.Sc., M.Sc., and D.Sc. degrees in chemistry all·from the University of Tokyo in 1962, 1964, and 1967, respectively.

Address: Department of Information Science, Faculty of Science, the University of Tokyo, 7-3-1 Hongo, Bunkyo-Ku,Tokyo, 113 Japan

Hironobu Gotoda is currently a master course graduate student at Department of Information Science, the University of Tokyo. His research interests include computer graphics, computer animation, and database systems. He received the B.Sc. degree in information science from the University of Tokyo in 1989. He is a student member of the IEEE Computer Society and ACM.

Address: Department of Information Science, Faculty of Science, the University of Tokyo, 7-3-1 Hongo, Bunkyo-Ku,Tokyo, 113 Japan

Command History in a Reversible Painting System

BRUCE A. STYNE

ABSTRACT

The combination of command history and history management functions provides a powerful adjunct to a reversible computing environment in which earlier versions of a command history can be easily edited and new versions can be built upon existing primitives. A reversible painting system illustrates the construction of one such environment which is based upon the integration of history management, reversible execution and a simple, but appropriate, application system.

Keywords: reversible computing, electronic painting, command management, command history, undo.

1. INTRODUCTION

Reversible computing has been implemented in a wide ranging set of environments which span the gamut from text editing to cricket scoring (Zelkowitz 1971; Flowers 1980; Archer 1884; Tichy 1985; Briggs 1987). Yet, in spite of this diversity a common feature in most reversible systems is an unlimited facility to *undo* (Burton 1980) commands all the way (if required) to the starting state of the system. This provides, in a rudimentary form, a means of correcting user errors which have occurred at any point in the lifetime of a system.

In the electronic graphics environment, a reversible painting system provides similar facilities for altering design elements which require retrospective correction or alteration. However, even greater advantages are to be gained by combining reversible painting with a command history and management system to yield a multi-version painting system in which several command histories of a graphic exist simultaneously and existing elements from each version may be used in the construction of new versions.

One form of a multi-version, reversible painting environment has been constructed and is based upon the facilities of a relatively simple, but powerful, command history and management system.

2. COMMAND HISTORIES

In an irreversible, i.e., conventional, computing system, a command history is a journal, listing all of the commands executed from the starting state, S_0, of some system to the current state, S_n, as in:

$$S_0 \xrightarrow{E} S_n,$$

where E represents the command string $C_0, C_1, C_2, ..., C_{n-1}$.

In reversible systems, where is is possible to 'undo' commands, it is necessary to differentiate between the execution history, E, and the history of all commands which have been issued, C. These two strings will differ if part of C has been unexecuted and not yet re-executed; a third string, U, may be used to store all such unexecuted commands. The commands which alter the contents of these strings are termed *meta* commands. Their actions constitute an *editing* of the history, but are not, at least in the present discussion, included in the history itself.

2.1 Irreversible Systems

In an irreversible computing system, editing of the command string can be modelled by a single operation, *append*, which concatenates a newly executed command, C_n, to both the command history and the execution history:

$$\textit{Append}(C_n)$$
$$E = C = C_0, C_1, C_2, ..., C_{n-1} \longrightarrow E = C = C_0, C_1, C_2, ..., C_{n-1}, C_n$$
$$U = \varnothing \longrightarrow U = \varnothing$$

In irreversible systems the unexecuted history is always empty.

2.2 Partially Reversible Systems

Extended editing facilities are provided in partially reversible systems (Apple 1984a, 1984b) where it is possible to reverse execution to a limited degree (e.g., once-only undo) and, in some cases, to 'redo' the most recently undone command.

For example, *undo*, which can be applied only if U is empty, truncates the rightmost element of E and places it in U:

$$\textit{Undo}$$
$$C = C_0, C_1, C_2, ..., C_{n-1}, C_n \longrightarrow C = C_0, C_1, C_2, ..., C_{n-1}, C_n$$
$$E = C_0, C_1, C_2, ..., C_{n-1}, C_n \longrightarrow E = C_0, C_1, C_2, ..., C_{n-1}$$
$$U = \varnothing \longrightarrow U = C_n$$

Redo can usually be applied only directly following an *undo:*

$$\textit{Redo}$$
$$C = C_0, C_1, C_2, ..., C_{n-1}, C_n \dashrightarrow C = C_0, C_1, C_2, ..., C_{n-1}, C_n$$
$$E = C_0, C_1, C_2, ..., C_{n-1} \dashrightarrow E = C_0, C_1, C_2, ..., C_{n-1}, C_n$$
$$U = C_n \dashrightarrow U = \emptyset$$

Neither operation affects the command history, C; only the partition of C between E and U is altered. This partition defines the extent to which the history may be edited without introducing inconsistency between the current state of the system and the record of commands, E, which were executed to reach this state. Although E may not be edited directly, U may be modified without restriction.

The set of editing primitives which are applied to U and E determines whether the editing is *constructive* or *destructive*. If following every operation, E is a prefix of a command history in C, and U is the remaining suffix of the history containing this prefix, then the editing can be termed as *constructive*. Otherwise, if this prefix/suffix property does not hold, the editing is destructive.

2.3 Fully Reversible Systems

Partially reversible systems limit the size of the partition of C into U. In a fully reversible system, this partition is unrestricted to the extent that U may be any suffix of C, including C itself. Management schemes for fully reversible systems have been implemented in both the constructive and destructive (Archer 1984) mould. However, even constructive systems (Singer 1981) have been limited by the fact that they are only selectively reversible to particular points in the command history which have been explicitly marked.

In contrast, the history management system which is presented here is a constructive editing, which is also 'piecewise' reversible. Consideration of this system begins with a simple instance of the *append* command which has been applied after undoing some number of commands. As before, *append* is applied implicitly with the execution of a new event. This creates a permanent division of the command history into three substrings which contain the prefix of the original history, its suffix, and a new suffix to which subsequent commands are appended:

$$\textit{Append}(C_r)$$
$$C = C_0, C_1, C_2, ..., C_{n-2}, C_{n-1}, C_n \dashrightarrow C = C_0, C_1, C_2, ..., C_{n-2}, (C_{n-1}, C_n + C_r)$$
$$E = C_0, C_1, C_2, ..., C_{n-2} \dashrightarrow E = C_0, C_1, C_2, ..., C_{n-2}, C_r$$
$$U = C_{n-1}, C_n \dashrightarrow U = C_{n-1}, C_n$$

The parentheses '(' and ')' denote a fork in the history (Fig. 1); the two branches of the fork are separated by the '+' sign.

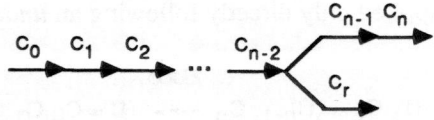

Fig. 1. $C = C_0, C_1, C_2, ..., C_{n-2}, (C_{n-1}, C_n + C_r)$.

As before, undo has the effect of reversing execution to an earlier state:

$$Undo$$
$$C = C_0, C_1, C_2, ..., C_{n-2}, (C_{n-1}, C_n + C_r) \longrightarrow C = C_0, C_1, C_2, ..., C_{n-2}, (C_{n-1}, C_n + C_r)$$
$$E = C_0, C_1, C_2, ..., C_{n-2}, C_{n-1} \dashrightarrow E = C_0, C_1, C_2, ..., C_{n-2}$$
$$U = C_n \dashrightarrow U = C_{n-1}, C_n$$

Generally, the use of *append* and *undo* give rise to a tree structured history. Branches in the history are formed where commands are appended within the existing command history following the use of *undo*.

Although, in the example given, **C** is a non-deterministic history containing a fork and two branches, we may without loss of generality, view **C** as a history **set** containing two deterministic histories:

$$C = \{C_0, C_1, C_2, ..., C_{n-2}, C_{n-1}, C_n; \ C_0, C_1, C_2, ..., C_{n-2}, C_r\}$$

which share a common prefix. In this view, only one string of the history is under execution at a given moment; the remaining strings represent alternative versions of the history. This clarifies the operation of the *redo* primitive when a fork is encountered in the history; *redo* is defined to execute the command which follows in the current version:

$$Redo$$
$$C = C_0, C_1, C_2, ..., C_{n-2}, (C_{n-1}, C_n + C_r) \dashrightarrow C = C_0, C_1, ..., C_{n-2}, (C_{n-1}, C_n + C_r)$$
$$E = C_0, C_1, C_2, ..., C_{n-2} \dashrightarrow E = C_0, C_1, C_2, ..., C_{n-2}, C_{n-1}$$
$$U = C_{n-1}, C_n \dashrightarrow U = C_n$$

However, where forks do occur, it is useful to be able to *select* an alternative version for execution:

$$Select \ (C_r)$$
$$C = C_0, C_1, C_2, ..., C_{n-2}, (C_{n-1}, C_n + C_r) \longrightarrow C = C_0, C_1, C_2, ..., C_{n-2}, (C_{n-1}, C_n + C_r)$$
$$E = C_0, C_1, C_2, ..., C_{n-2} \dashrightarrow E = C_0, C_1, C_2, ..., C_{n-2}$$
$$U = C_{n-1}, C_n \dashrightarrow U = C_r$$

which is denoted by the first command in the branch of the new version.

Formally, the *append* primitive is implemented in one of two forms, depending on the status of **U**. If **U** is non-empty then an insertion is made creating a new branch at the current point of execution:

$$Append(C_s)$$

$$\mathbf{C} = C_0,C_1,C_2,...,C_{n-2}, (C_{n-1}, C_n + C_r) \longrightarrow \mathbf{C} = C_0,C_1,C_2,...,C_{n-2}, (C_{n-1},(C_n+C_s) +C_r)$$
$$\mathbf{E} = C_0,C_1,C_2,..., C_{n-2}, C_{n-1} \longrightarrow \mathbf{E} = C_0,C_1,C_2,..., C_{n-2}, C_{n-1}, C_s$$
$$\mathbf{U} = C_n \longrightarrow \mathbf{U} = \varnothing$$

This has the effect of creating a new version in **C**,

$$C_0,C_1,C_2,...,C_{n-2}, C_{n-1},C_s$$

which is automatically selected as the current execution version.

Otherwise, the new command is appended to both **C** and **E** in the current version:

$$Append (C_s)$$

$$\mathbf{C} = C_0,C_1,...,C_{n-2}, (C_{n-1}, C_n + C_r) \longrightarrow \mathbf{C} = C_0,C_1,...,C_{n-2}, (C_{n-1}, C_n, C_s + C_r)$$
$$\mathbf{E} = C_0,C_1,C_2,...,C_{n-2},..., C_{n-2}, C_{n-1}, C_n \longrightarrow \mathbf{E} = C_0,C_1,C_2,...,C_{n-2}, C_{n-1}, C_n, C_s$$
$$\mathbf{U}=\varnothing \longrightarrow \mathbf{U} = \varnothing$$

Append, undo, redo, and *select* define a constructive management system in which a new version of the command history can be formed from any prefix of an existing version. This idea can be extended to the sharing of suffixes with the addition of two further primitives, *cut* and *paste*.

Cut provides a facility to remove an existing command from the history:

$$Cut$$

$$\mathbf{C} = C_0,C_1,C_2,...,C_{n-3}, C_{n-2}, (C_{n-1},C_n + C_r) \longrightarrow \mathbf{C} = C_0,C_1,C_2,...,C_{n-3},$$
$$(C_{n-2} + \Delta), (C_{n-1},C_n + C_r)$$
$$\mathbf{E} = C_0,C_1,C_2,...,C_{n-3} \longrightarrow \mathbf{E} = C_0,C_1,C_2,...,C_{n-3}$$
$$\mathbf{U} = C_{n-2}, C_{n-1}, C_n \longrightarrow \mathbf{U} = \Delta, C_{n-1}, C_n$$

The first element in **U** is bypassed by establishing a null command, Δ, in a branch parallel to the first element (Fig. 2). Under execution, the null command has no effect other than to advance execution through the next element. As the null command gives rise to a new version of the history, the original version of the history remains intact; both versions share a common suffix following the bypassed command.

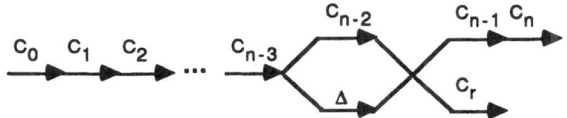

Fig. 2. $C = C0, C1, C2, ..., Cn-3, (Cn-2 + \Delta), (Cn-1, Cn + Cr)$

The *paste* command provides a facility for inserting existing substrings of a version into another location without explicitly reinserting each element:

$$Paste\ (C_s,...,C_z)$$

$$\mathbf{C} = C_0,C_1,C_2,...,C_{n-3}, C_{n-2}, (C_{n-1},C_n + C_r) \longrightarrow \mathbf{C} = C_0,C_1,C_2,...,C_{n-3}, C_{n-2},$$
$$(C_{n-1},C_n, C_s,...,C_z + C_r)$$
$$\mathbf{E} = C_0,C_1,C_2,..., C_{n-3}, C_{n-2}, C_{n-1},C_n \longrightarrow \mathbf{E} = C_0,C_1,C_2,..., C_{n-3}, C_{n-2}, C_{n-1},C_n$$
$$\mathbf{U} = \emptyset \longrightarrow \mathbf{U} = C_s,...,C_z$$

IF **U** is empty, then the pasted substring is appended to **C** and **U**. Otherwise, the string is contained in a fork which is parallel to a null command (Fig. 3).

$$Paste\ (C_s,...,C_z)$$

$$\mathbf{C} = C_0,C_1,C_2,...,C_{n-3}, C_{n-2}, (C_{n-1},C_n + C_r \longrightarrow \mathbf{C} = C_0,C_1,C_2,...,C_{n-3}, (C_s,...,C_z + \Delta),$$
$$C_{n-2}, (C_{n-1},C_n + C_r)$$
$$\mathbf{E} = C_0,C_1,C_2,..., C_{n-3} \longrightarrow \mathbf{E} = C_0,C_1,C_2,..., C_{n-3}$$
$$\mathbf{U} = C_{n-2}, C_{n-1},C_n \longrightarrow \mathbf{U} = C_s,...,C_z, C_{n-2}, C_{n-1},C_n$$

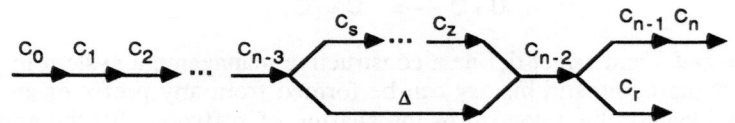

Fig. 3. $C = C0, C1, C2,...,Cn-3, (Cs,...,Cz + \Delta),\ Cn-2,\ (Cn-1, Cn + Cr)$

3. THE REVERSIBLE PAINTING ENVIRONMENT

The construction of a reversible environment requires a combining of history management function, reversible execution and an application system. Whilst the integration of these elements may be achieved in a variety of forms, the results of primary concern are the user level commands which contribute to the command history and the various functions which are available for managing these commands.

This suggests that command definition can serve as a useful starting point in determining the structure of a reversible environment. Indeed, this strategy has been pursued, here, in the design and implementation of the reversible painting environment, where elements of the command history correspond exactly to user selectable commands. Although these commands may appear spartan by comparison with conventional painting systems, it would seem to be a relatively minor task to expand the command set, significantly. The major emphasis of this work is necessarily concerned with the implementation of the command history and the history management system.

3.1 System Structure

The reversible painting system (Fig. 4) is a single BCPL (Richards 1979) program which is structured as separate modules to provide command selection and interpretation, management of the command history, and reversible emulation. This latter module (Styne 1988) is itself a BCPL program which emulates both forward and reverse execution of programs which are written in INTCODE (Richards 1972). INTCODE is an intermediate, machine independent object language which is optionally produced by most BCPL compilers.

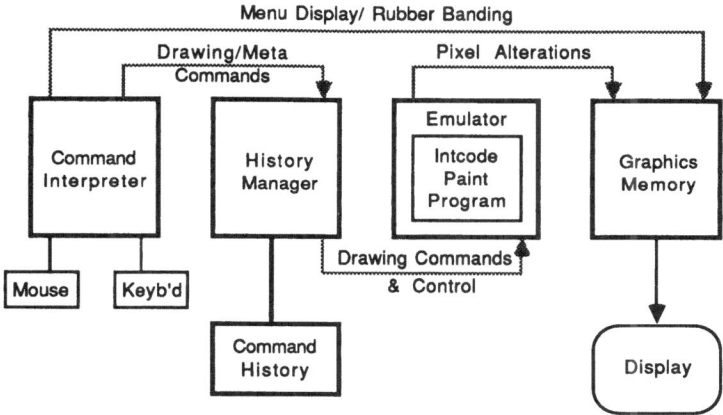

Fig. 4. The Reversible Painting System.

The command interpreter provides a user interface for command selection and, in the case of drawing commands, implements a complete mechanism for command specification. In line drawing, for example, this mechanism provides the routines required to 'rubber band' a line through various positions and directly reflect each position on the display. Once the position of the line is fixed, a command describing the line is forwarded to the history manager where it is appended or inserted within the command history. The command is then forwarded to the emulator for immediate execution.

Using this strategy, reversible emulation is applied only to the final specification of a line, rather than a set of intermediate positions used in line placement; as fewer lines are drawn, reversibly, the cost of emulation is a lesser proportion of the overall activity on the display.

The command interpreter also generates the meta commands which are used to control the command history. Meta commands are executed, locally, by the history manager, and have the effect of modifying the structure of the history and/or altering the location of emulator execution relative to the history.

The program under execution in the emulator is a construct of INTCODE drawing procedures which correspond to the user accessible drawing commands in the main menu. The overall structure of the program is that of a continuous loop:

```
// The Intcode Painting Program
    GET "LIBHDR"


//      Globals are loaded by the history manager before execution is invoked

        Global
        $( CommandIn : 200;  ComArg1 : 201; ComArg2: 202; ComArg3 : 203
           ComArg4 : 204;  ComArg5 : 206
        $)

        LET Start() BE
        $(
SW:     Switchon  CommandIn INTO
        $( CASE line:       DrawLine(ComArg1, ComArg2,
                                    ComArg3, ComArg4, ComArg5)

            ...

            CASE text:      DrawText( ComArg1, ComArg2,
                                    ComArg3, ComArg4, ComArg5)
        $)
        IntHalt()               // Force the emulator to halt
                                // and await the next command
        GOTO SW
        $)


//      Intcode drawing procedures:

        AND DrawLine(x1, y1, x2, y2, Colour) BE
        $(  // the line drawing procedure
            ...
        $)
        ...
```

At the top of the loop, the program determines which routine to invoke by examining a global area which is shared with the history manager. The history manager loads this area with the name and arguments of the command to be executed. Control of the program returns to the loop on completion of the drawing command. The loop then invokes a voluntary halt, which suspends operation of the emulator and returns program control to the history manager.

When traversing the history, it is crucial to maintain synchronisation between the history manager and the reversible emulator, i.e., the command being processed in the history must match the command which is under emulation. This problem of synchronisation arises because the emulator, by itself, cannot distinguish between the end of one drawing command and the start of another as each drawing command will be translated as several commands in INTCODE. Thus, in either mode of operation, the emulator would continue to undo or redo instructions without halting at the correct position.

A solution to this problem is provided by the special BCPL procedure, *IntHalt()*. When compiled into INTCODE, and subsequently interpreted by the emulator, *IntHalt* forces the emulator to cease operation after processing exactly one drawing command in the forward direction or undoing a command in reverse. Execution is resumed when the history manager issues a new command to the emulator.

3.2 Implementation Details

The history management system is an implementation of the constructive model presented in Section 2. The history itself is a relatively simple abstraction of two data types: commands and nodes. A path, which records the commands issued between nodes, consists of one or more commands. A command (Fig. 5) is a doubly linked element which contains a pointer to the node at the beginning and end of the path, and a set of fields which specify the type of command and its arguments. A system variable, **lastCommand**, points to the command which was most recently executed.

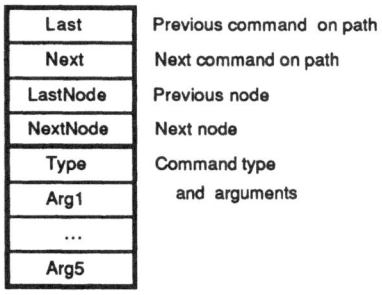

Fig. 5. Command structure.

A node is formed in the command history at every occurrence of a loop or path. Each node (Fig. 6) contains a field pointing to each of the commands which enter and/or leave the node. The commands entering and leaving the node in the current history version are also recorded, additionally, in separate fields, **VersionLast** and **VersionNext**.

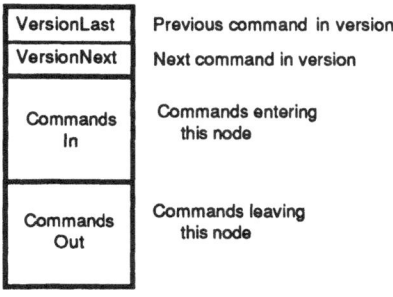

Fig. 6. Node structure.

At the start of operation, the history consists of only a root node. The first drawing command which is issued begins a path emanating from this node to which subsequent commands can be appended.

In general, the operation of *append* is dependent on the current point of execution in the history. If the previous command terminates in a node, then a new command begins a new path from the node. If, instead, the current point of execution is at the end of a path, then the new command is appended to the path. Otherwise, if the point of execution is within the interior of a path, a new node is formed at this point of execution.

Although several versions of the command history may co-exist, the *current version* of the history is a set of (node) connected paths defined by the current point of execution and each of the commands which have been executed to reach this point. Three user accessible meta commands are provided for traversing the current version. *Redo* and *undo* move the execution forwards and backwards, respectively, one command along the current path. *Select* is used to select a new path through the command history.

In the implementation of *undo* and *redo,* the value of **lastCommand** is incremented or decremented relative to the current version path as appropriate. *Undo* takes the command which is pointed to by lastCommand and forces its reverse emulation in the emulator. This process may be continued, if desired, all the way back to the root node.

Redo forces the emulator to move forward through the current version path and can be applied as far as the extent of the current version of the history. At the end of each path, the **VersionNext** field indicates the first command in the remaining suffix of the current version of the history. The **VersionLast** field fulfils a similar function when moving backwards.

In conjunction with *redo, select* can be used to choose an alternative version of the command history whenever the position of **lastCommand** immediately precedes a node. In subsequent applications of *redo,* the user must select a new path (to be incorporated in the current version) whenever a node is encountered.

Two additional meta commands, *cut* and *paste,* provide a primitive, but useful facility for editing the command history. *Cut* removes a command from the current version by inserting a null command in a parallel path. If they do not already exist, two new nodes are created immediately preceding and following the node which is to be cut. The version fields on both nodes effectively removes the node from the current version by inserting a null command in its place.

In a similar fashion, *paste* inserts commands from a marked sub-path of the history into the current version following **lastCommand**. The extent of the sub-path is determined by two commands, *startMark* and *endMark*, which are used in conjunction with *undo* and *redo* to establish a pair of temporary marks in the history.

3.3 System Operation

The reversible painting system has been implemented on a number of personal computers under the **Ms-DOS** operating system. The system occupies some 28K of compiled BCPL code.

Operation of the system is controlled by an icon driven menu (Fig. 7) which is implemented though a mouse and keyboard interface. The menu offers six drawing commands: **line, text, rectangle** (solid or unfilled) and **ellipse** (solid or unfilled) and seven meta commands: **undo, redo, select, cut, paste, startMark,** and **endMark** for traversing and editing the history.

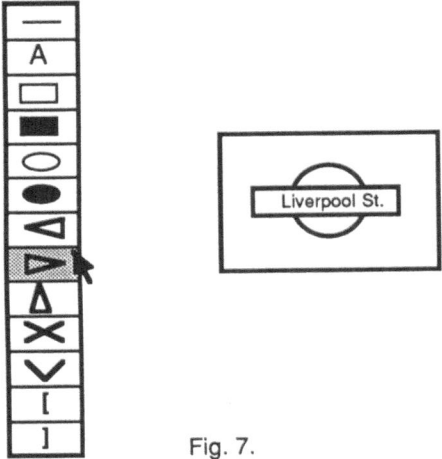

Fig. 7.

The operation of the system is best described with the aid of a simple example. Fig. 8 illustrates a drawing which is being prepared on the system.

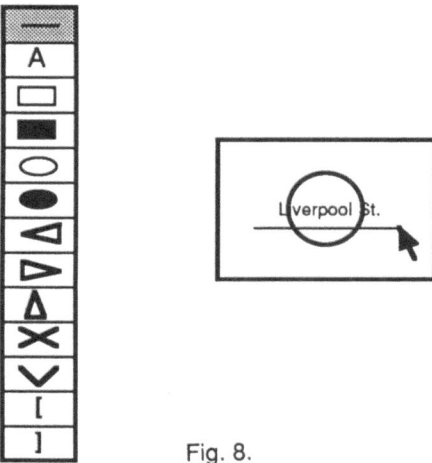

Fig. 8.

The command history of the system contains four elements:

E = C = Ellipse, Line, Text, Rectangle

It is decided to test an alternative design incorporating a filled, white rectangle in place of the line. This is accomplished by creating a new branch subsequent to the circle which will contain the new filled rectangle and a copy of both the existing text and the unfilled rectangle. This process proceeds in three stages.

In the first stage a marked sub-branch is created to copy the text and unfilled rectangle. To this end, the first command issued, **endMark**, places an end marker ']' in the history following the rectangle:

E = C = Ellipse, Line, Text, Rectangle]

Next, two **undo** commands are issued to reverse the point of execution prior to the text. A **startMark** command '[' (Fig. 9) is issued to complete the marking of the sub-branch:

C = Ellipse, Line, [Text, Rectangle]
E = Ellipse, Line
U = Text, Rectangle

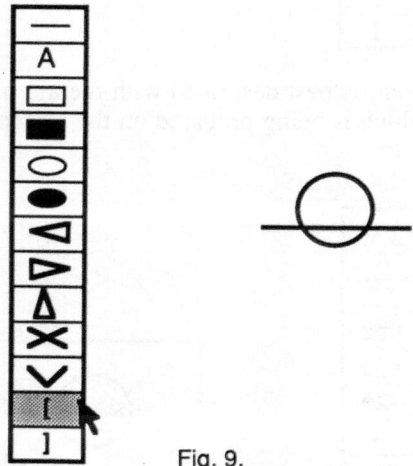

Fig. 9.

In the second stage, a new branch is created following the circle, which contains, initially, the new filled rectangle. This point of insertion is reached by one more application of **undo** (Fig. 10).

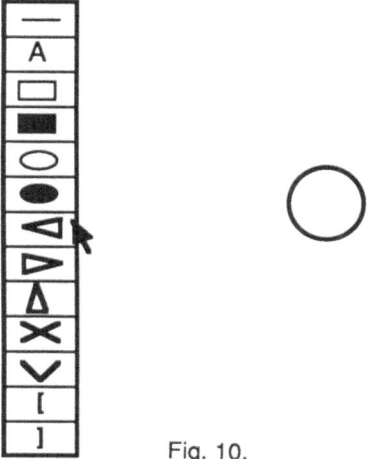

Fig. 10.

A filled rectangle command creates a node in the history, following the circle, and a new branch which emanates from this node (Fig. 11):

> **C** = Ellipse, (SolidRectangle + Line, [Text, Rectangle])
> **E** = Ellipse, SolidRectangle
> **U** = ∅

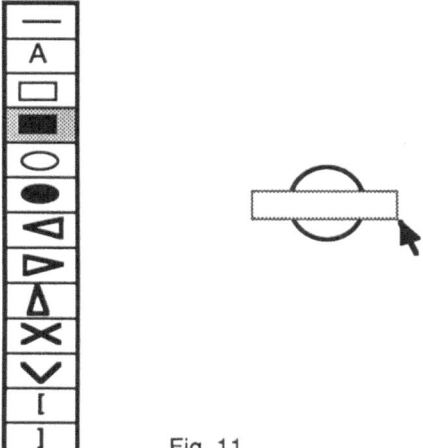

Fig. 11.

An application of the **paste** command appends the marked sub-branch to this new branch:

> **C** = Ellipse, (SolidRectangle, Text, Rectangle + Line, [Text, Rectangle])
> **E** = Ellipse, SolidRectangle
> **U** = Text, Rectangle

Two applications of **redo** execute the appended commands to produce the desired image (Fig. 12).

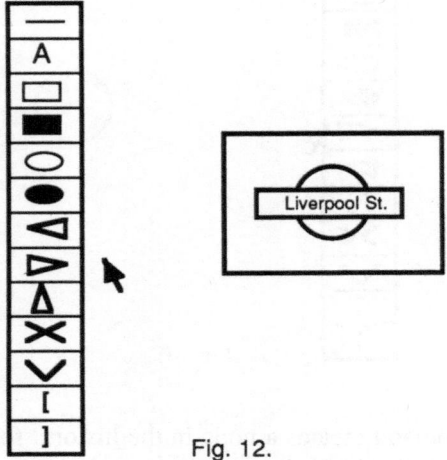

Fig. 12.

Should the user now decide that the original version is the preferred design, then, in the first instance, execution is undone until the filled rectangle is no longer visible. At this stage, the **select** icon is highlighted to indicate the presence of a node at the current point of execution.

The user may select which command to **redo** next by depressing the mouse button over the **select** icon. This has the effect of temporarily advancing execution exactly one command. When the button is released, execution retreats to the node. Depressing the mouse button again, selects the old branch for execution and displays the line (Fig. 13).

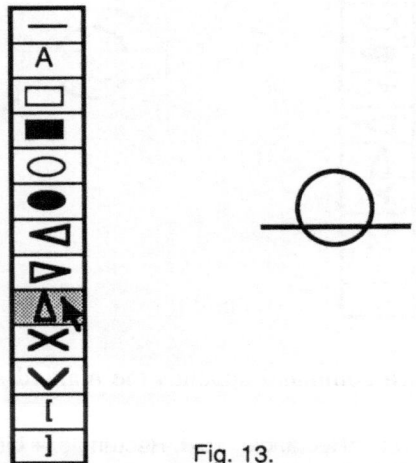

Fig. 13.

Once the mouse button is released, execution can be continued along the old branch.

4. CONCLUSION

In combination with reversible emulation, history management provides a powerful tool for the construction of an electronic painting system. In this environment, the user is offered virtually unlimited freedom to explore multiple versions of the same design without the usual cost of explicit checkpointing during the creation process.

The present history management system allows arbitrary partitions of the command history, in contrast with systems (Singer 1981; Tichy 1985) where partitions may be established only where marks are already present in the history. Thus, the user is freed from the burden of deciding in advance which states are likely to be revisited.

In contrast with other schemes which are piecewise reversible (Archer 1984), the present management scheme is fully constructive. Yet, the structure of the command history as an acyclic graph proves to be more powerful than other constructive schemes with are either linear (Archer 1984) or tree-structured (Singer 1981). Indeed, with the provision of the *cut* and *paste* primitives, the extended system offers the same degree of editing power which exists in hierarchically based image composition systems (Styne 1985).

REFERENCES

Apple Computers, Inc. (1984a), *Macwrite User's Manual*.

Apple Computers, Inc. (1984b), *Macdraw User's Manual*.

Archer, J.E., Conway, R., and Schneider, F.B. (1984), 'User Recovery and Reversal in Interactive Systems', *ACM Transactions on Programming Languages and Systems* **6**(1), 1-19.

Briggs, J.S. (1987), 'Generating Reversible Programs', *Software - Practice and Experience* **17**(7), 439-453.

Burton, R.R., Kaplan, R.M., Masinter, L.M., Sheil, B.A., Bell, A., Bobrow, D.G., Deutsch, L.P., and Haugeland, W.S. (1980), 'Papers on Interlisp-D', Report SSL-80-4, Xerox Palo Alto Research Center.

Flowers, P. (1980), 'RED - a Reversible Editor', Diploma Dissertation, University of Cambridge.

Richards, M. (1972), 'INTCODE - An Interpretive Machine Code for BCPL', University of Cambridge Computer Laboratory.

Richards, M. and Whitby-Strevens, C. (1979), *BCPL - The language and its compiler*, Cambridge University Press.

Singer, D.W. (1981), 'Scenarios: An Event Management Package', *Software - Practice And Experience* **11**(11), 521-529.

Styne, B.A., King, T.R., and Wiseman, N.E. (1985), 'Pad Structures For The Rainbow Workstation', *The Computer Journal* **28**(1), 68-72.

Styne, B.A. (1988), 'Management Systems for Computer Graphics', Ph.D. Dissertation, University of Cambridge, Computer Laboratory.

Tichy, W.F. (1985), 'RCS - A System for Version Control', *Software - Practice and Experience* **15**(7), 637-654.

Zelkowitz, M. (1971), 'Reversible Execution as a Diagnostic Aid', Ph.D. Dissertation, Cornell University.

Bruce A. Styne is currently Senior Lecturer in computer science at the University of Ulster. He joined the university in 1986 from the BBC where he was employed as a producer in Current Affairs television on <u>Newsnight</u> and as a senior member of the Computer Graphics Workshop (CGW). At CGW he was one of the team responsible for the BBC National Weather System and in charge of the bye-election graphics project. More recently, he has been involved in the implementation of election results and analysis systems for Radio Telefis Eireann. In work with Ulster Television, he has designed election systems, painting systems and implemented a weather system for Northern Ireland. Other research interests involve the design of broadcast quality frame store systems and video conferencing under the EC STAR Project. Dr. Styne received his B.A from Vassar College in 1974 and his M.A. from Columbia University in 1980. His Ph.D. (1988) was based on the Rainbow Display Project at the University of Cambridge.

Address: Department of Computing Science, University of Ulster, Cromore Road, Coleraine, Co. Londonderry, Northern Ireland, United Kingdom. BT52 1SA.

Computer Pinscreen Simulation

PEDRO FARIA LOPES and MÁRIO RUI GOMES

ABSTRACT

Seeking for new methods that enlarge the artists choice for expressing themselves we propose a computer model that simulates the traditional pinscreen image synthesis process. The pinscreen is a very particular and difficult 2D image synthesis device consisting of several hundred thousand headless pins arranged in an uniformly perforated frame, a pin per perforation. The frame is lit from an oblique angle and image synthesis is based in the shadows each pin casts, depending on how much each pin is pressed from beyond the frame. In this paper we first present some animation paradigms. Then we describe with some detail the traditional pinscreen technique, the way it is operated and related difficulties. The proposed computer model will be described. Finally we analise possibilities and problems of the method when compared with the traditional method.

Keywords: traditional animation, computer animation, computer expressiveness, pinscreen, pinscreen simulation

1. INTRODUCTION

Computer images, in the early days, were calligraphic or low resolution raster based, most of the time abstract oriented, mainly due to hardware limitations. Today the "de facto" standard for image synthesis is based on high resolution frame buffers with 24 color bit planes enabling the so called real color representation (more than 16 million colors) (Foley 1984). This capability, linked to the use of realistic oriented shading and texturing algorithms applied to 3D models, permits photorealistic image synthesis (sometimes one can not clearly state if a given picture is, or is not, a real photograph). Some artists think that computer synthesized images are too cold or that the human creative interpretation of reality is lost in the synthesis process. The problem with this approach is that computers are too precise and reality is not that precise. In the photorealistic approach one way to improve human control is by simulating optical and photographic effects like motion blur, focus distance, depth of field, etc., one area where some practical results have already been achieved (Magnenat-Thalmann 1985; Cook 1987).

In the 2D area paint programs spread as the tool for 2D image creation and composition. These programs simulate a painter's workbench by providing traditional based tools (brushes, color mixing capabilities, etc.). They also enable the user to access the "digital functionality" (cut, paste, image grabbing, fill area, ...). Nevertheless, once more, the basic expressiveness of the traditional tools is not yet completely available: digital brushes pressure and inclination dependent are difficult to achieve in the same way that artists feel and manipulate a real brush and research is being done in this area (Smith 1982; Magnenat-Thalmann 1985; Kochanek 1987).

When synthetinsing motion by computer two basic approaches exist [Magnenat-Thalmann 1985; Kochanek 1987]:

- 2D programs, computer assisted animation, that replicate the cel animation technique.
- 3D programs, computer modeled animation, that simulate the traditional 3D animation.

Each have strengths and limitations (Kochanek 1987; Lopes1988a; Lopes1988b; Lopes 1989b) and both replicate traditional animation methods. Research in both areas is normally conducted to overpass the limitations with better or new algorithms enlarging the tools already available (Platt 1981; Hofmann 1988; Pintado 1988). Next we present an introduction to traditional animation and to both computer animation approaches.

1.1 Traditional Animation

Like real image films, animation films usually tell stories. Each story is translated into cinema language by sequence, scene and plan decomposition. Characters are modeled taking into account shape, height, personality and other items. It is also necessary to build sceneries (backgrounds).

In traditional animation multiple 2D and 3D techniques can be used (Kochanek 1987; Lopes 1988b).

In commercial traditional animation the most important technique is character animation using transparent acetate sheets (cels).

Animators that are responsible for the motion specification, produce key frames, usually the first and last drawings defining a movement. This is done on paper sheets. The intermediate drawings, inbetweens, are executed by the inbetweeners. In the next phase the paper drawings are passed to cels by xeroxing. Each cel is then ink traced and painted by inkers and opaquers. Backgrounds are created. In the shooting phase, cels are overlayed on a background. Camera effects are simulated by manipulation of cels and background.

The transparency of the cels makes the production process easier. A character may exist in different cels and be reconstructed by overlaying. Nevertheless this has a drawback because cels are not totally transparent. The number of cels used in one frame is limited (5 or 6 cels) and it is necessary to use variations of the same color to achieve color continuity between cel levels (Kochanek 1987; Catmull 1979).

The intensive amount of work involved in the cel animation technique can be automated by the introduction of the computer, to assist in different levels of the process. This will be covered in the next section.

1.2 2D Computer Animation

Computer assisted cel animation includes scan-and-paint systems, paint programs and key frame interpolation (Kochanek87; Catmull79).

Inking, opaquing and recording the sequence into film or video can be done with scan-and-paint systems. Physical sheets are replaced by digital cels. The advantages are:

> - Digital cels don't get dusty, they can't be bent. Scratches don't affect them.
> - Digital cels are perfectly transparent. There is no limit for cel overlaying and no need to use color variations.
> - Color can be easily and automatically modified in all cels belonging to a sequence.
> - Recording can be automated.

Backgrounds can be either hand produced and afterwards digitized or they can be directly created in digital format by interactive use of a paint system.

Digital painting is faster than conventional painting. Colors are digitally mixed, not manually. There are no brushes to clean or paints to dry, but digital brushes expressiveness is yet weaker than that of a real brush.

The inbetweening process can be automated. The computer is fed with key frames and the linear interpolation process generates the inbetween drawings, calculating the position of each point from key to key.

1.3 3D Computer Animation

The meaning of key frame animation is different when applied to 3D Computer Animation. After modelling, the 3D object is set (translated, rotated, scaled) in key positions. Then a parametric interpolation is performed using the defined positions. The interpolated values are used to build transformation matrixes to be applied to the objects. 3D key frame animation is one of the methods to compute the values to build the matrixes.

Different approaches on the way how the transformation matrix is applied or calculated, in the motion specification process, are used by different 3D Computer Animation Systems. Skeleton animation systems imposes more restrictions than logo animation systems. Animation languages (Reynolds 1982), interactive methods (Catmull 1979), high-level motion specification (Zeltzer 1982), dynamics, inverse kinematics, constraints and key-frame animation are different approaches to the motion specification process.

An open question on 3D computer animation is the effective use of all the system capabilities toward high quality computer animation production. The animator, using a sophisticated system can easilly produce a "so called" film, based only on simple object transformations. Fundamental principals of traditional animation, as established at the Walt Disney Studio, and animator skill and experience should be used to produce high quality 3D Computer Animation (Lasseter 1987; Baerle 1987). Part of this knowledge could be inserted in an Inteligent 3D Computer Animation Systems but this is still a research topic.

A quite interesting research paper is [Hofmann 1988] where the author proposes a method to apply the scene-shifting technique of classical films to computer animation. For a specific frame parts of the preceding frame may be inserted with scaling and shifting transformations but with no need for perspective transformation or rendering, thus speeding up the rendering process in 3D computer animation. Particularly interesting is the way he gets into the problem: a scene from a Fellini's film (*La citta delle donne*) is used to show that if scene-shifting in real films illude the viewer then the same principle can be applied to computer generated scenes.

With today´s technology it is possible to create realistic images. It is now time to use knowledge not only from the photographic world but also from traditional animation areas. We follow this trend and, based on the experience in traditional animation of one of the authors [Lopes 1988b] and also studying traditional animation techniques [Russett 1976; Laybourne 1979; Salomon 1979], we realized that among all available animation techniques very few artists used the pinscreen animation technique. The explanation is that, inspite of the creative possibilities, it is a very time consuming technique and a not very easy one to deal with. We try to overcome these limitations with the computer model explained in this paper.

In the next chapter we describe the traditional pinscreen apparatus and operation techniques. Next we present a model for a computer modeled pinscreen and the visualization algorithm. Finally we discuss advantages of this approach over the traditional method.

2. TRADITIONAL PINSCREEN

Alexandre Alexeieff and Claire Parker invented the pinscreen between 1930 and 1935. Their goals were to build a system where one could produce images that, when animated, could resemble engraved pictures in motion [Salomon 1979].

The pinscreen technique is based on a white plate standing upright in a frame, with approximate A3 format or bigger. The plate is uniformly perforated perpendicularly to the surface by small holes where headless metal pins are inserted, one per hole, sliding easily through them. Depending on the size, a pinscreen may be composed from 80 thousand to one million pins. The pins are longer than the thickness of the plate. This means that each pin, or group of pins, can be pushed in the back surface of the plate emerging in the front surface. The reverse operation is also possible. Both surfaces are lighted at an angle by spotlights, one per surface.

The image creation in the pin screen is based in the shadow casting principle explained next, enabling the synthesis of black and white pictures with intermediate gray levels. Let's assume that we are looking to the front surface. When the pins are not emerging from a surface no shadows are cast and the surface appears white. If one of the pins is pushed from behind its shadow will be cast on the white surface. The further the pin is pushed the longer the shadow. Instead of a pin one can push a group of pins. Suppose we did it only halfway. The shadows cast will appear with white spaces between them and a medium gray tone will be obtained. If the pins are fully pushed each pin's shadow will overlap that of its neighbour. No light will reach the white surface and a black tone is formed. The back surface shows the reverse effect acting as a negative.

To animate images on the pinscreen a first one is synthesized using several tools to manipulate groups of pins, in both surfaces, until the desired gray tones are achieved to form the picture. This picture is photographed into a film frame. The next frame is obtained by slight modifications on the first image on the same pinscreen according to the desired motion.The complete animated film is a collection of images that were gradually and incrementaly produced, each one based on the previews one.

Few persons used this technique and few films were produced with it. Alexeieff and Parker made a total of six films with the pinscreen technique [Salomon 1979]. There are also few pinscreens in the world (one of them is at the National Film Board of Canada, Montreal, used by Jacques Drouin). The reasons for this are mainly two: frame construction and operation.

To build a pinscreen several thousands pins have to be assembled. If only one pin doesn't justify any particular concern when it amounts to hundreds of thounsands pins it turns into a heavy and expensive problem.

To operate a pinscreen it's not an easy task. It is almost impossible to exactly reproduce a given frame of an animated sequence, meaning that an error in one frame can easily throw away all the work involved in a complete animation sequence. Consequently, great amount of scene preparation, care and dedication are needed to produce a complete film.

Until now we saw how traditional pinscreen animation worked, the kind of results achieved with it and why there are so few artists using this technique. In the next chapter the model of a virtual pinscreen is presented.

3. COMPUTER MODELED PINSCREEN

3.1 First Steps

The pinscreen underlaying technique is a typical problem of casting shadows over a surface. With the first tests we tried to simulate the physical model of a pinscreen and apply raytracing to produce the shadows. We used a general purpose raytracer (the MTV public domain raytracing packge) enabling the specification of several kinds of primitives (spheres, cones, cylinders and mesh polygons). The pins were modeled as opaque cylinders placed vertically on a white polygon. The raytracer produced the expected shadows but, as we expected from the beginning, this approach is limited and only suitable for tests (rendering time is the major obstacle).

Next we present a model for the pinscreen and propose a visualization algorithm.

3.2 Model

The traditional pinscreen is really a simple device: pins in holes. The computer model should match the original simplicity and the time spent to compute the shadows should be inexpensive to enable interactive use, like in the real pinscreen.

The fundamental items in the pinscreen responsible for the image synthesis are the spot light, the pins and the white surface. They serve to produce the elements responsible for the image synthesis: the shadows and the white spaces inbetween. This means that the computer model only has to consider the minimum set of items that will simulate shadows.

We can identify the light and the white surface as elements to be supported in the model. What about the pins? In the real pinscreen, physical opaque pins interfere with light producing the shadows. In the computer model there is no need for a physical simulation. There is only need for each pins' position, high and thickness to calculate the cast shadow.

The pins' position distributed over the surface has to be also analised: there are moments when white spaces must be seen among the shadows so that intermediate tones of gray can be synthesized. For a particular image, the denser the pins' position the darker the image and vice-versa.

Resuming, the computer model supports:

- Light source (direction)
- White surface
- Pins (position, high, thickness, distribution)

3.3 Visualization

In the current version of the pinscreen model the thickness of a pin is approximated to the size of a pixel and the following algorithm is applied:

Initialize framebuffer to white
For each virtual pin
- read pin's position and high
- compute direction and length of shadow according to light position
- draw a black line starting in the pin's position with the shadow's direction and length.

3.4 Model Test

Tests were made with a black & white digitized image with 512 * 512 pixel resolution. For each pixel of the source image a virtual pin was assigned, its high being inversely proportional to the gray value of the pixel (the darker the pixel, low pixel value, the longer the pin, high pin length).

Different virtual pin densities were tried, from one to three pixel intervals. The resulting images, if compared with the original digitized one, lost definition and contrast, as it was easily predictable. The point is they aren't comparable because the reproducing techniques are different and the final goals are not the same: pinscreen is really intended to reproduce "chiaroscuro" images and, depending on the available resolution, more or less precise reproductions.

Nevertheless computer modeled pinscreen resolution is a problem with today's digital framebuffers. A 1024 * 768 pixel resolution digital framebuffer enables a pinscreen with 512 * 384 pin resolution, considering one pin interval between virtual pins. This gives a total of less than two hundred thousand pins, still a low resolution. To model the best traditional pinscreen available (one million pins) it would require a digital framebuffer with 2300 * 1740 pixel resolution. There are already digital film recorders that can record images up to 4000 * 4000 resolution but, for interactive use, this resolution is not yet available.

The results achieved till now show that the proposed model works: the images obtained aplying the proposed computer model are similar to those obtained on the traditional pinscreen with equivalent pin resolution. Inspite of the the good results, the best test possible will be to let a skilled artist to synthesize an image using a digital pinscreen and a traditional one, both with similar resolutions and tools (interactive virtual tools are under development).

3.5 Computer Model Possibilities

Based on the model described above we are currently developing a computer pinscreen system. The model advantages over the traditional pinscreen are now presented.

When compared to the traditional pinscreen the digital approach offers several advantages mainly related to automation.

Image synthesis and animation: As in the first tests we made, the user could begin an image synthesis session with any kind of digital image already in mass storage. Any subsequent changes can be easily recorded so that, at any time, any of the intermediate image states can be recovered. This approach can be generalized and the way traditional pinscreen animation is done, image by image synthesis, has much to gain from it. Any image of a given animation sequence can be recovered and manipulated, saving time and, most of all, avoiding the loss of the entire animated sequence, as it happened in the traditional method when an error occurred in the animation.

Real time playback: Using the right hardware pipeline it should be possible to show any sequence of images in real time for playback purposes, a feature absolutely impossible in the traditional method.

Automatic recording: Each image doesn't need to be recorded just after completed. It can be done later under computer control. This means time saving because it can be done without the animator being present and also that, if needed, it can be repeated error free.

Fig. 1
Original Image

Fig. 2
Part of a computer modelled pinscreen image with 640 x 512 pin resolution.

Fig. 3
Part of a computer modelled pinscreen image with 427 x 341 pin resolution.

4. CONCLUSIONS

In the present paper we described the traditional pinscreen technique, its possibilities and difficulties. We proposed a computer model for pin screen simulation which is intended to enlarge the artists choice for expressiveness when using computer based tools. The results achieved so far show that the proposed model works. Based on these results we are currently working on extensions to the basic pinscreen model.

The advantages of the digital pinscreen are enormous when compared with the traditional one, but the resolution of current digital framebuffers is a limitation to obtain top quality high resolution pinscreen.

ACKNOWLEDGEMENTS

Useful information about the traditional pinscreen device was provided by Doris Kochanek and Abi. Terry Higgins showed the pinscreen Jacques Droin is using at National Film Board of Canada. Carvalho Baptista provided some important reference entries in the traditional animation area.

REFERENCES

Baerle S Van (1987) Character Animation: Combining Computer Graphics and Traditional Animation. EUROGRAPHICS '87, Tutorial: Survey of Computer Graphics for Character Animation

Catmull E (1979) New Frontiers in Computer Animation. American Cinematographer

Cook R, Carpenter L, Catmull E (1987) The Reyes Image Rendering Architecture. Computer Graphics 21(4) : 95-102

Foley JD, Dam A Van (1984) Fundamentals of Computer Graphics. Addison-Wesley, Reading, MA

Hofmann GR (1988) The Calculus of Non-Exact Perspective Projection - Scene-Shifting for Computer Animation. In: Duce A and Jancene P (ed) EUROGRAPHICS'88 Conference Proceedings, North-Holland, Amsterdam, New York, Oxford Tokyo, pp 429-442

Kochanek D, Higgins T and ForseyD (1987) Introduction to Computer Animation. Tutorial Notes, CHI+GI'87 Conference

Lasseter J (1987) Principles of Traditional Animation Applied to 3d Computer Animation. CG 21(4) : 35-44

Laybourne K (1979) The Animation Book - a complete guide to animated filmmaking from flip-books to sound cartoons. Crown Publishers, New York

Lopes PF (1988a) Imagens Chave em Animação por Computador. 1º Encontro Português de Computação Gráfica, Eurographics Portuguese Chapter

Lopes PF (1988b) SARA: Um Sistema de Animação por Computador. Master of Science Thesis, Instituto Superior Técnico, Lisboa

Lopes PF, Gomes MR (1989a) Computer Animation in Portugal. C&G 13(3) : 381-387

Lopes PF, Gomes MR (1989b) A Computer Model For Pinscreen Simulation. Technical Report, INESC, Lisboa.

Magnenat-Thalmann N, Thalmann D (1985) Computer Animation: Theory and Practice. Springer, Tokyo Berlin Heildelberg, New York

Pintado X, Fiume E (1988) GRAFIELDS: Field-Directed Dynamic Splines for Interactive Motion Control. In: Duce A and Jancene P (ed) EUROGRAPHICS'88 Conference Proceedings, North-Holland, Amsterdam, New York, Oxford Tokyo, pp 43-54

Platt SM, Badler N (1981) Animating Facial Expressions. CG 15(3) : 245-252

Reynolds C (1982) Computer Animation with Scrips and Actors. CG 16(3) : 289-296

Russett R, Starr C (1976) Experimental Animation, An Illustrated Anthology. Van Nostrand Reinhold Company, New York

Salomon N, Fust J (1979) Entretien avec Alexandre Alexeïeff et Claire Parker.

Smith A (1982) Paint. Siggraph'82 Tutorial Notes: Two-Dimensional Computer Animation

Zeltzer D (1982) Representation of Complex Animated Figures. Graphics Interface'82 Proceedings : 205-211

Pedro Faria Lopes is currently a Teaching Assistant of Computer Science at the Instituto Superior de Ciências do Trabalho e da Empresa (ISCTE) and researcher at the Institute for Systems and Computer Engineering (INESC), in Lisbon, where he is the head of the Computer Animation area.

He received a B. Sc. in Electrical Engineering and a M. Sc. in Computer Science from Instituto Superior Técnico (IST) in 1985 and1989.

His main research area is Computer Animation.

From 1977 to 1979, he used different animation techniques to produce and direct nine three minute long traditional animated films. Some were selected, awarded or shown in several film festivals, workshops and television. Two of them represented Portugal at UNICA 80, 42.eme Reunion Mondiale du Cinema Non Professionnel, Baden, Switzerland.

He is the coauthor of the first computer animated film produced in Portugal (March 1987), a short experimental film, and also coauthor of the computer animation editor used to produced it, the ANIMED Editor. In 1988 he produced and co-directed the first computer generated advertising movie, shown in the Portuguese Television, completely produced with portuguese software, the SARA Animation System.

Address: Computer Animation Research Lab (CARL), Instituto de Engenharia de Sistemas e Computadores, Rua Alves Redol 9-2º, 1000 Lisboa , Portugal (pfl@inesc.uucp)

Mário Rui Gomes is a Teaching Assistant of Computer Graphics Master classes at the Instituto Superior Técnico (IST) and head of the Computer Aided Design / Computer Aided Manufacturing (CAD/CAM) group at Instituto de Engenharia de Sistemas e Computadores (INESC).

He received a B. Sc. in Electrical Engineering from IST (1981) and a M. Sc. in Computer Science from IST (1984). Graphical User Interfaces Development Environments is Mario's main research area.

Mário Rui Gomes is member of the Informatic Working Group of the Portuguese Engineering Association ("Ordem dos Engenheiros") and of the Technical Committee 14 (CAD/CAM) of the Portuguese Normalization Institute ("Instituto Portugues da Qualidade"). He is a member of Eurographics'90 Programme Committee, a founding member of Eurographics Portuguese Chapter and member of ACM, ACM-SIGGRAPH, IEEE Computer Society and Eurographics.

Address: Department of CAD/CAM, Instituto de Engenharia de Sistemas e Computadores, Rua Alves Redol 9-2º, 1000 Lisboa , Portugal (mrg@inesc.uucp)

An Object-Oriented Approach for Modelling Animated Entities

Mohammed Mahieddine and Jean Claude Lafon

ABSTRACT

In this paper we present why and how to construct object-oriented graphical animation packages from existing low-level graphics packages interfaced with an object oriented language supporting inheritance and dynamic binding.

Keywords: Animated entity, implementational sub-classification, inheritance, dynamic binding.

1. INTRODUCTION

Existing graphics standard like GKS and PHIGS or the windowing system X-WINDOW provide a collection of elementary functions which allow important capabilities of graphics modelling and display, but are too low-level. Software construction made directly from them is rather complex (Grant 1986).

Object-oriented programming provides a range of re-usable software construction and modelling features like behavioral conceptualisation, fast prototyping, best refinement of concepts, simultaneous multiple implementations, and incremental development (Stroustrup 1987; Trousse 1988; Beeker 1989).

Nevertheless, the straight construction of animated entities from the use of only an object-oriented language requires a supplementary effort and the result is often not very convincing.

In this paper, we present a method of using both an existing conventional graphical system and an object-oriented language supporting inheritance and dynamic binding to model animated entities, and discuss the relationship and difference between our approach and the object-oriented approaches proposed by Dietrich (1989) and Chmilar (1989). This new approach permits us to combine the advantage of object-oriented methodology with all the capabilities of existing graphics packages (no need to rewrite them) to model and implement the behavior of the animated entity. We introduce the notion of implementational sub-classification as a means of organizing classes. The implementational sub-classification is an implementational inheritance derivation depending only on classes representation and on low-level operations of class implementation and not on behavioral inheritance and common behavior like the commonly used approach proposed by Grant (1986). The implementational sub-classification is applied after deriving the behavioral inheritance and permits location of the implementational entities like the 3 by 3 or the 4 by 4 matrix used like geometrical transformation matrix, geometrical processing, splines (Mudur 1985), etc ... , the 4 by 4 determinant (Yamaguchi 1987), and the three-vector or the four-vector used for implementing color, geometric vector, and quaternions (Pletinckx 1989), etc ....

The rest of this paper is organized as follows : Part 2 introduces the notion of animated graphical data type. Part 3 deals with the combination of object-oriented language and conventional graphics packages to model animated entities and relates the new particular organization of class hierarchy by means of implementational inheritance and explores the advantages of using an object-oriented language supporting inheritance and dynamic binding like C^{++} (Stroustrup 1986) in the animated entities modelling. Finally, Part 4 offers some conclusions.

2. ANIMATED GRAPHICAL DATA TYPES

Graphical entities, have traditionally been handled by building structures from general-purpose data types. This approach requires the programmer to be aware of representation details that are not relevant to the task of modelling animated entities. Not only does this make programs difficult to write and to transform, but also the integrity of structures maintained at such a low level cannot be guaranteed.
A graphical data type is a data type providing an abstraction useful in graphical applications. Graphical abstract data types are a useful way to organise the special purpose concepts needed in a graphical programming language (Mallgren 1982; Magnenat-Thalmann 1983; Fiume 1988; Beeker 1989).
The direct provision of abstractions in a graphics language is needed in program development and improves the clarity of the final result. It is important to view animated entities as integral entities having a behaviour and a local shared state to store the effect of operations performed on them. We distinguish also between the general graphical entity and the animated entity.
Chmilar (1989) relates the benefits of the integration modelling and animation in a unified system.In our approach we have the same procedure but we want first; to characterize the animated entity through its behavior then incorporate the existing modelling and animating tools in this behavior. We do not want if possible, to use an independent scripting or modelling language.
The operators defined on animated entities can be divided into three groups, for creating, animating and examining objects:

1. geometrical modelling and rendering operators
2. animation modelling operators
3. inquiry operations; to get information about an object.

The animated entity is identified or characterized by its animation behavior.The animation behavior is principally expressed through animation modelling operators.

The animation modelling operators can be divided into four groups:

1.perspective and geometrical transformations (like scaling, translation and rotation),

2.interpolation and alteration or shape modification procedures (like in inbeetwinning and parameterized models),

3.motion physical laws, like dynamic laws,

4.sound and expression operator (for facial animation).

In geometrical and animation modelling, to provide optimal support for an operator, it is important to choose an efficient manner of representing the animated entity state specification. And it is often necessary to have simultaneous multiple representations of the same entity in order to make efficient the computation of operators.
It is not easy to match all these requirements using simple abstract data types.

The solution most often adopted is principally the actor model (Reynolds 1982, 1987; Magnenat-Thalmann 1985; Haumann 1988), just as few cases of using object-oriented methodology with conventional programming languages (Breen 1987).

We find that object oriented languages supporting, in addition to abstract data types, inheritance and dynamic binding (Cook 1987; Liskov 1987; Wilkinson 1988) offer good means to do that.

3. ADVANTAGES OF   INHERITANCE AND DYNAMIC BINDING

In the following, we explore the main advantages of the object oriented programming due principally to the inheritance and dynamic binding :

1.A better conceptualisation of the problem at the time of specification :
The data abstraction is used to conceptually partition the problem's domain in entities, and permits then to express the processing of the problem by initiating a communication between these entities.
The abstraction is a method for breaking a problem domain in independent entities that can be pursued independently.
Data   abstraction minimizes interdependence among entities, allowing an independent development of entities.
Processing is made by inter-object communication refered to as *message sending*.
The abstraction allows to focalise on what is really important, at the moment, regarding the behavior of the entities to be modeled.

2.Implementation details are postponed at the right time owing to the inheritance, they are implemented in the appropriate sub-classes. Inheritance allows data abstraction to be implemented in several related levels.

3.A better implementation with the implementational sub-classification .
The abstract data type is concerned by the behavioral specification of the entity.
The manner of organizing classes in an inheritance hierarchy is as important as the design of the abstract classes themselves, and by doing that we make effective the inheritance which is the most powerful property of object-oriented languages.
In (Grant 1986; Chmilar 1989) the organization of classes refered to as *(sub-)classification* is based on the factoring of common or similar behavior or methods.
With the inheritance a new form of classification appears which is the *implementational (sub-)classification*.
Behavioral inheritance deals with common conceptually similar behavior and relates the behavior of one type of entity to another, whereas the implementational sub-classification deals with the implementation of these behavioral operations.
The behavioral inheritance has nothing in common with the implementation.

The implementational classification is concerned by the similarities between the internal structures of the implementation (the representation of classes). This implementational classification is obtained by the following fourth steps:

Step 1: To model the real world with a set of behavioral entities as classes which cannot be further decompose in other abstract types,
Step 2: To make, at the implementation time, the list of the behavioral functions corresponding to the internal data structures on which they apply,
Step 3: To extract the similar data structures of the classes,
Step 4: Each extracted structure will be designed as the class having as behavior the union of operations that act on it when it was in its original classes. It is then necessary to create a link between the extracted class and the classes from which it has been extracted. In the animated graphical data types the implementation structures are mainly determined by the choice of algorithms implementing the behavior and by the subjacent data structure (list, tree, graph, ...).
Therefore, it is very important to obtain the final inheritance graph both from the behavioral inheritance graph(abstract level) and from the implementational inheritance graph (implementation level).

Example : The implementation of the geometrical transformations can be done in the following way :

```
// Examples given in this paper are written in C++, a superset of C
//providing abstract data types, inheritance and dynamic binding.

    void point_2d_core::translate(float tx,float ty){
        coord_x(coord_x()+tx);
        coord_y(coord_y()+ty);
    }
```
This way has the advantage of being fast, but does not permit to implement easily the compositions of transformations as by the means of matrix representation and homogeneous coordinates :

```
class matrix{
// ...
public:
void rotate(float);
void translate(float,float);//...
      };

class polygon{
matrix *transf;
   // ...
public:
matrix take_mat(){transf->take_mat();}
void put_mat(matrix m){transf->put_mat(m);}
void rotate(float a){transf->rotate(a);}
void translate(float xt, float yt){
transf->translate(xt, yt);
   }
void xform1();
   };
```

We first notice that a subset of the behavior of the *polygon* class applies straight only on the *matrix* data member. So, by decomposing the internal representation of the *polygon* class to extract from it the behavior applying straight on the *matrix* data member and by modelling this representational tool as a *matrix* entity, we finally have :

```
        class polygon : public matrix{
                //...
              public:
              void xform1();
                 };
```

Which means that the *polygon* object inherits the behavior of the *matrix* object. It is interesting to notice here that the *polygon* object is a veritable problem domain entity, whereas the *matrix* object it is not.

4. A best refinement of the concepts owing to the behavioral sub-classification, some behavior can be added, and some others re-defined. The polymorphism permits to answer differently to the same message with specific implementation.

5. The incremental development, which consists of adding the properties to a class progressively when they are identified or in appropriate time, and that only by adding the new methods.
In the early stages of the modelling phase only some of an entitys' behavior is known, when some additional behavior is identified it can to be added incrementally through the inheritance.

```
   class bresenham_line : public line{
      public:
   void draw();// a new manner of drawing lines
   };
```

6. The security : The security comes from the fact that the object particular data is private, and we can act on the private members of the object only by the public interface given by its class and not otherwise in the abstract classes.

7. The fast prototyping owing to the inheritance of superclass properties. Entities which differ only slightly can be cast as members of distinct sub-classes of the same class. Only the additional functionality is to be specified and the inheritance of the other behavior is done intrisicly (re-usability).

Example : to design the *camera* class the essential of the behavior requisited to the implementation is already done in the *matrix* class and can be then inherited from this class:

```
class camera : public matrix{
// ...
    public:
set_mat_pers();
point_2d perspective(point_3d);
};
```

8. The handiness in the implementation of heterogeneous data structures and multiple implementations of the same behavioral operation owing to the inheritance and dynamic binding.
Dynamic binding is the ability to operate against an entity without knowing exactly its type.
Dynamic binding lets the user not concerned by the operations' particularities applied to objects, in other terms the dynamic binding uniformize the use of the operations by processing them in the object's class itself rather than by the user.
Dynamic binding makes the implementational modelling easier to extend. If we want to implement the rotate behavioral operation by the use of the quaternions instead of transformation matrix, it is sufficient to add a sub-class comprising the desired implementational model to the abstract class.
The correspondence of the messages sent to the objects and the appropriate operation's implementation related to sub-classes of these objects can be automatically done when the true objects'nature is known.
For example:

```
class primitive{
    public :
virtual translate(float,float);
    };

class line : public primitive{// line is derived from primitive
    public :
void translate(float,float);
    private :
// ...
};

class module{
primitive *primi;
int num_primi;
    public :
void translate(float x, float y){
    for(int i=1;i<num_primi;i++)
    primi[i].translate(x,y); }   };
```

The implementation of the *translate* function is immediate, and allows to translate different objects of the *module* class by using a loop on the *translate* functions of different *primitive* object, and that with the same function syntax : This manner of writing is characterized by its reusability without change even if other primitives were added to the *primitive* class.

9. The simultaneous multiplicity of the implementation owing to inheritance :
Inheritance allows to maintain multiple implementations and permit the passing from one to the other in the same design phase.
For example : A polygon can be represented in several different ways, and several representations might well be used in a given application :

- in the explicit polygons representation (Foley 1982), a polygon is represented by an ordered list of vertices.
- in the explicit edges representation, a polygon is represented by a list of edges. An edge is represented by two vertices, and a list of polygons to which the edge belongs.

```
class edge{
point_3d vertex1;
point_3d vertex2;
polygon *poly;
};

class polygon_edge : polygon{
edge *edg;
int co_edge;
}
```

10. The merging of different graphics packages :
The modelling of the animated entity is facilitated by the object-oriented design through the use of the graphics capabilities of conventional graphics systems.
Dietrich and al.(1989) have interfaced an object-oriented language with a solid modelling system in the field of programming geometry. In their approach, although they have characterized a set of geometric entities, they permit the direct use of implementational entities like matrix and vector mixed with the veritable geometric modelling entities in the modelling interface provided for the designers. They do not separate the behavioral specification from the implementational tools and operations. On the other hand, in our approach we do not reveal our implementational entities having in mind that low-level implementational operations do not characterize the behavior of the modelling entity, and if they have to change nothing must be changed in the modelling interface supplied for the designer. The implementation of the behavior's specification must permit low-level implementation operations and object's data representation to be changed transparently to the public interface provided by the entity.
In addition in our approach we find that it is then more interesting to combine the particularities of many different graphics packages in the same application :
For example by using simultaneously the graphics standard CGI and CORE :

```
class point_2d : point_3d{
      public:
virtual void draw();
   };

// ...

class point_2d_cgi : public point_2d{
      public:
void draw();
      protected:
// ...
   };

class point_2d_core : public point_2d{
      public:
void draw();
// ...
   };
```

11. A natural specification by the preservation of the decomposition of the system design phase after applying the implementational sub-classification can be guaranteed through the use of the multiple inheritance (Wiener 1989; Shopiro 1989). The multiple inheritance permits the multiplicity of implementational derivations, and it is a way to mix behavioral inheritance with implementational classification.

12. A natural expression of a problem by the "confrontation", or the putting together of all objects of a given problem, which is expressed by the sending of appropriate messages. For example : We have a *plane* object and a *camera* object positioned somewhere, we move the *camera* according to a given path, and we look at the *plane* through the *camera*.

```
   main(){
polygon_3d plane(65,83);
plane.take_vertices();
plane.take_edges();
plane.init_3d_graphics();
plane.animate1(360.,1,0.,0,4.,1.,0,360,1,4.,1.,0,50.,1,1.,
        .5,0,,10.,1,.1);
plane.close_3d_graphics();
}
```

4. CONCLUSION

The essence of the object oriented programming is the preservation of the natural problem domain owing to the data abstraction and inheritance. The object oriented programming is also ideal for fast prototyping and for the incremental resolution of problems through inheritance and dynamic binding. Inheritance and dynamic binding are important tools useful for the designing phase of the animated entity by permitting the uniformization of similar behaviour as well as for its implementation phase. The object oriented programming encourages modelling of the world as a set of related entities and is then of great contribution to people who think about the design of a system rather than the resolution of algorithm problems that can be left later on. A great contribution of graphics software has been realized particularly by the conventional graphics packages or by the windowing user interfaces. Animated graphical entity is a super-graphical entity, there is great benefits for modelling it from powerful existing graphics packages, interfaced with object-oriented capabilities induced by inheritance and dynamic binding.

REFERENCES

BEEKER E (1989) Application de la programmation orientee objet a la CAO. Proceedings of the 8th international Conference, MICAD'89, Hermes 1:121-131

BREEN DE, GETTO PH, APODACA AA, SCHMIDT DG, SARACHAN BD (1987) The Clockworks: An Object-Oriented Computer Animation System. EUROGRAPHICS'87, Marechal G. edit., Amsterdam:275-281

CHMILAR M, WYVILL B (1989) A Software Architecture for Integrated Modelling and Animation. New Advances in Computer Graphics, Proceedings of CG International'89, Edit. Earnshaw RA, Wyvill B, Springer-Verlag:257-276

COOK S (1987) Varieties of Inheritance. OOPSLA'87 Addendum to the proceedings, Orlando:35-40

DIETRICH WC, NACKMAN LR, SUNDARESAN CJ, GRACER F (1989) TGSM: An Object-Oriented System for Programming Geometry. SOFTWARE-PRACTICE and EXPERIENCE 19(10):979-1013

FIUME E (1988) Object-Oriented Techniques in Computer Graphics. EUROGRAPHICS'88 Research, Practice and Experience, Tutorial

FOLEY JD, VAN DAM A (1982) Fundamentals of Interactive Computer Graphics. Addison-Wesley

GRANT E, AMBURN P, WHITTED T (1986) Exploiting Classes in modelling and Display Software. IEEE Computer Graphics & Applications 6(11):13-20

HAUMANN DR, PARENT RE (1988) The Behavioral Test-Bed: Obtaining Complex Behavior From Simple Rules. The VISUAL COMPUTER 4(6):332-347

LISKOV B (1987) Data Abstraction and Hierarchy. OOPSLA'87 Addendum to the Proceeding, Orlando:17-34

MAGNENAT-THALMANN N, THALMANN D (1983) The Use of High-Level 3-D Graphical Types in the MIRA Animation System. IEEE Computer Graphics & Applications:9-16

MAGNENAT-THALMANN N, THALMANN D (1985) Object-Oriented and Actor Languages and Systems. Computer Animation Theory and Practice, edit. Kunii TL, Springer-Verlag:135-142

MALLGREN WR (1982) Formal Specification of Interactive Graphics Programming Languages. ACM Distinguished Dissertation

MUDUR (1985) Mathematical Element for Computer Graphics. EUROGRAPHICS'85, Nice, Tutorial

PLETINCKX D (1989) Quaternion Calculus as a Basic Tool in Computer Graphics. The VISUAL COMPUTER 5(1/2):2-13

REYNOLDS C (1982) Computer Animation with Scripts and Actors.ACM Computer Graphics, SIGGRAPH'82 proceedings 16(3):289-296

REYNOLDS C (1987) Flock, Herds, and Schools: A Distributed Behavioral Model.ACM Computer Graphics, SIGGRAPH'87 proceedings 21(4):25-34

SHOPIRO JE (1989) An Example of Multiple Inheritance in C++: A Model of the Iostream Library. SIGPLAN Notices 24(12):32-36

STROUSTRUP B (1986) the C++ Programming Language. Addison Wesley

STROUSTRUP B (1987) What is Object-Oriented Programming?. BIGRE 54:45-54

TROUSSE B (1988) Benefices d'une approche orientee objets pour un environnement de CAO. Proceeding of the 7th Internatinal Conference, MICAD'88, Hermes,1:313-326

WIENER RS (1989) A practical Exemple of Multiple Inheritance In C^{++}. SIGPLAN Notices 24(9):112-115

WILKINSON NM (1988) Best Fit. UNIX Review 6(8):57-63

YAMAGUCHI F (1987) Theoretical Foundations of the 4x4 Determinant Method in Computer Graphics and Geometric Modelling. The VISUAL COMPUTER 2(3):88-97

Mohammed Mahieddine is a doctorate candidate in computer science at the university of Nice (France).He received an engineer degree in computer science from Houari Boumediene university (Algiers-Algeria).
Address: CNRS-I3S-LISAN, Bat. 3, rue A. Einstein, Sophia-Antipolis, 06560 Valbonne, France
E-mail: mahieddine@cerisi.cerisi.fr

Jean Claude Lafon is a professor of computer science at the university of Nice. His research interests include computer graphics, formal algorithmics and parallel processing. he leads actually the CNRS-I3S-LISAN graphics research team. Lafon received his engineer degree in 1969 and his doctoral thesis in 1976 from the university of Grenoble (France).
Address: CERISI, Avenue A. Einstein, B.P.132, 06561 Valbonne, France
E-mail: jcl@cerisi.cerisi.fr

Part V

Animation Techniques

Motion Comparison in Computer Animation

Myeong Won Lee, Tosiyasu L. Kunii, and Martin J. Dürst

ABSTRACT

As animating objects is becoming very popular in many applications, there is an increasing need to directly manipulate objects when generating an animation sequence. While manipulating objects, it will be indispensable to compare the difference in motion of the objects so that the validity of motion can be investigated. Motion comparison provides the basis to realize an object-oriented computer animation system with a reliable function to control the movement of objects. This paper presents an algorithm for motion comparison in a 4D environment, based on the construction of a motion-specific object coordinate system for each object.

Keywords: computer animation, motion comparison, object manipulation, motion-specific object coordinate system, geometrical movements

1. INTRODUCTION

Conventional animation systems only deal with representing and displaying motion. This is due to the fact that an incredible amount of time and effort is required just to generate a single animation sequence. Usually, such systems do not include any facilities for the analysis of motion. Also, they are generally application dependent. It is impossible for applications to share the objects generated by such animation systems. An application independent system, on the other hand, would permit the objects in the system to be reused. In addition, it is required that such objects can be handled without much training by the users.

To satisfy the above requirements, it is necessary to design animation systems in an object-oriented manner and to construct a database for common use (Lee and Kunii 1989). Our database is constructed according to the data structure shown in Fig. 1. The data structure includes features of the hierarchical, the relational and the network data model (Date 1975). The object data is organized in the form of nested lists. All the data required to represent the geometric entities which compose the object is organized hierarchically. In addition, an object composed of segments and joints has a tree structure, with the nodes denoting segments and links denoting joints between the segments. Therefore, when organizing segments, a network data structure is required to represent the relationships among the tree structures. The data of an object at each time instant can be stored and retrieved in relation to each frame. Thus, it becomes possible to compare the motion during animation by using the database to share these data structures. Such an animation system supported by the database can define and manipulate moving objects.

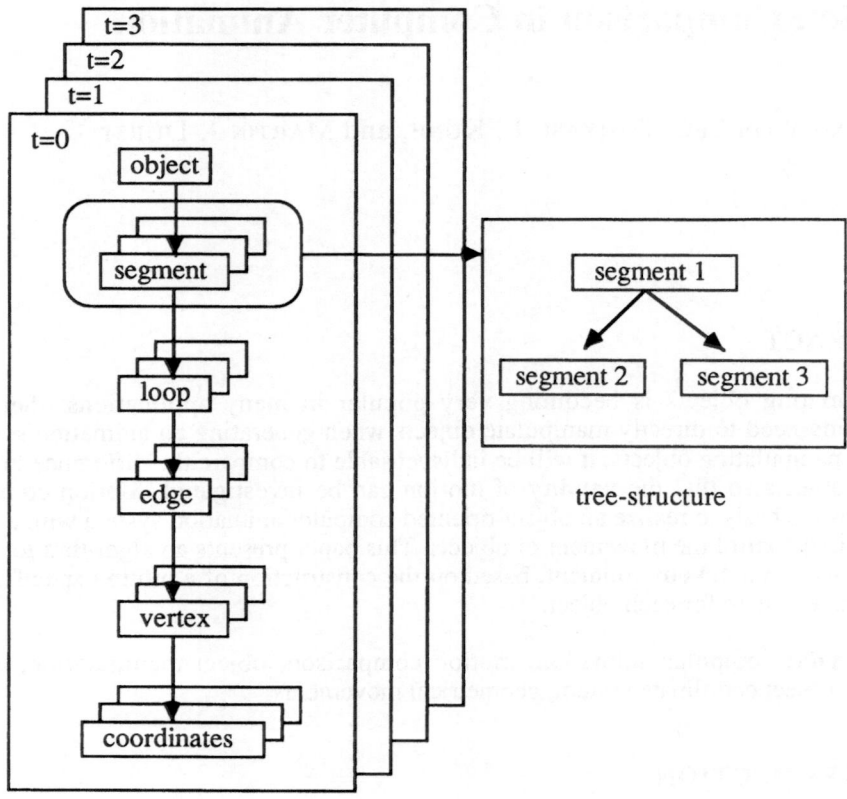

Fig. 1 Data structure for an animation database

There are many kinds of manipulation on objects in an animation system, but here we concentrate on motion comparison. This function can be used to maintain the validity of motion in an animation sequence and to find out differences in the motion of objects. The result of the motion comparison operation can also be used to control the movement of objects, in the same way as a condition in an **if** or **while** statement of a programming language is used to control the program flow.

If objects as well as their motion can be compared in a 3D or 4D environment, an animation system can generate more reliable motion. Furthermore, it is possible to analyze the motion of objects by checking the difference in geometry. The importance of difference checking lies in its power to overcome the difficulty to analyze motion when there are several degrees of freedom. For example, consider the case where an object has been transformed by rotation about several axes based on degrees of freedom at joints. Although individual parameters such as degrees of rotation are known during the generation of animation, it is difficult to estimate the effect of each of them on the overall motion. In this case, motion comparison can be of great help.

In this paper, the operation of motion comparison is defined and implemented as a function on the objects of a computer animation system. It is based on the comparative operations on solid models discussed in (Lee, Satoh and Kunii 1989).

2. DEFINITION OF COMPARATIVE OPERATIONS

When we consider comparative operations in computer animation, motion comparison as well as object comparison can be involved. Firstly, we briefly discuss the comparison of objects since motion comparison is an extension of object comparison. Compared with other works (Karasick 1989; Sugihara 1984; Tilove 1984; Turner 1988), the algorithm discussed here can accomplish object comparison even when the objects are composed of any number of connected components and even when they are positioned in any location and orientation.

2.1 Object Equality

Definition 2.1: Two objects are said to be equal if the objects positioned in any location of the global coordinate system are equivalent topologically and geometrically.

If the objects are compared during animation, besides the x, y, and z coordinates the time coordinate must be included in the comparison. The time coordinate must be carefully specified with relation to the x, y and z coordinates because motion can be analyzed differently depending on the selection of time instants. If in Fig. 2, for example, we select the time instants t_1 and t_3, ignoring t_2, it is difficult to recognize any difference in the motion of the two cubes. Therefore, it is important to specify the time coordinate at the same time intervals during animation.

Generally, the objects in an animation sequence can be classified into the following categories:

• segmented objects
• non-segmented objects

Segmented objects denote objects that are composed of segments and joints, such as human figures represented by a tree structure. Non-segmented objects denote objects that do not include any joints. It is also possible to say that non-segmented objects are composed of a single segment with no joints.

We use a boundary representation to represent both segmented and non-segmented objects because it helps to find out the difference in the geometry of objects. The boundary representation used in this paper is described in Fig. 3 (Lee, Satoh and Kunii 1989).

A connected component in the boundary representation corresponds to a segment of a segmented object. Non-segmented objects consist of one single connected component. The conditions for object equality are as follows:

Condition 2.1: The objects to be compared must be equivalent in topology. This can be checked by comparing the boundary representation of the two objects at the respective time instants.

Condition 2.2: All corresponding connected components which compose the objects must be equivalent in their quantitative and qualitative characteristics.

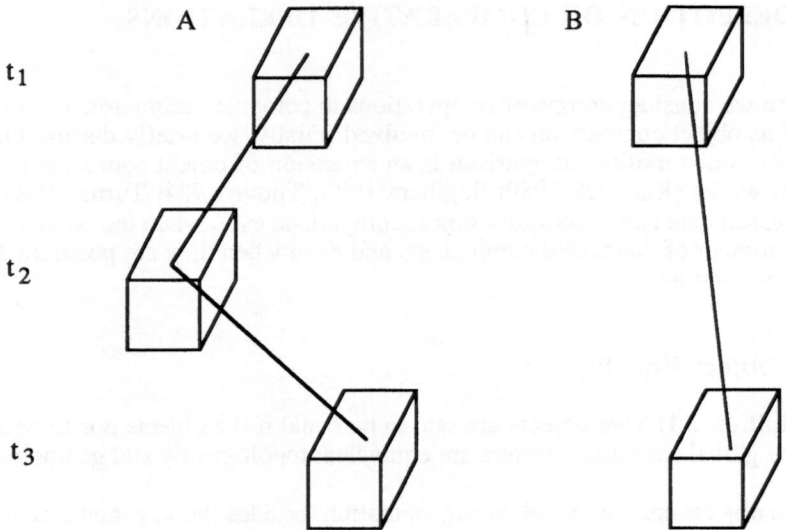

Fig. 2 Different time intervals

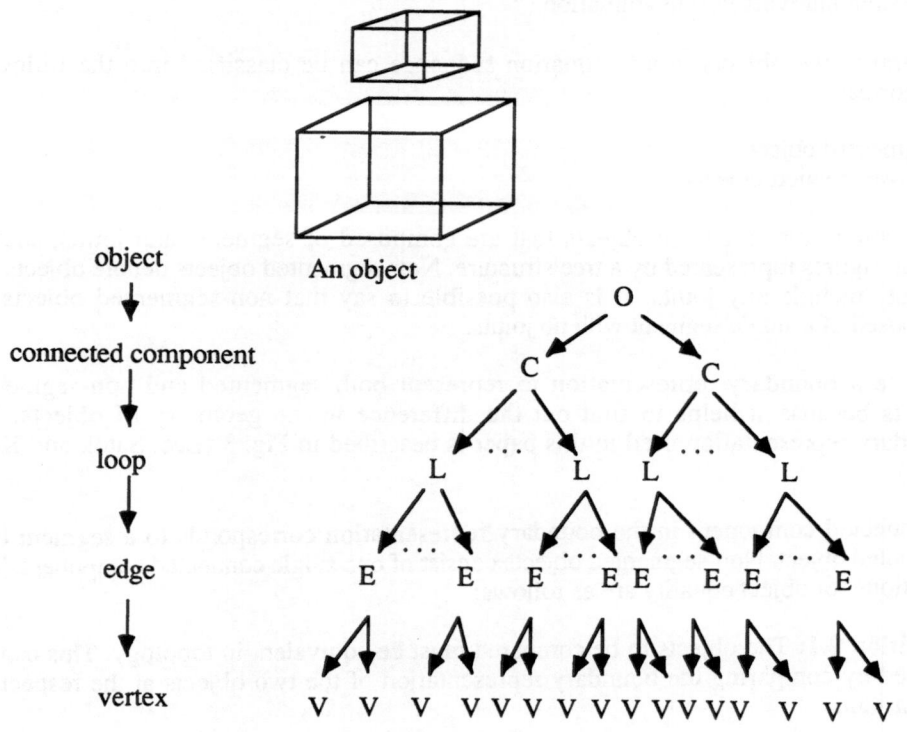

Fig. 3 A boundary representation

Condition 2.3: All relationships between corresponding connected components must be equivalent.

All the above conditions are described in detail in (Lee, Satoh and Kunii 1989).

2.2 Motion Equality

It may be thought that the motion of two objects can be compared using the various parameters that define an animation sequence. However, it is possible that different sets of parameters generate the same motion, and so this approach is not feasible. Also, there are cases where the motion is different although the angles about corresponding global axes are equal.

Consider the case of the motion of a human figure. Strictly speaking, a movement to the left produces different motion than a movement to the right, even though the motion as shown in Fig. 4 (a) (at the end of this paper) appears to be symmetrical. In geometrical modeling, however, it is unnecessary to recognize the direction of motion described above. As shown in Fig. 4 (b), the motion of two cubes is clearly equal, although the directions of motion are not equal.

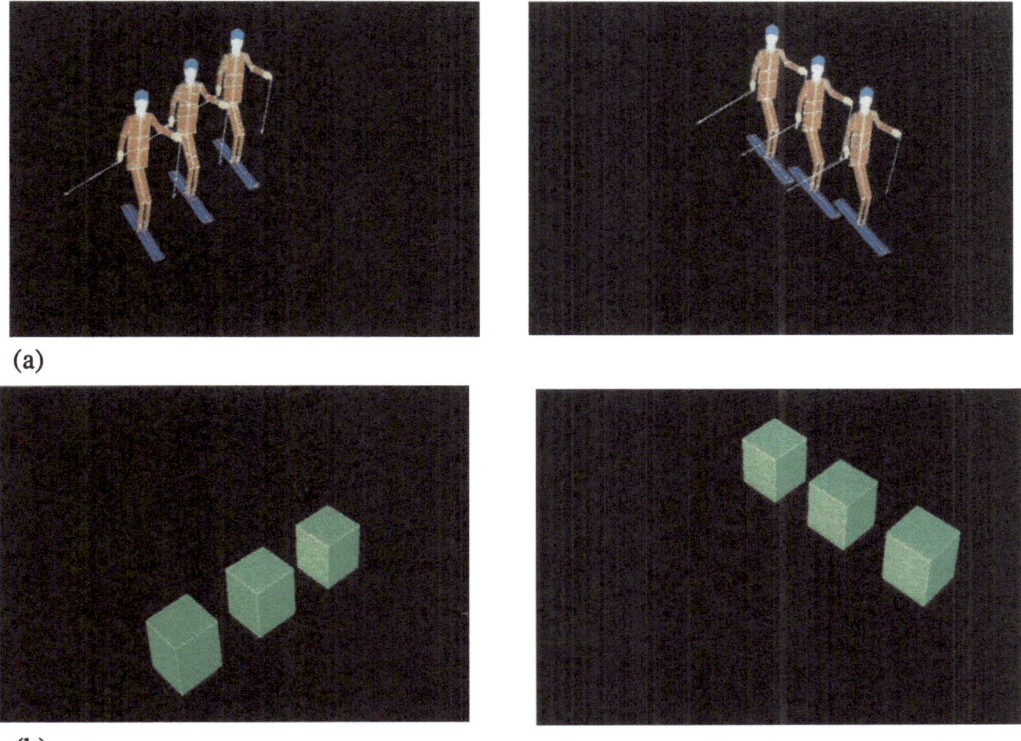

(a)

(b)

Fig. 4 Motion comparison

From the above analysis, motion comparison in computer animation must be done irrespective of the direction of motion in a global coordinate system. It must also not be concerned with the object position in the global coordinate system. In addition, it is also necessary to be able to compare the motion of objects if their geometrical composition is completely different. Therefore, the following definition is obtained for motion comparison:

Definition 2.2: The motion of two objects is equal if their geometrical movements are equal irrespective of the direction of motion.

From Definition 2.2, we can conclude that the motion of the skiers in Fig. 4 (a) is equal because the geometrical movements of the skiers are equal. Geometrical movements of objects in an animation system are composed of rotations and translations. Other transformations such as scaling could also be considered, but for simplicity, we limit the discussion to translation and rotation.

3. THE MOTION-SPECIFIC OBJECT COORDINATE SYSTEM

As we have shown above, if the direction of motion is not considered, it is difficult for the global coordinate system to recognize the difference of motion. In addition, if a local coordinate system for each object, as shown in Fig. 5, is used at every time instant, it is impossible to recognize the difference of motion, especially when the objects to be compared are composed of a number of identical loops (see also Fig. 3). Also, if such local coordinate systems are used, it is impossible to detect that the motion of two objects is equal although the directions are different.

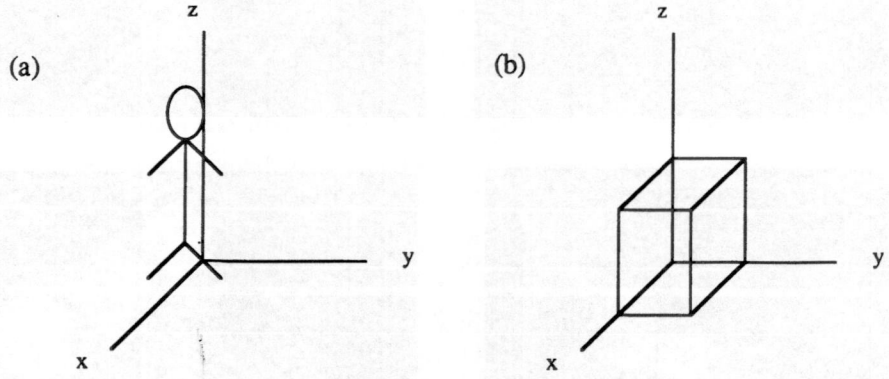

Fig. 5 Local coordinate systems

As an example, consider Fig. 6. The two cubes are equal, and one of them rotates 90° about the x-axis and the other 90° about the y-axis. In this case, it is difficult to recognize that the motion is equal if a local coordinate system such as that in Fig. 5(b) is used. Therefore, a specific coordinate system is required. It has to be both motion-specific and object-specific and therefore is called motion specific object coordinate system.

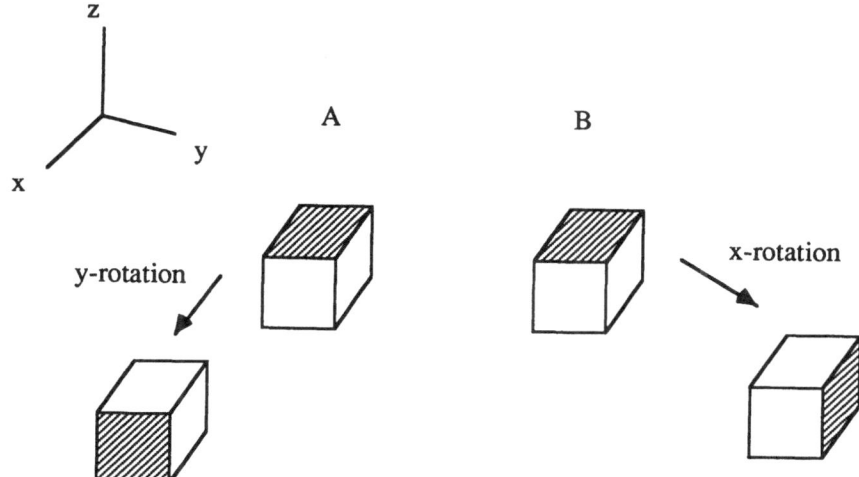

Fig. 6 Different rotations but equal motion

Now, we illustrate how this coordinate system is determined. The motion-specific object coordinate system requires at least three time instants for representing the topology and geometry of an object at a specific time instant.

Given serial time instants t_1, t_2 and t_3, let C_1, C_2 and C_3 represent the center points of the object at the time instants t_1, t_2 and t_3, respectively. As the center of an object, we can chose its barycenter, the barycenter of its vertices, or any other readily and unambiguously determined point. This has to be done in the same way for all objects and all time instants. Also, C_1, C_2 and C_3 must not be collinear. If they are, other time instants have to be chosen. The motion-specific object coordinate system for the object is then determined as follows (see Fig. 7):

- C_1 is the origin of the coordinate system.
- The x-axis of the coordinate system is defined by the vector from C_1 to C_2.
- The y-axis of the coordinate system is determined by the normal vector of the plane through C_1, C_2 and C_3.
- The z-axis of the coordinate system is perpendicular to both the x-axis the y-axis.

If the motion of two objects is equal at the time instants, the rotational transformation of the objects with respect to the motion-specific object coordinate system must be equal. The motion specific object coordinate system has the following features:

- Since it is independent of the position of an object, it can represent the topology and geometry of the object uniquely at any time instant.
- It is also independent of the direction of motion. Therefore, it can recognize whether the motion of objects is equal or not, even if the objects move in different directions.
- Although it is dependent on the time coordinate, it does not mean that one coordinate system must be constructed for an object at every time instant. Constructing only one coordinate system from the initial three time instants is enough to recognize the differences of motion. The coordinate system at all other time instants can be obtained simply by moving the origin.

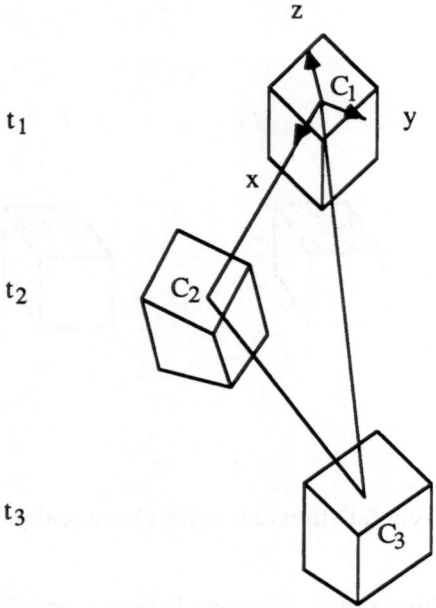

Fig. 7 A motion specific object coordinate system

4. COMPARISON OF MOTION

This section presents the algorithm that compares the motion of two objects and checks if it is equal throughout an animation sequence. We assume that since objects are modeled by a boundary representation, all the loops and vertices composing an object are distinguishable. This means that even if an object is symmetric, we know which loops and vertices at different time instants correspond to each other.

4.1 Motion Comparison of Non-Segmented Objects

The procedure for comparing the motion of non-segmented objects is as follows:

First, a motion-specific object coordinate system is established for each object as described in section 3, using the center points of the object at three time instants.

The second step is to determine the translation of the objects for any time instant, represented by the location of the center points in the motion-specific object coordinate system at the initial time instant t_1.

The third step is to determine the rotation of the objects for each time interval. The rotation is represented by a homogeneous matrix. This matrix differs from the matrix used when generating the animation because the coordinate system used is different. For any interval between two time instants t_1 and t_2, it is obtained as follows:

(a)   (b)

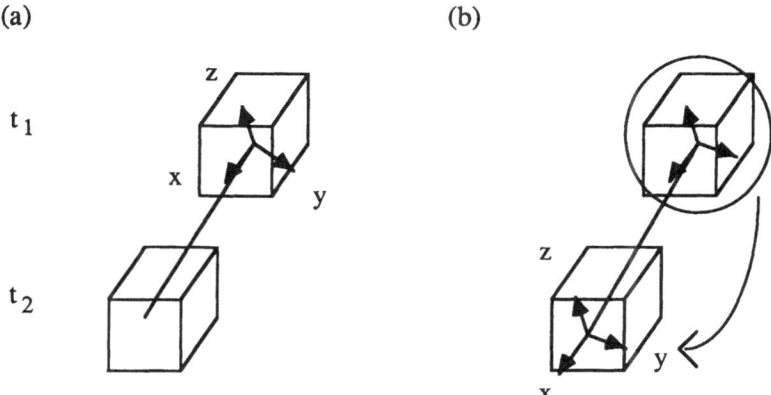

Fig. 8 A motion specific object coordinate system for non-segmented objects

- For each object, the coordinates of two vertices, which together with the center point must not be collinear, are represented in the motion-specific object coordinate system at time instant t_1 (Fig. 8 (a)).
- Next, the motion-specific object coordinate system is translated to the center of the object at the next time instant t_2 (Fig. 8 (b)).
- The corresponding vertices are represented in the motion-specific coordinate system moved to the center of the object at time instant t_2. If the coordinates of a vertex at t_1 are represented by v and the coordinates of the corresponding vertex at t_2 by v', the following equation is obtained:

$$v' = [R]_{t2} \cdot v \qquad\qquad (4\text{-}1)$$

where the rotation matrix $[R]_{t2}$ is of the following form:

$$[R]_{t2} = \begin{bmatrix} a_{11} & a_{12} & a_{13} & 0 \\ a_{21} & a_{22} & a_{23} & 0 \\ a_{31} & a_{32} & a_{22} & 0 \\ 0 & 0 & 0 & 1 \end{bmatrix} \qquad (4\text{-}2)$$

For each vertex, equation (4-1) decomposes into three scalar equations. So together with the conditions $a_{11}^2 + a_{12}^2 + a_{13}^2 = 1$, and so on, which hold due to the fact that $[R]_{t2}$ does not include scaling, we have the necessary number of equations to calculate all the elements of $[R]_{t2}$. For practical purposes, it might be simpler to choose three vertices, which together with the center point must not be coplanar, and to solve a completely linear system of equations. Finding the necessary number of vertices poses no problems if the object is truly 3-dimensional.

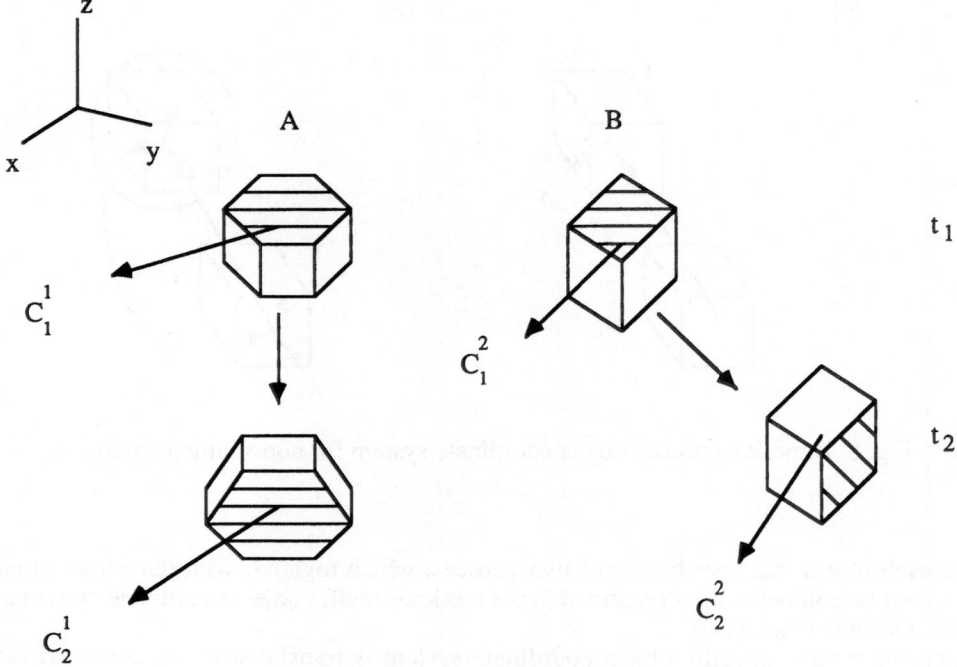

Fig. 9 Equal motion

The last step of the algorithm is to compare the translations and rotations obtained before at all time instants. For the comparison of translations, the coordinates of the center points at each time instant are compared according to their motion-specific object coordinate system. For the comparison of rotations, the elements in the corresponding homogeneous matrices are compared. If any differences are found, the motion is different. Otherwise, it is equal.

Fig. 9 shows an example where the center point of object A is moved from C_1^1 to C_2^1, and the center point of object B is moved from C_1^2 to C_2^2. We suppose that the translational movements of A and B are equal. In addition, object A is rotated 90° about the global y-axis and object B is rotated 90° about the global x-axis. When the rotations are represented by the motion-specific object coordinate system for each object, the movements are equal because both object A and object B have been rotated 90° about the y-axis of their own motion-specific object coordinate systems. The homogeneous matrices representing these rotations will thus be equal. Therefore, the algorithm concludes that the motion of object A and object B between time instant t_1 and t_2 is equal.

4.2 Motion Comparison of Segmented Objects

When we compare the motion of segmented objects, the motion at each joint has to be analyzed in addition to the motion of the whole object. If the number of joints for the two objects is different, it is difficult to find criteria for motion comparison. Therefore, we suppose that the number of joints and the tree structure of the segments for the two objects are equal. The basic algorithm is the same as that for non-segmented objects, but the following points must be considered carefully.

To compare the global motion of two segmented objects, the motion of their root segments is compared, as this motion is transmitted to the whole object. Thus, the motion-specific object coordinate system is constructed based on the center points of the root segments, and not on the center points of the whole object.

To analyze the rotation of each segment, a homogeneous matrix for each joint is prepared as follows:

- For each joint, a coordinate system is established by moving the motion-specific object coordinate system to the joint (Fig. 10).
- For each joint, the coordinates of at least two vertices chosen from the vertices of the segment connected by the joint are converted to this coordinate system. The rotation matrix for this joint is then obtained using equations (4-1) and (4-2).

In the last step, the rotation matrices have to be compared for each joint separately and if any differences are found, the motion of the two segmented objects is different. Fig. 11 shows an example of equal and different motion as detected with our algorithm.

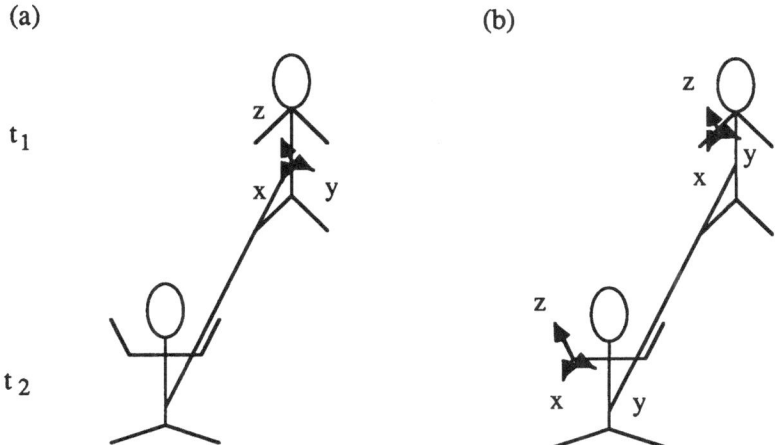

Fig. 10 A motion specific object coordinate system for segmented objects

 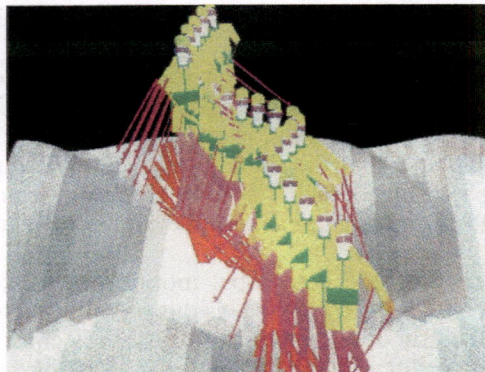

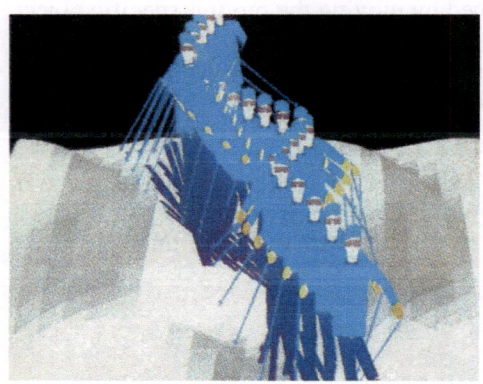 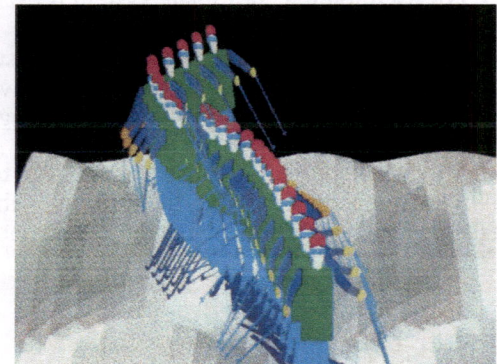

Fig. 11 Equal motion (top) and different motion (bottom)

5. DETERMINATION OF ROTATION ANGLES

Using the motion-specific object coordinate system, it is possible to check if the motion of two objects is equal. It is in this case sufficient to compare the rotation matrices at each time instant. But the rotation matrices can be used for other applications, like calculating the axis and angle of rotation.

Although the animation system may have transformed an object by several rotations about various rotation axes, depending on the degree of freedom at each joint, these rotations are combined to a single homogeneous matrix. On the other hand, any combination of rotations about the center of the object will keep at least one axis fixed, and so can be interpreted as a rotation about this arbitrary axis.

Given a rotation axis, represented by a normal vector n, and a rotation angle θ, the homogeneous rotation matrix is constructed as follows (Rogers and Adams 1976):

$$[R] = \begin{bmatrix} n_1^2 + (1-n_1^2)\cos\theta & n_1n_2(1-\cos\theta)+n_3\sin\theta & n_1n_3(1-\cos\theta)-n_2\sin\theta & 0 \\ n_1n_2(1-\cos\theta)-n_3\sin\theta & n_2^2+(1-n_2^2)\cos\theta & n_2n_3(1-\cos\theta)+n_1\sin\theta & 0 \\ n_1n_3(1-\cos\theta)+n_2\sin\theta & n_2n_3(1-\cos\theta)-n_1\sin\theta & n_3^2+(1-n_3^2)\cos\theta & 0 \\ 0 & 0 & 0 & 1 \end{bmatrix}$$

$$(5\text{-}1)$$

where n_1, n_2, and n_3 represent $\cos\alpha$, $\cos\beta$ and $\cos\gamma$ respectively as shown in Fig. 12.

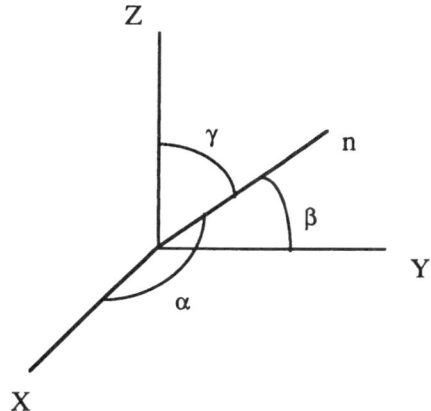

Fig. 12 An arbitrary axis

In section 4, we can assume that the rotation matrix $[R]_{t2}$ was obtained by the rotation about an arbitrary axis for an interval between two time instants. Therefore, the rotation matrix $[R]_{t2}$ corresponds to the matrix (5-1). After the rotation matrix in the section 4 is calculated, we can determine the rotation axis and the angle of rotation by solving for all the variables in the matrix (5-1).

6. APPLICATIONS

Since the algorithm of motion comparison is based on the analysis of geometrical movements in an animation sequence, it is well suited for precisely detecting differences of motion when their geometry has to be compared exactly. Thus the algorithm is well suited for research areas such as assembly, robot motion and simulation.

In some applications, however, geometrical precision may not be so important. An example is the comparison of the movements of human figures. Our algorithm can easily be modified for such a case by introducing comparison ranges for angles and distances, globally or if necessary for every joint separately.

7. CONCLUSIONS

This paper introduced the concept of motion comparison in computer animation and presented an algorithm to compare the motion of two objects, independent of the directions of motion or the position of the objects in a given coordinate system. This method provides an animation system with the ability to verify and control object motion.

To compare the motion, the coordinates of an object, and parameters such as rotation angles and translation vectors, which define the states of an object at various time instants, have to be readily available. For that, we believe that an object-oriented database storing the data for the animated objects in a 4D environment is needed.

The algorithm has been developed and tested with various objects, including human figures as well as mechanical solids, using the SKI animation system at Kunii Laboratory of the University of Tokyo, and the library facilities of DESIGNBASE (ver. 2.0) of Ricoh Co., Ltd, under the UNIX operating system on a Personal IRIS workstation.

ACKNOWLEDGEMENTS

We would like to thank Ms. Deepa Krishnan for her comments. Our thanks are also due to Dr. Hideko S. Kunii, the director of the Software Research Center of Ricoh Co., Ltd., for her support to this research, and to Silicon Graphics International for providing a Personal IRIS workstation.

REFERENCES

Date CJ (1975) An Introduction to Database Systems. Addison-Wesley, Reading, MA

Karasick M (1989) The Same-Object Problem for Polyhedral Solids. Computer Vision, Graphics and Image Processing 46(1):22-36

Lee MW, Kunii TL (1989) Design Methodology for Computer Animation Database Systems. Proceedings of the International Symposium on Database Systems for Advanced Applications 1:73-79

Lee MW, Satoh T, Kunii TL (1989) Comparative Operations in Solid Modeling. Proceedings of the 1989 IFIP WG 5.10 International Working Conference on Workstations for Experiments. to appear

Mäntylä M (1988) An Introduction to Solid Modeling. Computer Science Press, Rockville, MD

Requicha AAG (1980) Representations for Rigid Solids: Theory, Methods, and Systems. Computing Surveys 12(4):438-464

Ricoh (1988) DESIGNBASE Library Manual. Ricoh, Tokyo

Rogers DF, Adams JA (1976) Mathematical Elements for Computer Graphics. McGraw-Hill, New-York

Sugihara K (1984) An *nlogn* Algorithm for Determining the Congruity of Polyhedra. Journal of Computer and System Sciences 29(1):36-47

Tilove RB (1984) A Null-Object Detection Algorithm for Constructive Solid Geometry. Communications of the ACM 27(7):684-694

Turner JU (1988) Accurate Solid Modeling Using Polyhedral Approximations. IEEE Computer Graphics and Applications 8(3):14-28

Myeong Won Lee is currently a doctor course graduate student of the Department of Information Science at the University of Tokyo. Her research interests include computer animation, computational geometry, computer graphics, computer aided design and database systems. She received the BS degree in 1981 and MS degree in computer science in 1984, all from Seoul National University. She is a member of IEEE, ACM SIGGRAPH and Information Processing Society of Japan.

Address: Department of Information Science, Faculty of Science, the University of Tokyo, 7-3-1 Hongo, Bunkyo-ku, Tokyo,113 Japan.

Tosiyasu L. Kunii is currently Professor and Chairman of Information and Computer Science, the University of Tokyo. At the University of Tokyo, he started his work in raster computer graphics in 1968 which was let to the Tokyo Raster Technology Project. His research interests include computer graphics, database systems, and software engineering. He authored and edited more than 30 computer science books, and published more than 100 refereed academic/technical papers in computer science and applications areas.

Dr. Kunii is Honorary President and Founder of the Computer Graphics Society, Editor-in-Chief of The Visual Computer: An International Journal of Computer Graphics, and on the Editorial Board of IEEE Transactions on Knowledge and Data Engineering and IEEE Computer Graphics and Applications. He is on the IFIP Modeling and Simulation Working Group, the IFIP Data Base Working Group and the IFIP Computer Graphics Working Group. He organized and was chairing the Technical Committee on Software Engineering of the Information Processing Society of Japan from 1976 to 1981. He also organized and was President of the Japan Computer Graphics Association (JCGA) from 1981 to 1983. He served as General Chairman of the 3rd International Conference on Very Large Data Bases (VLDB) in 1977, Program Chairman of InterGraphics in 1983, Organizing Committee Chairman and Program Chairman of Computer Graphics Tokyo in 1984, Program Chairman of Computer Graphics Tokyo in 1985 and 1986, Organizing Committee Chairperson and Program Chairperson of CG International '87, Program Co-Chairman of IEEE COMPSAC '87, and Honorary Committee Chairperson of CG International '88. He served as Organizing Committee Chairperson and Program Chairperson of IFIP TC-2/WG 2.6 Working Conference on Visual Database Systems in 1989 and Program Chairperson of IFIP TC-5/WG 5.10 Working Conference on Modeling in Computer Graphics in 1991.

He received the B.Sc., M.Sc., and D.Sc. degrees in chemistry all from the University of Tokyo in 1962, 1964, and 1967, respectively.

Address: Department of Information Science, Faculty of Science, the University of Tokyo, 7-3-1 Hongo, Bunkyo-ku, Tokyo,113 Japan.

Martin J. Dürst is currently a doctor course graduate student of computer science at the University of Tokyo, with a Monbusho (Japanese Ministry of Education, Science, and Culture) scholarship. His research interests include computer graphics, geometric modeling, image processing, and computational geometry. He received a lic. oec. publ. (speciality: computer science) from the University of Zürich, Switzerland. He is a student member of the ACM and the Computer Society of the IEEE, and a member of the Information Processing Society of Japan.

Address: Department of Information Science, Faculty of Science, the University of Tokyo, 7-3-1 Hongo, Bunkyo-ku, Tokyo,113 Japan.

A Definition of Frame-to-Frame Coherence

Danièle Tost and Pere Brunet

ABSTRACT

Some hidden surface/line removal algorithms may be called "Window Algorithms", because instead of processing the scene globally, they divide it into subspaces and solve the visibility problem in each subspace. These algorithms may capitalize on a special form of coherence , called "predictive coherence", in which information is passed from each sub-space to the next in order to speed up the calculations. This paper establishes a parallel between these algorithms and the process of animation and describes frame-to-frame coherence as predictive coherence. A model of frame-to-frame algorithms based on these definitions is presented and discussed.

Keywords: computer graphics, hidden surface removal, computer animation, coherence, frame-to-frame coherence.

1. INTRODUCTION

Hidden surface removal algorithms can be considered as a mapping that converts the R^3 (x,y,z) space of the scene into the two dimensional (x,y) display space. They can be classified into four categories which main characteristics are summarized in table 1:

1. Contour Algorithms (edge-edge), are based on the computation of areas of constant visibility, and include the methods of Appel (1967), Loutrel (1970), Galimberti and Montanari (1969), and Hornung (1984)

2. List-Priority Algorithms (face-face) obtain by different methods a sorted list of the polygons of the scene allowing them to be displayed back-to-front, and include the Newell, Newell and Sancha works (1972), along with those Shumacker (1969), and finally the Binary Space Partition method (Fuchs et al., 1980, 1983).

3. Edge-face Algorithms compute the visibility, comparing the relevant edges against the faces of the scene and include the Roberts method (1963) and its subsequent adaptations.

4. Finally, Window Algorithms which which we will analyse below in more depth, compute the visibility of the scene through a set of windows.

Hidden surface removal algorithms consist mainly of one or more sort processes and capitalize on some forms of coherence in order to speed up the computations (Sutherland and al., 1974). This paper is concerned with the hidden surface removal of 3-D animated scenes for which, as will be described in section 4, there is a real lack of specific solutions. The goal of this paper is to give a theoretical definition of a form of coherence that is likely to be used in computing animated scenes: the frame-to-frame coherence.

In section 2 we will analyse the window algorithms for static environments and in section 3, the coherence on which they are based. In section 4 we will show that animation may be defined as a window algorithm in 4-D and we will give a formal definition of frame-to-frame coherence. In section 5, a theoretical model of temporal algorithms will be proposed and compared to previous work. Finally, in section 6, we will conclude by proposing directions for future work in this field.

Although it is assumed in this paper that the scenes studied are made up of planar polygons, most of our conclusions can be generalized to sculptured surfaces or mixed scenes.

2. WINDOW-ALGORITHMS FOR STATIC SCENES

Definition 1 : Window algorithms are methods that compute the visibility of the scene by dividing the R^3 space into a set of working sub-spaces in each of which the scene information is reduced and therefore the problem is easier to solve.The two dimensional display is partitionned into windows and the working sub-spaces are the volumes swept from these windows in the z direction.

Calling wd the dimension of the windows, the dimension of each work sub-space is wd+1. The algorithms consist of two steps: first the intersection of the scene with each work-space must be computed, we thus obtain a set of wd dimensional elements that must be then depth sorted for a later display. The windows may be one-dimensional or more. The full set of windows allows the computation of the visibility of the whole scene with a resolution that may depend on the size of these windows.

Table 1. Classification of hidden surface/line algorithms for scenes made up of plannar faces

NAME	ALGORITHMS	SPACE	COMPARISIONS	INPUT	OUTPUT
Contour	Appel, Loutrel, Hornung...	Object	edge/edge	edges	visible segments
List Priority	Newell et al., Fuchs et al...	Object+ Image	face/face	polygons	sorted list of polygons
Edge-Face	Roberts	Object	edge/face	edges+polygons	visible segments
Window	Ray-tracing	Image	face/workspace	faces+windows	points
	Scan-line	Image	edge/workspace	edges +windows	visible seg.
	Warnock,	Image	face/workspace	faces+windows	visible
	Weiler et al.	Object			polygons

There are three main families of hidden surface/line removal algorithms based on this strategy. The first group of algorithms includes ray-tracing (ray-casting) algorithms which study the visibility of the scene in image space, pixel by pixel, by tracing a set of rays in the Z-direction, across the screen (Fig.1.a) (Appel, 1968; Kay and Greenberg, 1979). The intersections of the scene with each ray are computed and a depth sort of the intersection points is performed. As can be seen, in fact the pixels constitute 0-D windows and determine the 1-D work sub-space (the rays) which intersect the scene in 0-D points. The precision of the representation depends on the size of the pixels ∂p, (resolution of the screen).

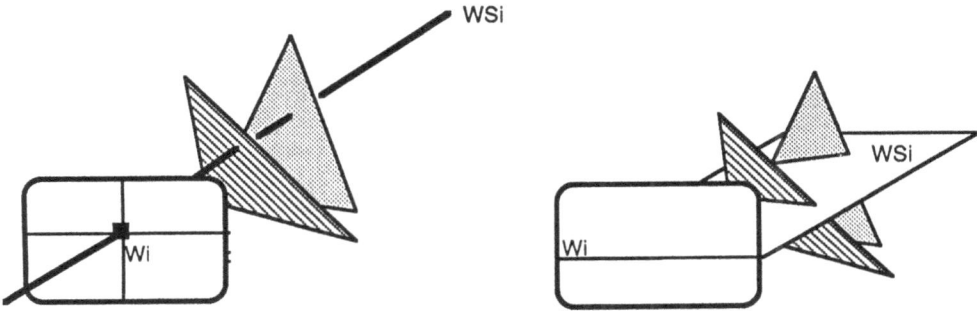

Fig.1 Window algorithms: a) ray-tracing; b) scan-line.

The second family consists of scan-line algorithms (Watkins, 1970). These study the visibility of the scene in image-space through a set of 1-D windows (the scan-lines). The scene is thus intersected by 2-D scan-line planes in which the depth sort is performed between 1-D segments. (Fig. 1.b). The precision of the representation depends on the width of the scan-lines: ∂sl.

Finally, two other algorithms must be mentioned: the Warnock algorithm (1969) in image space, and the Weiler and Atherton algorithm (1977), in object-space. Although they are very different from one another, they share the same principle: the use of 2-D windows. In Warnock's algorithm, the screen is recursively divided into 2-D windows until in the depth classification of the polygons in each sub-space (paralelpipeds) is easy to solve. In Weiler and Atherton's algorithm a recursive clipping between the faces of the scene is made, leading to a final division of the scene into 3-D volumes in which the polygons or subpolygons of the scene are z-sorted and have been clipped against the top polygon, which can be considered as a 2-D window.[1]

In an initial simplified approach the structure of the "window-algorithms" can be outlined as a repetitive process as follows, where :

CWS(Wi) symbolizes the computation of the intersection of the scene with the work sub-space (Compute the Work Sub-space) for a window Wi ,

---

[1] In fact, Weiler and Atherton algorithm does not save this data structure, but keeps only the top polygon of each window for its display.

HER(Wi) symbolizes the operation of Removal of the Hidden wd-dimensional Element in the work sub-space and,

DSP(Wi) is the display of the visible elements in Wi

for each window wi

CWS(wi)

HER(wi)

DSP(wi)

endfor

Three data structures are involved in these processes:

WS(wi) the Work-Space (tube) associated to each window Wi and constituted by the wd dimensional elements computed in CWS,

VM(wi) the Visualization Model consisting of the elements of the work space, after these have been modified (cut and sorted) in the HER process and,

VE(wi) the Visible Elements (VE) of the scene, either a set of points, segments or polygons.

In table 2 these data structures are described for the three families of window algorithms. In 1-D window algorithms, for instance, the work spaces WS are constituted by a set of segments, intersections of the scan-line planes and the scene, while the VM (Visualization Model) consists of the spans in which the scan lines are divided in the HER process, along with the list of sorted segments associated to each span. The Visible Elements (VE) are the segments nearest to the observer in each span.

Table 2: Data stuctures in static window algorithms

DIM.	WINDOWS	ALGORITHMS	WS(Wokspaces)	VM(Visual. Model)	VE(Visible Elem
0-D	Pixels	Ray-tracing	Set of points	List of sorted points	Visible point
1-D	Scan-lines	Scan-line	Set of segments	Spans+ sorted segm.	Visible segments
2-D	Screen Areas	Warnock	Set of polygons	List of sorted polygons	Visible polygons
	Polygons of the scene	Weiler and Atherton			

3. USES OF COHERENCE IN STATIC SCENES

3.1 Definitions

Definition 2: Objective coherence is the use of the set of properties based on the logical relationships between the different geometric entities of a scene, in order to speed up a hidden surface/line removal algorithm.

In general, the structure of a scene is not arbitrary. A scene is made up of a collection of interrelated objects, forming mechanisms, bodies, or buildings, and set in the space at specific locations in order to carry out given functions. In most mathematical representations of a scene, and moreover, in the data structures used in most of the hidden surface/line algorithms, this logical knowledge is lost. Objective coherence is aimed precisely at recovering this information by relating the elements with which it deals as forming regions of the scene, objects, faces or edges. As a result, some logical sets of data can be processed globally, avoiding the treatment of each element separately. An example of objective coherence is, as we will show in the next section, the use of bounding boxes or spatial divisions.

It should be noted that objective coherence is the unique form of coherence used in most hidden surfaces/lines algorithms. In the next section, for our purposes, we will discuss various uses of objective coherence in Window Algorithms, but similar uses can be described in the other categories of algorithms. Contour Algorithms for example, try to recognize the visible areas of the projection of a scene using area coherence and edge coherence, which are both objective forms of coherence. So are cluster coherence and frame coherence on which List Priority algorithms capitalize, in order to identify the logical order between faces of the scene.

> Definition 3: Predictive coherence is the use of the set of properties based on the relationships between successive windows due to their neighbourhood, in order to predict the state of the work-subspace associated with one window based on the state of the work-subspace associated with the previous window.

In window algorithms, in addition to the loss of information mentioned above and due to the mathematical modelling of the scene, more general information is lost because the scene is cut-off into sub-spaces regardless of its real structure. Predictive coherence uses the fact that the window algorithms are based on the repetition of the same proces for each window, and tries to avoid the repetition of the whole treatment by saving useful information in each iteration for the next one, and thus reducing the treatment of each iteration to an update process.

The use of predictive coherence requires a modification of the structure of window algorithms as follows. The first window will be processed completely, while subsequent ones will be only updated from the previous windows. Thus, throughout the algorithm the two data structures WS and VM must be saved and updated at each iteration.

$$CWS(W1)$$
$$HER(W1)$$
for each window Wi
    $UCWS(Wi-1,Wi)$
    $UHER(Wi-1,Wi)$
    $DSP(Wi)$
endfor

where $CWS(W1)$ and $HER(W1)$ symbolize the whole process applied to the first window, and $UCWS(Wi-1,Wi)$ and $UHER(Wi-1,Wi)$ symbolize the Update processes of computing the workspace and removing the hidden element for each window, which depend both on the current window Wi and the previous one.

Predictive coherence is used in each loop for both the UCWS and the UHER operations. In computing the work-space, the elements of the scene intersecting the previous work space can be examined, and four operations can be performed:

1. Copy the elements that have not been modified from one window to the other.

2. Update the elements that intersect the previous work space and the current one: compute the new intersections.

3. Add   the new elements that appear

4. Remove those which no longer belong to the current work-space.

Predictive coherence may use criteria based on geometrical or statistical properties in order to perform these four operations more efficiently.

There are deep differences between one form of coherence and the other:

1. While objective coherence may be used in all the hidden surface/line algorithms, predictive coherence is unique to window algorithms.

2. Objective coherence analyses   real, known data while predictive coherence deals with hypothetical   similarities concerning continuity between neighbour windows. This explains our use of the terms of objective and predictive.

3. The information that objective coherence uses is known since the beginning of the process while the predictive coherence is based on data analysed dynamically from window to window.

In window algorithms for non-animated environments, the objective and predictive forms of coherence can be used at two stages: first, in the determination of the intersection of the scene and the work sub-spaces (CWS), and next, in the removal of hidden elements in each work sub-space (HER).

3.2 The Use of Objective Coherence In Static Window Algorithms

In the CWS process, if no coherence is used all the faces (edges) of the scene must be checked against each workspace: the number of computations increases depending on the number of faces (edges) of the scene and the number of windows, while the complexity of the comparisons depends on the dimension of the workspaces (1D, 2D or 3D). Thus, the goal of coherence takes two forms: to avoid computing some of the workspaces and to reduce the number of faces to be checked against each window.

The use of bounding boxes around the objects (extents), allows to skip over some of them with only a few tests (Hall and Greenberg ,1983). Alternatively, as stated by Rubin and Whitted (1980), hierarchical models of the scene can provide an efficient way of determining which regions of the scene are likely to be intersected by each workspace, allowing the algorithm to skip over the empty workspaces and, for the non-empty ones, computing their intersection with only the regions of the scene that are in their neighborhood. These techniques involve objective forms of coherence such as object coherence, clustering coherence and what has been called hierachical coherence (Clark, 1976). For 0-D Window (ray-tracing) algorithms especially, the most costly operation is CWS, because it is performed for each pixel. Thus, using extents and/or hierachical models is a common practice (Goldsmith and Salmon, 1987, Arvo and Kirk, 1987)).   The early research herein is centered on combining ray tracing with BSP (Kaplan, 1985) and also octree data structures (Matsumoto and Murakami, 1983; Glassner, 1984; Fujimoto et al., 1986, Cleary and Wyvill, 1988). The CWS in scan-line algorithms (1-D) can also be improved by using object and area coherences. Instead of processing each scan-line, horizontal strips of the screen can be considered (Hamlin and Gear,

1977; Bronsvoort, 1987). Finally, Warnock (1969) suggested the use of bounding boxes to improve his method, and Weiler and Atherton (1977) proposed two possible extentions of their solution in order reduce the CWS's cost (reduce the number of clippings): first by combining their partition with a Warnock one , and second , by using "consolidation" (processing the area comprised within the silhouettes of the objects, rather than each of their faces separately).

In the HER processes, objective coherence avoids repeating some computations for all the elements of the work spaces. In 0-D algorithms no further relationships can be found from single points, but in the 1-D algorithms the segments properties can be very useful (Pueyo, 1986). Due to point to point coherence, in a segment it is only necessary to process the start point, the end point and the intersection points because the visibility between these points along the segment is constant (Atherton, 1983). On the other hand, the visibility of a vertex can be deduced from the visibility of the segments that start/end in it because of object coherence. The transitivity of relative depths of segments also avoids a lot of depth comparisons. Along with the segment properties, the polygon properties are useful in a similar way in 2-D window algorithms.

3.3 The Use of Predictive Coherence In Static Window Algorithms

Warnock's algorithm capitalizes on one form of predictive coherence: when it processes sub-windows, it uses the results of their parent-windows. So in the CWS process of a sub-window, only the intersector polygons and contained polygons of its "parent" are checked: the area coherence allows us to "predict" that the disjoint polygons and the surrounding polygons of the "father" will also be disjoint or surround the "child-window", respectively.

Weiler and Atherton algorithm uses the same principle. Its CWS process consists of a clipping of a list of polygons against the polygon at the top of the list. At the first step of the algorithm, all the polygons are checked against the first clipper, but in the following steps, as this process is performed recursively, only a partial list of polygons (the inside list of the previous step) is checked against the clipper. In addition, we also use the fact that the order of this list is almost correct, and therefore the sort process is an uodate (UHER).

Speer et al. (1986) capitalized on ray coherence which is the predictive coherence between successive rays in a ray-tracing algorithm, by updating the intersection tree at each pixel but they failed in reducing the total computational cost of the standard algorithm.

However, the main example of predictive coherence in window algorithms, is the scan-line coherencein the 1-D window family. Scan line coherence assumes that from one scan-line to the next, only a few changes may occur, and thus the visibility in a scan-line plane can be computed on the basis of the visibility of the previous one. Five properties can be stated, allowing probable predictions (Atherton, 1983) :

1. the list of active edges (edges intersecting the current scan-line) is almost the same as that of the previous scan-line. This list is kept throughout the algorithm and updated at each step (UCWS) (Watkins, 1970).

2. the x-order of the segments in the scan-plane is assumed to be similar, and so generaly a bubble sort is enough (UHER) (Romney,1970) and the segments can be computed incrementally.

3. the depth order of the segment is almost identical in neighbourhood scan-lines, and can thus be used and updated thoughout the algorithm (UHER).

4. if the segments in two consecutive scan-planes belong to the same faces, and their x-order is identical in the two scan-planes, then the z-sort is also the same, as long as there are no penetrations (UHER).

5. finally, the visibility is not likely to change: the spans of the previous scan-line can thus be checked as a first good approximation (UHER).

4. COHERENCE IN DYNAMIC SCENES

4.1 Animation

Computer animation of 3-D scenes can be considered as a mapping that converts the $R^4(x,y,z,t)$ space of the moving scene into a 3-dimensional space (x, y, t). As in practice, it is not possible to generate the whole continuous 3-D space (x,y,t), the temporal dimension is discretized and a finite number of sequential 2D frames (x,y,t1), (x,y,t2)...(x,y,tn) is generated. Computer animation is thus a generalization of the 1-D window processes for a 4-D environment (3D space + 1D time). The 4-D work space is studied through a set of 1-D temporal windows (instants). The animation consists of two stages: first the 3-D static workspaces corresponding to the state of the scene at each of the given instants are computed, and next the visibility of the scene is studied in each of them. The whole temporal evolution is represented through the full set of temporal windows, with a precision that depends on the difference in time between successive windows: ∂t.

The major drawback of this sampling is that it may produce temporal aliasing: the hight speed movements may have a jerky appearance. Traditionally the algorithms that incorporate motion blur to reduce this aliasing (Korein and Badler 1983; Potmesil and Chakravarty 1983, Glassner,1988) are based on a super sampling of the temporal dimension at located pixels of the screen, plus some filtering effects. We will discuss later the importance of the use of coherences in these algorithms.

Using the same notation as in the previous section, the structure of an animation process can be represented as follows :

                        for each instant ti
                                CWS(ti)
                                HER(ti)
                                DSP(ti)
                endfor

where:
        CWS(ti) symbolizes the Computation of the Work Subspace (scene at the instant ti) and
        HER(ti) symbolizes the process of visualization - Hidden Elements Removal- of the scene at
                ti. In this process, for each 3-D static work subspace, a 2-D projection of the
                scene (frame) will be produced as the final result.
        DSP(ti) is the display of the frame

The important point of this definition is the establishment of a parallel between the scan-line algorithms for 3-D static workspaces and the animation for 4-D animated environments. In both cases the windows are 1-dimensional (scan-line and time) and the dimension of the work spaces is reduced by one in each of the work sub-spaces (2-D scan-line planes or 3-D static states of the scene). A sampling of the work-spaces is made along one of their axes: the y-axis in scan-line methods and the t-axis in animation (Fig. 2) . In each case, y and t are treated as

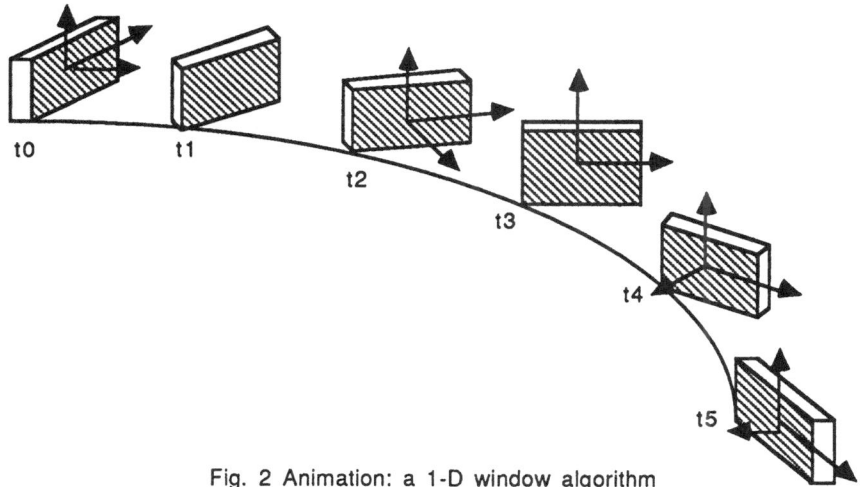

Fig. 2 Animation: a 1-D window algorithm

discrete variables. The continuity of the representation depends on the separation ("width") between successive windows: ∂sl or ∂t (Pueyo and Brunet, 1987). In scan-line methods this continuity means precision, accuracy and quality of the representation. In animation, the interval of time between successive temporal windows affects also the illusion of continuous changes, the illusion of movement (Magnemat-Thalmann and Thalmann, 1985).

In the next section we will focus on this parallel between animation and scan-line methods in order to establish a similar comparision between frame-to-frame coherence and scan-line coherence.

4.2 The Use of Objective Coherence in Animation

One major problem in 3-dimensional animation is that the number of calculations that must be done is very high: in the worst case the cost of the visualization is the number of frames times the cost of the visualization of a single static frame. Temporal coherence, objective as well as predictive, is aimed to reduce this cost. We will first analyse objective coherence in animation and in the next section predictive temporal coherence.

The algorithm of Binary Space Partition (Fuchs et al, 1980; Fuchs et al., 1983) is the major example of temporal objective coherence for static scenes and changing viewpoint. The authors observed that in a static scene, the faces can be sorted according to their relative priorities regardless of the viewer's position. Thus, they perform this sort prior to any visualization and use this information directly for each different observer position. They invest in a pre-processing of the scene in order to reduce the per-frame computations, but they do not preserve information from one frame to the next. This form of coherence is thus objective and not predictive.

More recently Glassner (1988) proposed a ray-tracing algorithm for animated scenes also based on temporal coherence. The whole 4-dimensional space is hierarchically divided at the beginning of the algorithm along the x, y, z and t axes. This significanlty reduces the number of intersections to be computed for each ray at each frame. This spacetime structure is also suitable for the extra sampling that may be done when motion blur is incorporated to the algorithm.

Matsushita (1972) in an earlier work, studied the relationships between pairs of polygons of a rotating object and proposed to compute a rotation table in a pre-process and to use it at each frame in order to speed up the computations.

Finally two algorithms of temporal anti-aliaiing (Korein and Badler,1983; Grant, 1985))   may be referenced because they involve objective temporal coherence in a way that may be generalised to the whole process of hidden surface removal of the animated scene.

4.3 The Use of Predictive Coherence in Animation: Definition of Frame-to-Frame Coherence

Definition 4: Frame-to-frame coherence is the predictive temporal coherence of animation algorithms. Frame-to-frame coherence assumes that from one instant to the next, only a few changes may occur in a scene, thus various properties (geometical, kinematic or dynamic) may be stated that allow to deduce the visibility of the scene at a given instant on the basis of its visibility at the previous instant.

It is important to observe that a parallel can be established from this definition, between scan-line coherence and frame-to-frame coherence. As far as animation is a 1-D window process in a 4-D environment, it may capitalize on predictive (frame-to-frame) coherence between 1-D successive windows (instants), just as scan-line algorithms in a 3-D environment capitalize on predictive (scan-line) coherence between successive 1-D windows (scan-lines). In the CWS process scan-line coherence allows one to predict which faces of the scene will be intersected by a scan-plane. Similarly, when computing the state of the scene at each instant, frame-to-frame coherence may allow us to predict which objects the scene will be composed of at this instant and where they will be. In addition, whereas scan-line coherence in the HER process is used to predict the depth order of the segments in the scan-plane, frame-to-frame coherence may be used to predict the relative priorities of the faces of the scene at a given instant, or other analog visualization data.

The use of frame-to-frame coherence modifies the structure of an animation algorithm, just as the use of scan-line coherence modifies scan-line algorithm structure. Using the notation of the previous section, this structure is :

```
            CWS(t1)
            HER(t1)
            for each instant ti
                    UCWS(ti-1,ti)
                    UHER(ti-1,ti)
                    DSP(ti)
            endfor
```

In the next section we will focus on this model and the data structures related to it.

The algorithm of Hubshman and Zucker (1980, 1982) is perhaps the first attempt to identify some geometrical properties -constraints- between successives frames. The authors showed that changes in the visibility of the objects occur only within a restricted area bounded by their silhouette and the silhouette of the objects occluding them, in the current frame and in the previous one. The removal of hidden surfaces at each frame can thus be considered as a contour algorithm (see section 1).   This algorithm presents two major drawbacks: first, it is restricted to convex, closed, nonintersecting polyedra and second it is difficult to implement.

More recently Crocker (1987) used frame-to-frame coherence using a scan-line technique for the visualization of CSG trees. Crocker's algorithm restricts the computation at each frame to the modified nodes of the CSG tree. It determines an area of probable changes for each frame (the AOI: Area Of Interest), and within it only performs hidden-surface computations on modified spans (the MSE : Modified Span Extent).

Finally, Badt (1988) proposed two ray-tracing algorithms based on frame-to-frame coherence. The first one is more convenient for a moving scene, whereas the second one is better adapted to a moving viewpoint, but they may be combined. The originallity of these solutions is that they based on a probabilistic approach of the problem. In the first solution, changes are detected by re-computing a certain number of pixels randomly selected. The second solution reprojects in the image plane the first intersection point of each ray with the scene at the prior instant. It then filters the frame, detects inconsistencies and recomputes a limited number of erroneous pixels. The major drawback of these solutions is that they are approximate, thus a manual touch-up is necessary.

In addition to these three main algorithms, other works use some properties of the movement as a particular application of the frame-to-frame coherence. First, it can be shown that in a parallel motion the silhouettes of the objects do not change. Based on this property, in the engineering animation system ANIMENGINE (Noma, 1985), the visualization of the solids with parallel motion is studied in the projected plane. A second similar property is that the silhouette of cilinders, elipsoids and spheres does not change if they rotate around their axis. Herbison-Evans (Herbison-Evans, 1982) created an animation system in which all the objects are modelled with spheres and ellipsoids, allowing the use of a specific algorithm of visualization based on this property. In both cases the visualization capitalizes on frame-to-frame coherence. It is a particular case in which, the information saved from frame-to-frame (the silhouettes of the objects) does not need to be modified but just copiied , because it is constant throughout the whole period considered.

Finally Shelley and Greenberg (1982) introduced path coherence which is predictive, in the path specification in animation and the back-buffer algorithm (Baum et al. 1986) uses also predictive coherence in radiosity calculations in dynamic environments.

5. THE STRUCTURE OF THE ALGORITHMS BASED ON FRAME- TO- FRAME COHERENCE

We have shown that all algorithms based on predictive coherence share a similar structure. We here describe this structure and show how it can be adapted to static as well as dynamic window algorithms based on predictive coherence.

At the heart of the algorithm are the update processes UCWS and UHER. They are shown in figure 3 : after the Workspace (a) or the Visualization Model (b) of the prior window have been analysed, the Identical Elements (IE) are Copiied, the New Elements (NE) are added, the Modified Elements (ME) are updated and the Deleted Elements (DE) are removed.

Figure 4 illustrates the general schema of the algorithm. At each frame new information concerning the elements to be added must be input in the UCWS process. This information is stored the Reference Model which we define below.

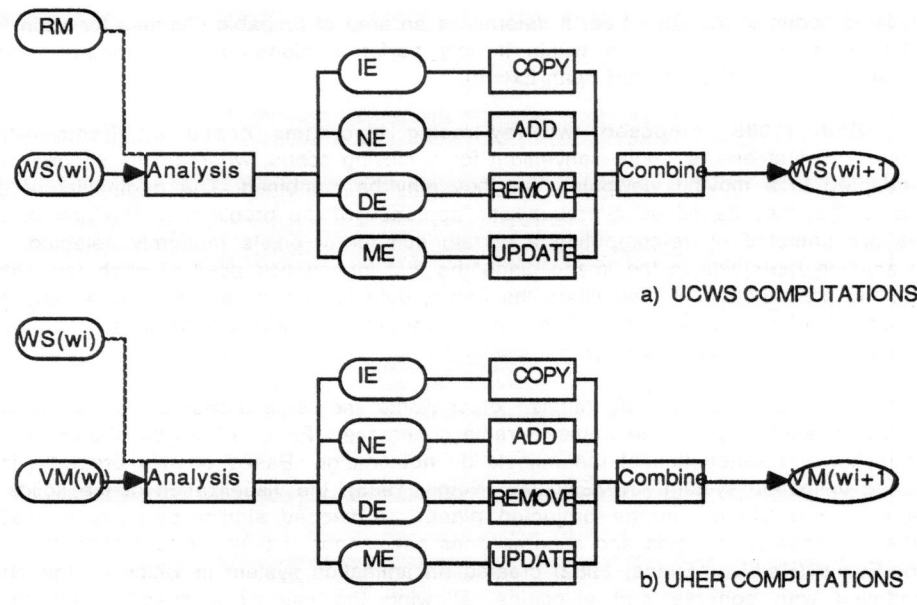

a) UCWS COMPUTATIONS

b) UHER COMPUTATIONS

Fig. 3 Update processes

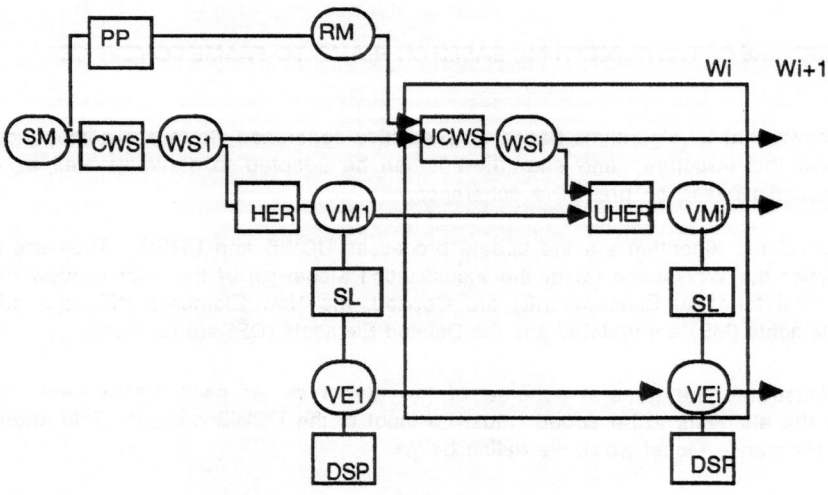

Fig.4 Structure of a window algorithm capitalising on predictive coherence

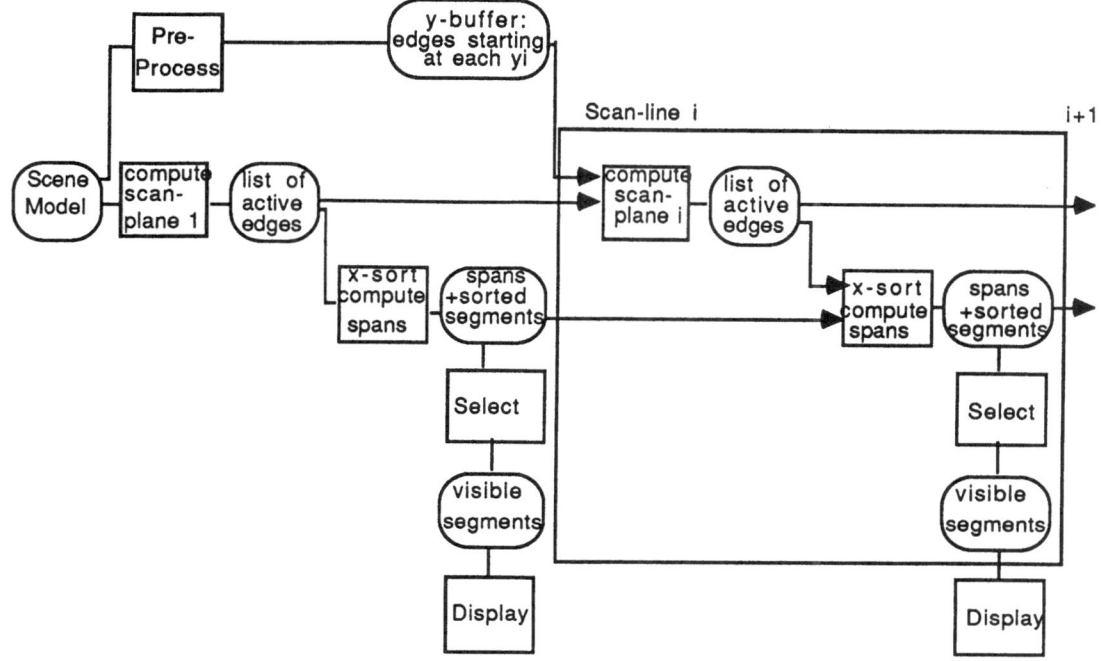

Fig. 5 : Structure of Scan-line algorithms

Definition 5 : The Reference Model in window algorithms is the expression of the intersections of the elements of the scene with the working spaces, which may be computed at the beginning of the algorithm and used in the update of the working spaces.

The Reference Model is computed in a Pre-Processing (PP). It involves an analysis of the scene throughout the whole set of workspaces. It therefore remains constant, unmodified during the whole algorithm. The model can be either deterministic or stochastic, depending on whether it provides exact information or only probable information. Depending on the solution it may be complex to calculate, thus   only partial expressions may be computed.

The structure proposed above is also adapted to scan-line algorithms (Fig. 5). Following Watkins algorithm (1970) it can be seen that:

1. In Watkins the Reference Model (RM) is the data structure computed at the beginning of the algorithm (faces and edges inter-related) that associaties to each scan-line the set of edges starting in it. (It should be noted that here, the full scene is studied throughout the full set of scan-lines, just as in animation the Pre-Process (PP) will study the scene throughout the period of time studied).

2. The   Work Sub-spaces (WS) are constituted by all the segments of the scan-line planes. The Visualization Model (VM) are made up of the visible segments structured in spans.

3. In the UCWS process, for each scan-line, the elements in the scan line plane (WS) are updated from the previous one. The process includes the operations of ADD, COPY, MODIFY, REMOVE active edges from the list of active edges of the scan-plane. The

knowledge needed in the ADD and REMOVE computations is provided by the Reference Model (RM): when an edge appears, the number of scan-lines in which it will appear is computed. The MODIFY operation is possible due to the property 1 (section 3) of the scan-line coherence : the new segments can be computed in an incremental form (dx=tg(slope)/dy).

4. The UHER process is also an update: it modifies the spans of the previous scan-line and in particular capitalizes on properties 2 to 4 of the scan-line coherence.

At the same time it can be shown that the frame-to-frame algorithms described above are also adapted to this structure. Figures 6 and 7 represent the structure of Hubshman's algorithm and Crocker's algorithm respectively. Hubshman uses the terms of Static data structure and Dynamic data structure for the two main data structure of his algorithm (fig.6). The static data structure (RM) is a static description of the scene: structured list of polygons and edges of the scene. It is valid during all the considered period because the scene is fixed and only the observer's position changes. The dynamic data structure corresponds to our VM, Visualization Model. It is composed of the list of visible polygons , the list of visible silhouette edges, the list of visible interior edges and the list of boundary segments of the visible areas. In Hubshmann's algorithm the Working Subspaces (WS) of our structure are inexistent and the Visualization Model is updated directly from the previous Visualization Model and the Reference Model. This is due to the fact that only the viewer's position changes, therefore only the visualization information need to be computed or saved.

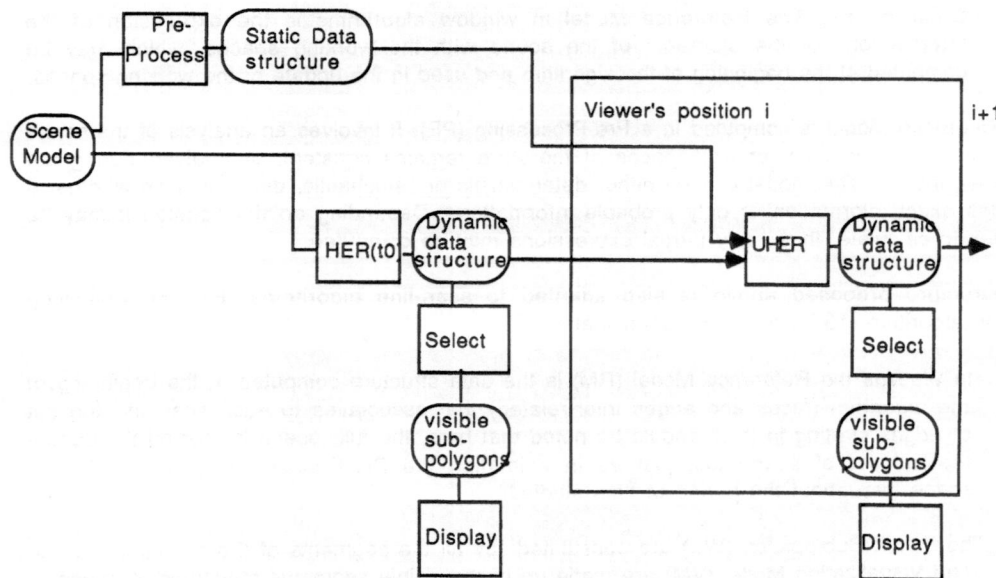

Fig 6 Hubshman and Zucker's algorithm

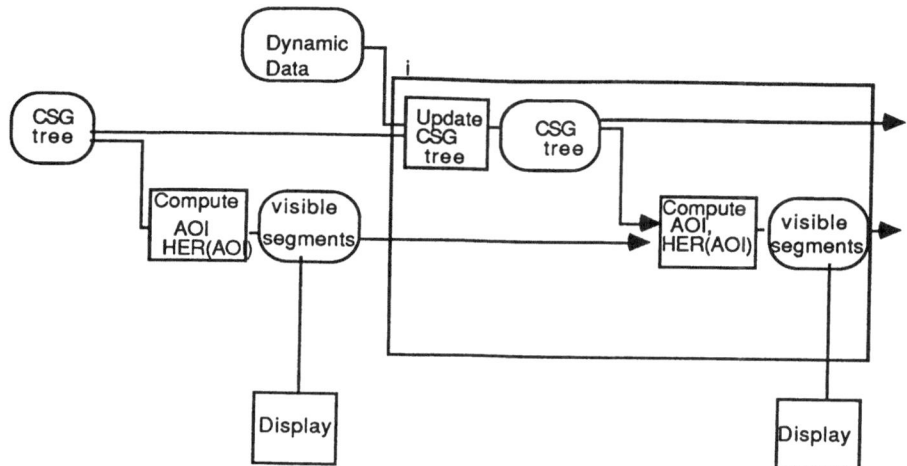

Fig. 7 Structure of Crocker's Algorithm

In Crocker's algorithm (fig. 7) the Work Sub-Spaces are constituted at each frame by the CSG models of the objects. The CSG trees are computed by an update process which saves the unchanged nodes (COPY) and processes the added geometry (ADD) and the deleted geometry (REMOVE) along with the transformed geometry and changes in the tree (MODIFY). At each instant the projection of the scene in the screen (frame) constitutes the visualization model (VM). The algorithm consists of updating only the modified areas of the frame and thus performing the operations of COPY and MODIFY. The area of changes in the screen (AOI: Area Of Interest) is deduced directly from the CSG model at each frame but, as suggested by the author, it could be deduced from the previous AOI capitalizing on more frame-to-frame coherence. In the areas of changes a scan-line algorithm is used for the removal of the hidden surfaces, handling with dynamic information. This algorithm capitalize also in frame-to-frame coherence by computing the SOI (Spans of Interest), taking into account the changes in the CSG trees.

6. CONCLUSIONS

We first studied the existing hidden surface/line removal algorithms for static scenes and we divided them into four classes (section 1). We defined "Window Algorithms", as grouping the methods based on the division of either the screen or the environment into sub-spaces where the problem is generaly easier to solve. Generalizing this definition, we concluded that the visualization of animated scenes can be understood as a 1-D window process for 4-D environments, or more precisely, as an extention in 4-D of the scan-line (1-D window for 3-D worlds) methods.

We also showed (section 3) that the coherence of the environment can be used in two different forms: the "objective" one, dealing with the data known in order to solve the current step of the problem, and the "predictive" form, unique to Window algorithms, that allows us to work in an incremental form, deducing the state of a window from the state of the previous one. Generalizing the scan-line coherence (predictive coherence for 1-D window algorithms in 3-D environment) we defined the frame-to-frame coherence as a predictive coherence of 1-D window processes in a 4-D environment.

Finally we showed that the algorithms which capitalize on predictive coherence share a special structure, perform similar computations and involve specific data structures. We analized this structure and proposed a model of it which is valid either for static or changing environments (section 5).

The evidence of some coherence between successive frames is not easy to express in an algorithmic form. Very few solutions have been found and they are sometimes very complex o partial . It is our feeling that more efficient solutions could be developed on the basis of a more theoretical preliminary study of coherence. Our paper is an initial approach to this study. Based on the conclusions stated above, our future goal is to develop specific algorithms of visualization of animated scenes which capitalize on both temporal objective and predictive coherence.

Acknowlegments : We wish to thank Dr. Pueyo X., of our Department, for his valuable help in preparing this paper.

REFERENCES

Appel, A (1967) The notion of quantitative invisibility and the machine rendering of solids. Proceedings ACM National Conference: 387-393.

Appel, A (1968) Some Techniques for Shading Machine Rendering of Solids. Proceedings AFIPS, Spring Joint Computer Conference, 32: 37-45, AFIPS, Thompson Books, Washington D.C. (1968)

Arvo J, Kirk D (1987) Fast ray-tracing by ray classification . ACM Computer Graphics 21(4):55-63

Atherton P (1983). A scan-line hidden surface removal procedure for Constructive Solid Geometry. ACM Computer Graphics 17(3) pp. 73-82.

Badt SJ (1988) Two algorithms for taking advantage of temporal coherence in ray tracing. The Visual Computer (4): 123-132

Baum DR, Wallace JR, Cohen M, Greenberg D. (1986) The back-buffer algorithm: an extention of the radiosity method to dynamic environments. The Visual Computer (2): 298-306

Bronsvoort W (1987) An algorithm for visible-line and visible surface display of CSG models. The Visual Computer, 3:176-185.

Clark JH (1976) Hierarchical geometric Models for Visible Surface Algorithms. Com. of the ACM 19(10): 547-554.

Cleary JG , Wyvill G (1988) Analysis of an algorithm for fast ray tracing using uniform sapce subdivision. The Visual Computer 4: 65-83

Crocker GA (1987) Screen-area coherence for interactive scan-line display algorithms IEEE Computer Graphics and Applications: (9)10-17

Fuchs H., Abram G., Grant B. (1983) Near Real-Time shaded display of rigid objects, ACM Computer Graphics, 17(3): 65-69

Fuchs H., Kedem Z., Naylor B. (1980) On visible Surface Generation by a priori Tree structures. ACM Computer Graphics, 14(3): 124-133

Fujimoto A, Tanaka T, Iwata K (1986) ARTS: an accelerated Ray-tracing system IEEE Computer Graphics and Applications, (4):16-25..

Galimberti R, Montanari U (1969) An Algorithm for Hidden-line Elimination. Com. of the ACM, 12 (4):206-211

Glassner A (1984),   Space division for fast ray tracing. IEEE Computer Graphics and Applications, (10) 15-22.

Glassner A (1988) Spacetime raytracing for animation. IEEE Computer Graphics and Appl. : 60:70

Goldsmith J, Salmon J (1987) Automatic creation of object hierarchies for ray tracing, IEEE Computer Graphics and Applications, (5): 14-20.

Grant C (1985) Integrated Analytic and temporal antialiasing for polyhedra in 4-D space, Computer Graphics 19(3)

Hall R, Grenberg D (1983) A testbed for realistic image synthesis. IEEE Computer Graphics and applications, (11):10-19

Hamlin G., Gear W. (1977) Raster-Scan Hidden Surface Algorithm Techniques. Computer Graphics, 11(2):206-213

Herbison-Evans D (1982) Real time animation of human figure drawings with hidden lines omitted. IEEE Computer Graphics and Applications (11):27-33,.

Hornung C. (1984), A method for solving the visibility problem IEEE Computer Graphics and Applications

Hubshman H. (1980) Frame-to-frame coherence and the hidden surface computations Master Thesis, Mac Gill University, Montreal, Canada.

Hubshman H, Zucker S (1982) Frame-to-frame coherence and the hidden surface computations: constraints for a convex world . ACM Transactions on Graphics, 1(2): 129-162 .

Kaplan M. (1985) Space tracing: a constant time ray tracer. ACM Computer Graphics, Siggraph'85 : tutorial notes.

Kay D., Greenberg D. (1979) Transparency for Computer Synthesized Images" ACM Computer Graphics, Vol 13, pp 158-164.

Korein J, Badler N (1983) Temporal Anti-Aliasing in Computer Generated Animation. ACM Computer Graphics, Proceedings Siggraph 83, 17(3): 377-388.

Loutrel P., (1970) A solution to the Hidden Line Problem for computer drawn Polyhedra, IEEE transactions on Computers, C19, 3.

Matsumoto H., Murakami K. (1983), Ray-tracing with Octree data structure, Proc. 28th Information Processing Conference, pp. 1535-1536.

Matsushita Y. (1972), Hidden Lines Elimination for a rotating object. Communications of the ACM, 15 (4):245-252.

Magnemat-Thalmann N., Thalmann D. (1985) Computer Animation: Theory and Practice Springer-Verlag

Newell M, Newell R, Sancha T (1972) A solution to the hidden surface problem Proceedings ACM National Conference: 443-450.

Noma T, Kunii T (1985), ANIMENGINE: an Engineering Animation system , IEEE Computer Graphics and Applications (10): 24-101.

Roberts L. (1963), Machine Perception of Three dimensional Solids, MIT Lincoln laboratory, TR 315.

Reeves W. (1983) Particle systems - A technique for Modeling a Class of Fuzzy Objects ACM Transactions on Graphics, Vl. 2, No. 2, pp 359-376

Romney G (1970), Computer Assisted Assembly and Rendering of Solids , Department of Computer Science, University of Utah, TR-4-20.

Rubin S, Whitted T (1980). A 3-dimensional representation for fast rendering of complex scenes ACM Computer Graphics, 14(3):110-123.

Potmesil M, Chakravarty I (1983) Motion Blur in Computer generated images ACM Computer Graphics 17(3)

Pueyo X (1986) Estudi dels algorismes de visualitzacio d'escenes tridimensionals formades per superficies corbes i mixtes utilitzant el principi d'escombrat linia a linia. Tesi Doctoral, Universitat Politecnica de Catalunya

Pueyo X., Brunet P. (1987) A parametric space based scan-line algorithm for removal of bicubic surfaces. IEEE Computer Graphics and Applications (11): 17-25

Shelley Kl, Greenberg DP (1982) Path specification and path coherence. ACM Computer Graphics, Proceedings Siggraph 82, 16(3): 157-166

Schumacker R., Brand B, Gilliland M., Sharp W. (1969) Study for applying Computer Generated Images for Visual Simulation AFHRL -TR -69-14, US Air Force Human Resources Laboratory.

Speer RL, DeRose TD, Barsky BA (1986) A Theoretical and Empirical Analysis of Coherent Ray-Tracing. Proccedings Graphics Interface 86: 11-25.

Sutherland IE, Sproull RF, Shumacker RA (1974) . A characterization of 10 Hidden-Surface Algorithms. ACM Computing Surveys, 6 (1):1-55

Watkins C. (1970), A real time Visible Surface Algorithm, Computer Science Department, University of Utah, UTECH-CSC-70-101, June 1970.

Warnock J, (1969) A Hidden Surface Algorithm for generated halftone Pictures , C.S. Tech. Report 4-15, University of Utah.

Weiler K, Atherton P (1977) Hidden Surface removal using Polygon area sorting   ACM Computer Graphics, 1: 214-222.

Whitted T (1980) An Improved Illumination Model for shaded display , Communications of the ACM,   23(6): 343-349.

Whitted T., Weimer D. (1982), A Software Testbed for the development of 3-D Raster Graphics Systems, ACM Transactions on Graphics, Vol 1, pp 43-58.

Wyvill G, Kunii T, Shirai Y (1986) Space division for Ray tracing in CSG, IEEE Computer Graphics and Application, (4): 28-34.

Danlèle Tost is a PhD student at the Polytechnical University of Catalunya, in Barcelona. She is currently teaching computer science at the Engineering school of the same University. She obtained the degree of engineer in 1985. Her research interests include computer graphics, computer aided design, image synthesis and computer animation. She is a member of the Eurographics association.

Pere Brunet is currently a professor of computer science at the Polytechnical University of Catalonia in Barcelona. He obtained the degree of engineer in 1971 and his PhD in 1976. His research interests include computer graphics, computer aided design, computer aided geometric design and geometric modelling of solids. He has published a total of 50 odd scientific papers in these fields. Brunet is president of` the Spanish Chapter of the Eurographics association and member of the excutive commitee of the same assocition. He is also a founding member of the working group 5.10 of IFIP, on Computer Graphics. He is a member of the Editorial Board of Computer Aided Design and Computer & Graphics and he has been a member of the programme commitee of Eurographics 86, 88 and 90, Computer Graphics International'88, Pixim'88 and Micad 88 and 90 conferences, among others.

Address: Departament de Llenguatges i Sistemes Informatics. Universitat Politècnica de Catalunya. Diagonal 647 (ETSEIB) 08028 BARCELONA, SPAIN

Automating View Function Generation for Walk-through Animation Using a Reeb Graph

YOSHIHISA SHINAGAWA, TOSIYASU L. KUNII, YASUYA NOMURA, TAEKO OKUNO, and YI-HO YOUNG

ABSTRACT

A new method is presented to automate view function generation for walk-through animation from cross sectional data. A view function is a function of time that shows the location of the view point. First, a Reeb graph, which describes the "skeleton" of an object, is used to determine the topological shape of the locus of the view function. The Reeb graph is extended to be able to cover the cases containing the number of holes of each equivalence class. Then, the method to find the geometrical location of the view point on each cross section is presented. Using this location as the representative in each equivalence class of the Reeb graph, the view function is generated.

Key Words and Phrases: computer animation, view function, homotopy, Reeb graph

INTRODUCTION

There is often a need for a walk-through animation of objects. In medicine, for example, a walk-through animation of human organs is of great interest [Nomura et al. 1989]. To simulate the effect of a gastroscope or needle otoscope [Nomura 1982] when the CT data of the patient is given using computer graphics, it is necessary to first reconstruct the 3-D objects and then to walk through the organs. The object to be walked through is usually reconstructed from its cross sectional data, for example, CT images or photographs of serially sectioned celloidin specimens. Also in speleology, walking through caves reconstructed from topographic data is of great significance. A walk-through animation can be also used for passing through a 3-D maze. There are two models for 3-D object reconstruction from cross sectional data; surface and solid models. For walk-through animation, surface models are advantageous. Surface models reconstruct objects by formulating surfaces between the digitized contour lines on each cross sectional plane [Fuchs et al. 1977, Christiansen et al. 1988, Kaneda et al. 1987, Boissonnat et al.1988, Shinagawa et al. 1989]. Therefore, for walk-through animation, it is necessary to generate a view function that passes through the objects where data is given by their contour lines on each plane. The view function gives the location of the view point as a function of time. The situation is totally different from ordinary path planning where it is necessary to move among objects and the motion is restricted to a plane. As with a walk-through, the path is inside complicated objects and is not restricted onto a plane. Also it is difficult to constitute good cost functions[e.g. Breen 1989] because the objects consist of a large number of surface patches. This paper presents a new method to generate this view function. First, a Reeb graph is introduced to determine the topological shape of the locus of the view function. Then a method to compute the geometrical location of the view point on each cross section is proposed. Combining the topological and the geometrical information, the view function is generated.

TOPOLOGICAL PRELIMINARIES

In this section, the concept of "homotopy type" [Armstrong 1983] is described. First of all, a homotopy is defined as follows.
DEFINITION: Let f,g: X → Y be maps where X and Y are topological spaces. Then f is

homotopic to g if there exists a map $F:X \times I \rightarrow Y$ such that $F(x,0) = f(x)$ and $F(x,1) = g(x)$ for all points $x \in X$. Here $I = [0,1] \subset \mathbf{R}$. This map F is called a homotopy from f to g and we shall write $f \cong g$. If for some subset A of X

$$F(a,t) = f(a) \text{ for all } a \in A, \text{ for all } t \in I$$

holds, f is said to be homotopic to g relative to A and is written $f \cong g$ rel A.

DEFINITION: Two spaces X and Y have the same homotopy type if there exist maps

$$f : X \rightarrow Y, g : X \rightarrow Y$$

such that $g \bullet f \cong 1_X$ and $f \bullet g \cong 1_Y$.

REEB GRAPH

In this section, a Reeb graph is introduced to determine the topological shape of the view function. A Reeb graph represents the topological "skeleton" of the 3-D object. Therefore, the locus of the function is decided according to the Reeb graph. George Reeb first introduced this graph in his thesis [For details, cf. Thom 1988].

DEFINITION: Let $f : M \rightarrow \mathbf{R}$ be a real valued function on a manifold M [e.g. Armstrong 1983]. The Reeb graph of f is the quotient space of the graph of f in $M \times \mathbf{R}$ by the equivalence relation $\tilde{}$ given below: $(X_1, y_1) \tilde{} (X_2, y_2)$ holds if and only if $y_1 = y_2$ and X_1, X_2 are in the same connected component of $f^{-1}(y_1)$ where $y_1 = f(X_1)$ and $y_2 = f(X_2)$. We represent by the notation $[(X, y)]$ the equivalence class that includes the point (X, y).

First of all, the 3-D objects to be walked through are considered to be 3-dimensional manifolds in $\mathbf{R}^3$. Then the Reeb graph of the height function $h(X)$ on these manifolds is considered. Here, $h(X)$ gives the height of the point on the manifold $X = (x_1, x_2, x_3)$ where $x_1, x_2, x_3 \in \mathbf{R}$. and the x_3 axis is set to be perpendicular to each cross sectional plane of the objects. i.e. $h(x_1, x_2, x_3) = x_3$

For simplicity, we assume that the equation of the i-th cross sectional plane from the bottom is $x_3 = z_i$ and this plane is referred to as the i-th frame. For example, the Reeb graph of the height function of the torus shown in the Fig. 1a is as in Fig. 1c. This is easy to see when we consider the cross sectional planes as in Fig. 1b; all the contour lines on each plane are represented by a point in the Reeb graph. The graph shows the "skeleton" of the manifold and so the topological shape of the locus of the view function.

The Reeb graph itself is incapable of showing the homotopy type of the object. For example, a disk and an annulus are represented by a point in the Reeb graph. They do not, however, have the same homotopy type. This is easy to see when we think of the deformation retraction [1] of a disk and an annulus. The deformation retraction of a disk is a point while that of an annulus is a circle S^1 (see Fig. 7). The homotopy type of each connected component on the cross sectional plane is not needed for a usual walk-through. It is necessary for the "horizontal walk-through" discussed later. Therefore we assign this information to the node (equivalence class) of the Reeb graph. Each connected component has the same homotopy type as a disk with n holes (surface with $n+1$ boundaries). Thus, the number of holes n is added to each equivalence class.

The Reeb graph loses its geometrical information on the $x_1 x_2$ plane. We recover this information by choosing a representative value from each equivalence class; we associate a point with each contour line on the plane and the locus of the view function passes through this point. For example, we can associate with each contour line its center. The choice of the representative value is discussed in the next section.

Computation of the Reeb graph is instantaneous when the surface is already reconstructed. That is, when there is a surface patch between two contours on the i-th frame and the i+1-th frame, there is a path from the equivalence class of the one contour to that of the other. On the other hand, the Reeb graph can be used to reconstruct a surface when the reconstruction has not yet taken place. Therefore, automatic computation of the Reeb graph from the cross sectional data is of great significance. We succeeded in doing so and also expanded the expressive capability of the graph. The details are beyond the scope of this paper. Hereafter, we assume that the surface of the object is given. The computation of the number of holes in each connected component on a frame is not difficult in our case where the contours are approximated by polygons.

---

[1] "Deformation retract" is defined as follows. Let A be a subspace of X. A homotopy $G : X \times I \rightarrow X$ which is relative to A and for which $G(x,0) = x$, $G(x,1) \in A$ for all $x \in X$ is called a deformation retraction of X onto A.

If there is a deformation retraction of X onto A, then X and A have the same homotopy type.

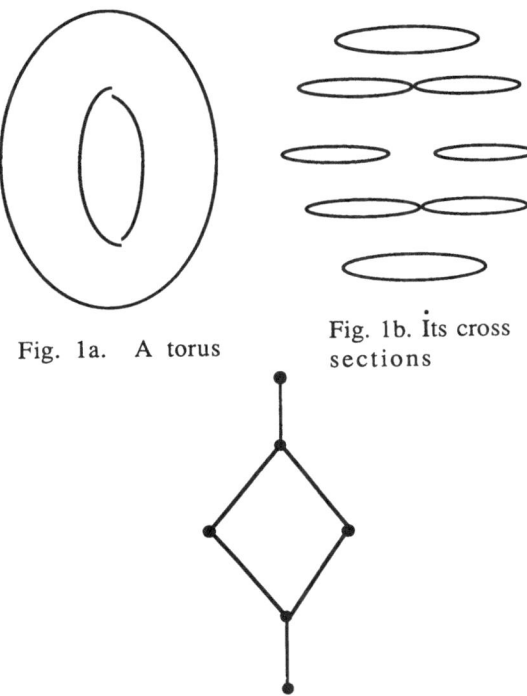

Fig. 1a.   A torus

Fig. 1b. Its cross
sections

Fig. 1c. Its Reeb graph

CHOICE OF REPRESENTATIVE VALUES

The locus of the view function must lie in the interior of the object. Therefore, the representative point of each equivalence class must lie in the interior of each contour line that it represents. We assume that the contours are approximated by polygons unless otherwise noted. The easiest choice is the center of gravity of each polygon. However, it is not always in the interior as shown in Fig. 2. The center of the kernel [Preparate & Shamos 1985] of the polygon that approximates a contour line seems to be a reasonable choice because from that point we can view the whole contour. The kernel of a polygon P is the locus of the points Z not external to P such that for all points p of P the line segment $\overline{Zp}$ lies entirely within P. Each edge of a polygon P determines a half-plane in which the kernel must lie. These half-planes are referred to as the interior half-planes and the kernel is the intersection of them. As illustrated in Fig. 3., there are, however, cases where the kernels do not exist. The the maximum circle contained in the polygon [Aonuma et al. 1989] [2] is another choice. When the contours differ widely in shape, however, the center also moves rapidly from a frame to a frame. Therefore, we choose the representative point as follows. In the following part, each cross sectional plane $x_3 = z_i$, which is determined by the CT images or the slices of specimens, is referred to as the i-th frame (i = 0,1,..,n). First of all, the representative value of the bottommost frame (0-th frame) is computed. Next, we compute the representative value of the contours on the upper frame. This process is iterated until the topmost frame and the representative values are determined on all the frames. Finally, the representative points on the frames are linearly interpolated to get the path of the view point. In other words, the view point moves along the line segments that connect each representative point on the frames. Instead of a linear interpolation, a cardinal spline [Clark 1981] can be used , but this complicates the implementation. The pseudo-Pascal code for this procedure is given below.

---

[2] It is the case where the L_2-distance is used instead of L_∞-distance in ACPF (automatic character placing function).

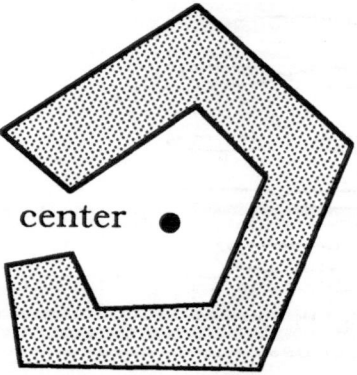

Fig. 2. An example where
the center does not lie on
the inside

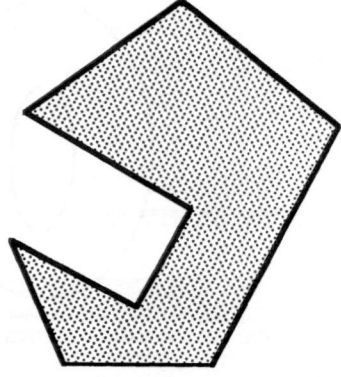

Fig. 3. The kernel is absent

```
procedure main()
begin
        Compute representative of the 0-th frame;
        for i:= 1 to n do
                Compute representative of the i-th frame using the value
                of the i-1-th frame;
        for i:= 1 to n-1 do
                Interpolate the representative points
                on the i-1-th and the i-th frame;
end.
```

Computation of each representative point of the contour on the frame is done as follows. First, we map the polygon that represents the contour (i-th frame) onto a unit square centered at the origin by translating and scaling (see Fig. 4). This process is referred to as the normalization v_i. The normalized image of the representative point of the previous frame (i-1-th frame) by the map v_{i-1} is also brought in to the unit square. This point is referred to as R. For the bottommost frame (i = 0), R is set to the origin. Then, R is tested to see if it lies inside the normalized polygon of the i-th frame. The method presented by Guibas et al. was used for the point-in-polygon test. [Guibas et al. 1983, Dobkin et al. 1988]. If R is contained in the normalized polygon, it is chosen as the representative of its equivalence class. Otherwise, the point inside the polygon near R is chosen. To be precise, we search for the edge of the polygon that is nearest to R first. Here, the distance between an edge E and a point R is defined as

$$\min_{p \in E} (p, R);$$

i.e., minimum distance between R and a point included in E. Then an open ray from R that passes through the middle of the edge referred to as the point N is computed. The intersection of the ray and each edge of the polygon is then calculated. The intersection second nearest to R is referred as the point F. The representative of this contour is the midpoint of line joining the point N and F (see Fig. 5). Finally, the representative R' is obtained by v_i^{-1}. The pseudo-Pascal code for this procedure is given below.

```
procedure Compute_representative(frame No.)
POINT          F,N,P,R;
LINE SEGMENT   E;
OPEN RAY  L;
begin
        R := normalized image of the representative of the previous frame;
        Map the contour onto a unit square centered at the origin;
        if (R is in the polygon)
                representative := R;
```

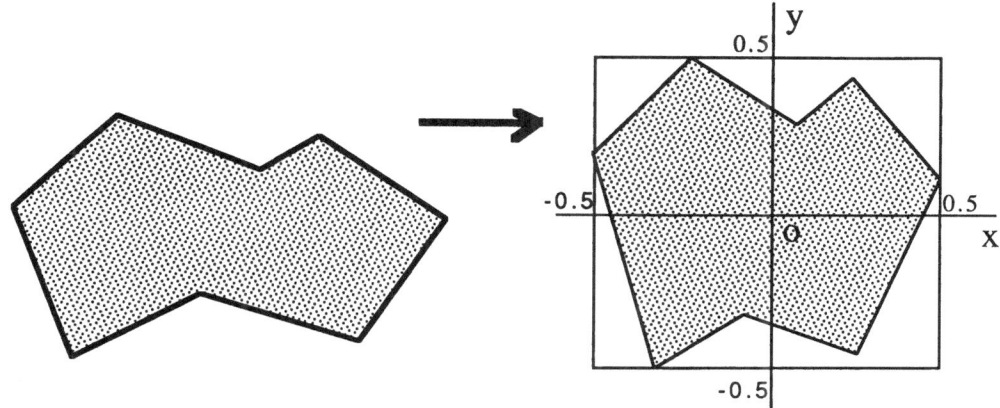

Fig. 4. Normalization

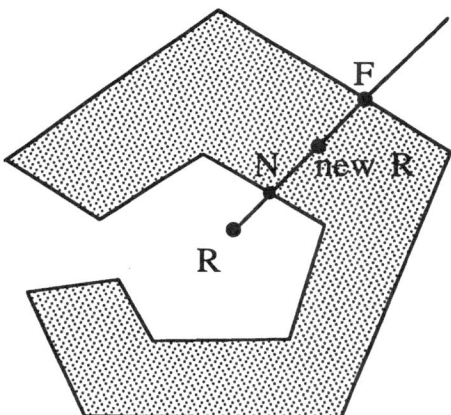

Fig. 5. Selection of the representative
point

```
        else
        begin
                for each edge of the polygon do
                begin
                        d := distance(the edge, R);
                        if (d = minimum) then E := the edge;
                end;
                L := open ray from R that passes through the midpoint of E;
                for each edge of the polygon do
                begin
                        P := intersection(the edge, L);
                        d := distance(P, R);
                        if (d = minimum) then begin
                                F := N; N := P;
                        end;
                end;
                representative := midpoint of N and F;
        end;
        This algorithm is trivial.  For simplicity, we do not discuss the efficiency of the algorithm.
```

HORIZONTAL WALK-THROUGH

There are cases where tracing the Reeb graph is not adequate. For example, the Reeb graph of a torus laid horizontally as in Fig. 6a is shown in Fig. 6b. It is not desirous to trace this graph. For these cases, we trace the object on the horizontal plane; i.e. on the frame. We shall call this a "horizontal walk-through." If the cross section is an annulus (1 hole), the locus of the view function is a circle (see Fig. 7). When there are more than two holes, we choose one hole and the view point moves around that hole. If there is no hole in the cross section, the horizontal walk-through is not effective. In this section, the discussion is limited to those cases where there are holes. In order that the locus of the view function be inside the object, it is decided as follows. First of all, the hole around which the walk-through is done is selected. Let the contour of that hole be represented by a polygon T.

Case 1: T is convex;

The minimum distance λ between T and other contours is calculated. The locus of the view function is set to a polygon larger than T by $\lambda / 2$ (see Fig. 8a). This polygon is similar to dilation in the image processing [Serra 1982]. We also call this "Dilation of T" and is denoted as $T \bigcirc (\lambda / 2)$ in this paper. It is constructed as follows. First, each edge of T is moved outward by $\lambda / 2$. Then the endpoint of these edges are connected by linear line segments as in Fig. 8b.

Case 1: T is not convex;

For ease of implementation, locus of the view function is set to T where ε is a very small number. When ε is very small, dilation process can be ignored.

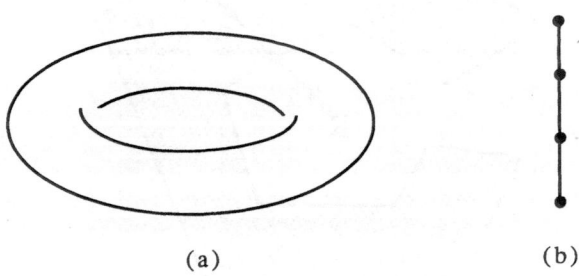

(a)   (b)

Fig. 6. A torus laid horizontally (a) and its Reeb graph (b)

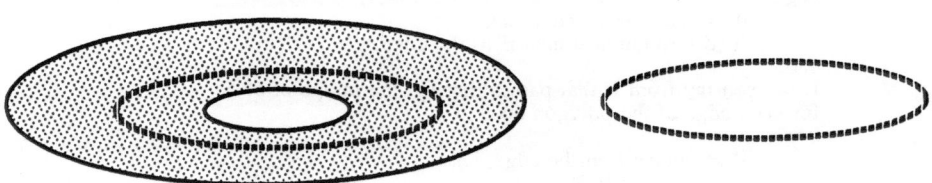

Fig. 7. Horizontal walk-through of an annulus

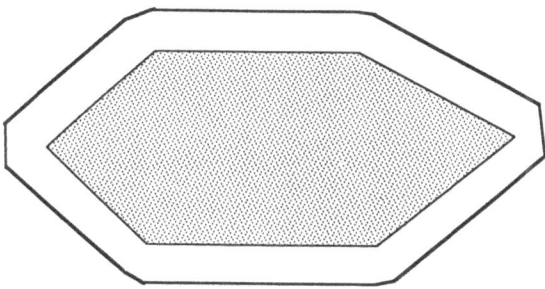

Fig. 8a. Dilation of T

Fig. 8b. The dilation process

LINE OF SIGHT, TWIST ANGLE AND VELOCITY

The line of sight and the twist angle at the view point are essentially independent of the view function. In this paper, however, they are defined using the view function.

There are several ways to define the line of sight. One way is to use the tangent line of the view function, i.e., $\frac{df}{dt}$, where $f : \mathbf{R} \to \mathbf{R}^3$ is a view function. Since the locus of the view function consists of linear line segments, the line of sight at the view point is made to coincide with the line segment that the view point is on. When the view point is at an end point of a segment, the tangent line is not defined. In order to avoid a jump in the line of sight at each end point, the line of sight changes smoothly from the direction of the previous line segment to the present one (see Fig. 9). When a cardinal spline is used instead of a linear interpolation, the line of sight is just the tangent line of the curve at the view point.

When the interval between the adjacent frames is small, the direction of the tangent line changes rapidly. In this case, the direction of the line of sight at the time t is set to be
$$f(t + \Delta t) - f(t)$$
where Δt is a constant. This corresponds to "always looking ahead." It is also possible to set the direction of the line of sight to
$$\mathbf{X} - f(t)$$
where $\mathbf{X}$ is a fixed point. This corresponds to "always gazing at a fixed point." This is useful when the part of the object around $\mathbf{X}$ is important.

The twist angle is defined to be the right-hand rotation about the line of sight. In our implementation, it is kept constant during the walk-through. The time needed to move from one frame to another is kept constant in the implementation. This defines the velocity of the view point.

TRAVERSAL OF THE REEB GRAPH

Traversing the Reeb graph is trivial when there is no branch in it. However, when there are branches, it is necessary to decide which branch is to be traversed for an effective walk-through. In this paper, this choice of the branch is made interactively.

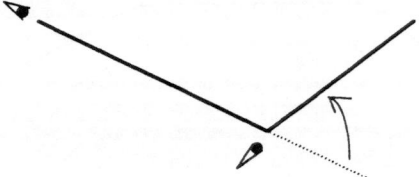

Fig.9. Movement of the line of sight

HUMAN EAR DATA

A human temporal bone with the ear lobe was obtained from a cadaver and subjected to the conventional celloidin processing. A motor-driven drill was used to place reference marks in a celloidin block [Nomura et al. 1989]. The celloidin block was serially sectioned into slices 20 μm thick. All slices were stained with hematoxylin and eosin (H-E) and mounted in glass slides. A color photograph was taken of each of the H-E stained specimens.

The photographs were converted to image data by a drum scanner G-225C (Graphica Co., Japan) and outline curves of the objects to be reconstructed were plotted with a stylus pen. The computer used here was HP9000 series model 550 (Hewlet-Packard Co., USA). Finally the modified contour data were fed into IRIS 4D/70GT (Silicon Graphics Co., USA), where the three dimensional reconstruction was performed.

DISPLAY EXAMPLE

We now present examples of the finished product. Fig. 10 shows the organs in the external, the middle and the inner ear. Fig. 11 shows the walk-through in the organs.

CONCLUSIONS AND FUTURE WORK

A new method is presented to automate view function generation for walk-through animation from cross sectional data. First, a Reeb graph, which describes the "skeleton" of an object is used to determine the topological shape of the locus of the view function. Then, the method that finds the geometrical location of the view point on each cross section was presented. Using this as the representative of each equivalence class of the Reeb graph, the view function is generated. When the shape of the consecutive contours differ widely, there is a possibility that the locus of the view function may be partially outside the object. A spatial containment test to check if the locus lies inside the object is part of our future research. The usual walk-through and the horizontal walk-through are treated separately in this paper. Combining these two is another extension that we have in mind. The dilation process for concave polygons is also left as a problem for future research.

ACKNOWLEDGMENTS

We wish to express our gratitude to Mr. Kansei Iwata, the president of Graphica Co., Ltd. and Mr. Norimasa Koyama, the executive director of Cadtech Inc. for offering the drum scanner, G-225C, Yokogawa Hewlet Packard Co., Ltd. for HP900 model 550 and Silicon Graphics Co., Ltd. for IRIS 4D/70GT.

Special thanks are extended to Dr. Yannick L. Kergosien of Mathematiques, Universite de Paris-Sud, Mr. Martin Durst, Ms. Deepa Krishnan, and Mr. Yasuto Shirai of the Kunii Laboratory of Computer Science, the University of Tokyo.

Fig. 10. Organs in the external, the middle and the inner ear

Fig. 11. Walk-through in the organs

REFERENCES

Aonuma H, Imai H, Kambayashi Y A Visual System of Placing Characters Appropriately in Multimedia Map Databases. (1989) In: Kunii TL (ed) *Visual Database Systems.* Elsevier Science Publishers B.V., Amsterdam New York Oxford Tokyo, pp. 525-546

Armstrong MA (1983) *Basic Topology.* Springer, New York Berlin Heidelberg Tokyo, p.88, pp.103-105, p.169

Boissonnat JD (1988) Shape Reconstruction from Planar Cross Sections. *Computer Vision, Graphics, and Image Processing,* Vol.41, No.1, pp.1-29

Breen DE (1989) Choreographing Goal-Oriented Motion Using Cost Functions. In: Magnenat-Thalmann N, Thalmann D (ed) *State-of-the-art in Computer Animation.* Springer, New York Berlin Heidelberg Tokyo, pp. 367-380

Christiansen HN, Sederberg TW (1978) Conversion of Complex Contour Line Definitions into Polygonal Element Mosaics. *Proc. ACM SIGGRAPH'78,* pp.187-192

Clark JH (Nov. 1981) Parametric Curves, Surfaces and Volumes in Computer Graphics and Computer-Aided Geometric Design. *Computer Systems Laboratory, Technical Report No.221,* Stanford University.

Dobkin D, Guibas L, Hershberger J, Snoeyink J (Aug. 1988) An Efficient Algorithm for Finding the CSG Representation of a Simple Polygon. *ACM Computer Graphics, Vol 22, No. 4,* pp.31-40

Fuchs H, Kedem ZM, and Uselton SP (Oct. 1977) Optimal Surface Reconstruction from Planar Contours. *Comm. ACM Vol.20, No.10,* pp.693-702

Guibas L, Ramshaw L, Stolfi J (1983) A Kinetic Framework for Computational Geometry. *Proc. 24th Annual IEEE Symposium on Foundations of Computer Science,* pp.100-111

Kaneda K, Harada K, Nakamae E, Yasuda M, and Sato AG (1987) Reconstruction and Semi-Transparent Display Method for Observing Inner Structure of an Object Consisting of Multiple Surfaces. In: Kunii TL (ed) *Computer Graphics 1987.* Springer, New York Berlin Heidelberg Tokyo, pp. 367-380

Nomura Y (1982) A Needle Otoscope. *Acta Otolaryngol 93,* pp.73-79

Nomura Y (1982) Effective Photography in Otolaryngology-Head and neck Surgery: Endoscopic photography of the middle ear. (Jul.-Aug. 1982) *Otolaryngol Head Neck Surg 1982; 90,* pp.395-398

Nomura Y, Okuno T, Hara M, Shinagawa Y, Kunii TL (1989) Walking through a Human Ear. *Acta Otolaryngol (Stockholm) 107,* pp.366-370

Serra J (1982) *Image Analysis and Mathematical Morphology Vol. 1.* Academic Press, London San Diego New York Boston Sydney Tokyo Toronto

Shinagawa Y, Kunii TL, Nomura Y, Okuno T, Hara M (1989) Reconstructing Smooth Surfaces from a Series of Contour Lines Using a Homotopy. In: Eanshaw RA, Wyvill B (ed) *New Advances in Computer Graphics.* Springer, New York Berlin Heidelberg Tokyo, pp.147-161

Thom R (1988) *Esquisse D'une Semiophysique.* Inter Editions, Paris, p.57

Preparata FP, Shamos MI (1985) *Computational geometry: an introduction.* Springer, New York Berlin Heidelberg Tokyo

Yoshihisa Shinagawa is currently a master course graduate student of information science at the University of Tokyo. His research interests include computer graphics and its applications. He received the B.Sc. degree in information science from the University of Tokyo in 1987. He is a student member of the IEEE Computer Society, ACM and the Information Processing Society of Japan.
Address: Department of Information Science, Faculty of Science, the University of Tokyo, 7-3-1 Hongo, Bunkyo-Ku,Tokyo, 113 Japan

Tosiyasu L. Kunii is currently Professor of Information and Computer Science, the University of Tokyo. At the University of Tokyo, he started his work in raster computer graphics in 1968 which was let to the Tokyo Raster Technology Project. His research interests include computer graphics, database systems, and software engineering. He authored and edited more than 30 computer science books, and published more than 100 refereed academic/technical papers in computer science and applications areas.

Dr. Kunii is Honarary President and Founder of the Computer Graphics Society, Chairman of the Board of the Handheld Computer Society, Editor-in-Chief of *The Visual Computer: An International Journal of Computer Graphics* and on the Editorial Board of *IEEE Transactions on Knowledge and Data Engineering* and *IEEE Computer Graphics and Applications*. He is on the IFIP Modeling and Simulation Working Group, the IFIP Data Base Working Group and the IFIP Computer Graphics Working Group. He organized and was chairing the Technical Committee on Software Engineering of the Information Processing Society of Japan from 1976 to 1981. He also organized and was President of the Japan Computer Graphics Association(JCGA) from 1981 to 1983. He served as General Chairman of the 3rd International Conference on Very Large Data Bases(VLDB) in 1977, Program Chairman of InterGraphics '83 in 1983, Organizing Committee Chairman and Program Chairman of Computer Graphics Tokyo in 1984, Program Chairman of Computer Graphics Tokyo in 1985 and 1986, Organizing Committee Chairperson and Program Chairperson of CG International '87 in 1987, Program Co-Chairman of COMPSAC 87 in 1987, and Honorary Committee Chairperson of CG International '88 in 1988. He served as Organizing Committee Chairperson and Program Chairperson of IFIP TC-2/WG 2.6 Working Conference on Visual Database Systems in 1989 and Program Chairperson of IFIP TC-5/WG 5.10 Working Conference on Modeling in Computer Graphics.

He received the B.Sc., M.Sc., and D.Sc. degrees in chemistry all from the University of Tokyo in 1962, 1964, and 1967, respectively.
Address: Department of Information Science, Faculty of Science, the University of Tokyo, 7-3-1 Hongo, Bunkyo-Ku,Tokyo, 113 Japan

Yasuya Nomura is currently Professor and Chairman of the Department of Otolaryngology, the University of Tokyo. He received his M.D. in 1956 and Dr.Med.Sci. in 1975 from the University of Tokyo.

Address: Department of Otolaryngology, Faculty of Medicine, the University of Tokyo, 7-3-1 Hongo, Bunkyo-Ku,Tokyo, 113 Japan

Taeko Okuno is currently an instructor in the Department of Otolaryngology, the University of Tokyo. She received her M.D. in 1977 from Chiba University Medical School and Dr.Med.Sci. in 1984 from the University of Tokyo.

Address: Department of Otolaryngology, Faculty of Medicine, the University of Tokyo, 7-3-1 Hongo, Bunkyo-Ku,Tokyo, 113 Japan

Yi-Ho Young is currently a postgraduate student in the Department of Otolaryngology, the University of Tokyo. He received his M.D. in 1981 from National Taiwan University.

Address: Department of Otolaryngology, Faculty of Medicine, the University of Tokyo, 7-3-1 Hongo, Bunkyo-Ku,Tokyo, 113 Japan

Author Index

Keyword Index